CBSE Term II
2022

English Core

Class XI

- Chapterwise Summary in all Sections
- Extract Based Questions
- Short/Long Answer Type Questions
- 3 Practice Papers

Author
Srishthi Agarwal

arihant

ARIHANT PRAKASHAN (School Division Series)

ARIHANT PRAKASHAN (School Division Series)

ॐ **Administrative & Production Offices**

Regd. Office

'Ramchhaya' 4577/15, Agarwal Road, Darya Ganj, New Delhi -110002
Tele: 011- 47630600, 43518550

ॐ **Head Office**

Kalindi, TP Nagar, Meerut (UP) - 250002, Tel: 0121-7156203, 7156204

ॐ **Sales & Support Offices**

Agra, Ahmedabad, Bengaluru, Bareilly, Chennai, Delhi, Guwahati, Hyderabad, Jaipur, Jhansi, Kolkata, Lucknow, Nagpur & Pune.

ॐ **ISBN :** 978-93-25796-76-8

ॐ **PRICE :** ₹ 200.00

PO No : TXT-XX-XXXXXXX-X-XX

Published by Arihant Publications (India) Ltd.

For further information about the books published by Arihant, log on to www.arihantbooks.com or e-mail at info@arihantbooks.com

Follow us on   

Contents

Syllabus

CBSE Term II Class XI

Section		Weightage
A	**READING COMPREHENSION** • Unseen passage (factual, descriptive or literary /discursive or persuasive) • Unseen passage for Note Making and Summarising	13 (8+5 Marks)
B	**CREATIVE WRITING SKILLS AND GRAMMAR:** **Short Writing Tasks** • Posters **Long Writing Tasks(One)** • Official Letters: e.g. to school/college authorities (regarding admissions, school issues, requirements / suitability of courses) • Debate **Grammar** • Determiners • Tenses • Re-ordering of Sentences *{MCQs on Gap filling/ Transformation of Sentences }*	08 (3+5+4 Marks)
C	**LITERATURE** • Questions based on extracts/texts to assess comprehension and appreciation, analysis, inference, extrapolation **Book-Hornbill:** • The Voice of the Rain (Poem) • The Ailing Planet: The Green Movement's Role (Prose) • The Browning Version(Play) • Childhood (Poem) • Silk Road (Prose) **Book-Snapshots:** • Albert Einstein at School (Prose) • Mother's Day (Play) • Birth (Prose)	9 Marks Hornbill + 6 Marks for Snapshots=15 marks
	Total	40
	ASL	10
	Grand Total	40+10 = 50

केन्द्रीय माध्यमिक शिक्षा बोर्ड

(शिक्षा मंत्रालय, भारत सरकार के अधीन एक स्वायत संगठन)

CENTRAL BOARD OF SECONDARY EDUCATION

(An Autonomous Organisation under the Ministryof Education, Govt. of India)

Term I Examinations:

- At the end of the first term, the Board will organize **Term I Examination** in a flexible schedule to be conducted between November-December 2021 with a window period of 4-8 weeks for schools situated in different parts of country and abroad. Dates for conduct of examinations will be notified subsequently.

- The Question Paper will have Multiple Choice Questions (MCQ) including case-based MCQs and MCQs on assertion-reasoning type. Duration of test will be **90 minutes** and it will cover only the rationalized syllabus of **Term I only** (i.e. approx. 50% of the entire syllabus).

- Question Papers will be sent by the CBSE to schools along with marking scheme.

- The exams will be conducted under the supervision of the External Center Superintendents and Observers appointed by CBSE.

- The responses of students will be captured on OMR sheets which, after scanning may be directly uploaded at CBSE portal or alternatively may be evaluated and marks obtained will be uploaded by the school on the very same day. The final direction in this regard will be conveyed to schools by the Examination Unit of the Board.

- Marks of the **Term I** Examination will contribute to the final overall score of students.

Term II Examination/ Year-end Examination:

- At the end of the second term, the Board would organize **Term II or Year-end Examination** based on the rationalized syllabus of Term II only (i.e. approximately 50% of the entire syllabus).

- This examination would be held around **March-April 2022** at the examination centres fixed by the Board.

- The paper will be of **2 hours duration** and have questions of different formats (case-based/ situation based, open ended- short answer/ long answer type).

- In case the situation is not conducive for normal descriptive examination **a 90 minute MCQ based exam** will be conducted at the end of the Term II also.

- Marks of the Term II Examination would contribute to the final overall score.

केन्द्रीय माध्यमिक शिक्षा बोर्ड

(शिक्षा मंत्रालय, भारत सरकार के अधीन एक स्वायत संगठन)

CENTRAL BOARD OF SECONDARY EDUCATION

(An Autonomous Organisation under the Ministryof Education, Govt. of India)

Assessment / Examination as per different situations

A. In case the situation of the pandemic improves and students are able to come to schools or centres for taking the exams.

Board would conduct Term I and Term II examinations at schools/centres and the theory marks will be distributed equally between the two exams.

B. In case the situation of the pandemic forces complete closure of schools during November-December 2021, but Term II exams are held at schools or centres.

Term I MCQ based examination would be done by students online/offline from home - in this case, the weightage of this exam for the final score would be reduced, and weightage of Term II exams will be increased for declaration of final result.

C. In case the situation of the pandemic forces complete closure of schools during March-April 2022, but Term I exams are held at schools or centres.

Results would be based on the performance of students on Term I MCQ based examination and internal assessments. The weightage of marks of Term I examination conducted by the Board will be increased to provide year end results of candidates.

D. In case the situation of the pandemic forces complete closure of schools and Board conducted Term I and II exams are taken by the candidates from home in the session 2021-22.

Results would be computed on the basis of the Internal Assessment/Practical/Project Work and Theory marks of Term-I and II exams taken by the candidate from home in Class X / XII subject to the moderation or other measures to ensure validity and reliability of the assessment.

In all the above cases, data analysis of marks of students will be undertaken to ensure the integrity of internal assessments and home based exams.

Dr. Joseph Emmanuel
Director (Academics)

CHAPTER 01

Reading Comprehension

(Factual, Descriptive or Literary/ Discursive or Persuasive Passages)

Comprehension involves a thorough understanding of the given passage consisting of one or more paragraphs. It is meant to test the understanding power and intellectual skill of a student. In class XIth Term II examination, passage carrying a total of **8 marks** will be asked from Reading Section.

Types of Passages

Type of Passage	Examples		Sources from where passages are taken	
Factual passage	▪ A set of facts	▪ Instructions	▪ Newspapers and magazines	▪ Brochures
	▪ Report	▪ Description	▪ Reference books	▪ Encyclopaedias
Discursive passage	▪ Opinions	▪ Persuasive text	▪ Newspapers and magazines	
	▪ Argumentative text	▪ Interpretative text	▪ Reference books	
Literary passage	▪ Extract from fiction, drama, essay, biography, etc		▪ Novels ▪ Short stories ▪ Dramas	
			▪ Biographies ▪ Other literary books	
Case based Factual passage	Passage with visual and verbal inputs of		▪ Newspaper reports ▪ Magazines ▪ Reference books	
	▪ Statistical data ▪ Charts ▪ Graphs			

Points to be Kept in Mind

- Read the passage carefully and thoroughly to understand its contents. Underline the main ideas and instances, examples and arguments supporting them.
- Underline the words you don't understand and try to guess their meaning from the context. Check the vocabulary related questions and try to find the answers from the context.
- In Multiple Choice Questions, analyse the questions and options carefully before selecting the correct option because some of the four options are closely related.
- Quickly go through the subject matter questions and mark the parts of the passage you feel are the answers to the questions. Make sure you have understood the questions.
- Read the passage again to counter check your answers.

Chapter Practice

• Factual, Descriptive or Literary/Discursive or Persuasive Passages

Read the passages given below.

Passage 1

1. 'Amitabh Bachchan', who left an indelible mark in the history of Indian cinema, was born on 11th October, 1942 in the city of Allahabad, Uttar Pradesh. His father, Dr. Harivansh Rai Bachchan, was a famous Hindi poet. His mother, Teji Bachchan, was a highly educated and modern-minded woman. Amitabh's primary education was in St. Mary's School, Allahabad. He was then sent to Sherwood, a famous school in Nainital. He graduated from Kirori Mal College, Delhi University. While studying in this college, he decided to make 'acting' his career. Amitabh moved to Bombay (Mumbai) in 1969 at the age of twenty-seven.

2. Amitabh Bachchan started his career in films with the film 'Saat Hindustani' directed by Khwaja Ahmad Abbas in 1969. He was awarded the Filmfare Award for Best Supporting Actor for the film 'Anand'. A new twist in Amitabh's career came in 1973 after the release of the film 'Zanjeer'. He came to be called the 'Angry Youngman' due to the performance of a police inspector in this film.

3. The film 'Sholay' set new records of success and became the most successful commercial film in the history of Hindi Film Industry. After this, Amitabh Bachchan became famous and popular as a superstar. Amitabh Bachchan entered politics in 1984. He was elected M.P. from Allahabad Lok Sabha seat. He resigned from his post in 1987, after 3 years without completing his term as an M.P. and made a distance from politics.

4. Through the television reality show 'Kaun Banega Crorepati' in 2000, Amitabh Bachchan entered the world of television and not only strengthened his financial position but also reached a new height of fame and success. He has worked in more than 150 films.

5. For his achievements, he was honoured with 'Padma Shri' award in 1983 and 'Padma Bhushan' in 2005. He was voted Actor of the Millennium in 1999 by a BBC poll. In 2002, he was awarded the 'Personality of the Year' award by the International Films Academy. He has received 12 Filmfare Awards so far. Apart from this, he has also received 'Best Actor' award from Filmfare 5 times. Amitabh Bachchan was conferred the Dadasaheb Phalke Award on 29th December, 2019 by President Ram Nath Kovind.

6. Amitabh Bachchan is the pride of India. He is rich in versatility. Apart from acting, he has also performed playback songs for many films and has also produced some films as a producer. It is because of his immense success that he is called 'Big B' and 'the great hero of the century'. Amitabh always emphasised that life, time and opportunity do not get repeated. Therefore, we should not lose the courage to succeed even in difficulties.

Questions

Based on your understanding of the passage, answer **any eight** out of the **ten** questions by choosing the correct option.

(i) Which trait of Amitabh's personality helped him in leaving an indelible mark on the Indian cinema?
   (a) Steadfastness
   (b) Irresolution
   (c) Indolence
   (d) Audacity

(ii) A phrase is a small group of words standing together as a conceptual unit.

The writer mentions that Amitabh 'made a distance from politics.'

Select the words from the options that is a correct phrase using 'distance'.
   (a) Beyond walking distance
   (b) Within walking distance
   (c) Off a distance
   (d) Distance coaching

(iii) Select the option that suitably completes the given dialogue as per the context of the passage.

    X. I just want to earn and live my life to the fullest.

    Y. That's why, you are (1) ....

    X. Why do you say that?

    Y. (2) you .... for others.

    (a) (1) so valuable and famous (2) are an antithesis

    (b) (1) so pertinent and gracious (2) are an exemplar

    (c) (1) so selfless and caring (2) are so aggressive

    (d) (1) so competitive and combative (2) are so apathetic

(iv) Which option represents the award that was awarded to Amitabh Bachchan by the President Ram Nath Kovind in the year 2019?

    1. Padma Vibhushan   2. Dadasaheb Phalke

    3. Padma Bhushan   4. Padam Shri

    (a) Only 1   (b) Only 2

    (c) Only 3   (d) Only 4

(v) Select the option that is correct with reference to the given passage.

    (a) Amitabh was just 19 years old when he moved from Allahabad to Bombay (Mumbai) to start his career in films.

    (b) Amitabh's mother was not so opened-minded in nature.

    (c) Amitabh has also received 'Best Actor' award from Filmfare 7 times.

    (d) In 2002, he was awarded the 'Personality of the Year' award by the International Films Academy.

(vi) What is the relationship between (1) and (2)?

    1. He not only strengthened his financial position but also reached a new height of fame and success.

    2. Through the television reality show 'Kaun Banega Crorepati' in 2000, Amitabh Bachchan entered the world of television.

    (a) (2) is the cause of (1)

    (b) (1) and (2) are independent of each other

    (c) (2) elaborates upon the premise of (1)

    (d) (2) sets the stage of (1)

(vii) "He came to be called 'Angry Youngman' due to the performance of a police inspector in this film." Which film and role is being referred to in given line?

    (a) The role of a young policeman dissatisfied with and outspoken against the existing social and political structures in the movie 'Zanjeer'.

    (b) The role of a critic and a protector against existing social and political structures in the movie 'Agneepath'

    (c) The role of a young struggler who helps a woman awaiting surgery with seven other countrymen in the movie 'Saat Hindustani'.

    (d) The role of a young gangster dissatisfied, who helps the people of Ramgarh against existing cruelty in the movie 'Sholay'.

(viii) Which of the following options accurately describes Amitabh Bachchan as 'The Pride of India.'?

    1. Versatile and skillful

    2. Thoughtful and observant

    3. Gracious and Painstaking

    4. Problem solver and caring

    (a) 1 and 3

    (b) 2 and 4

    (c) 3 and 4

    (d) 1 and 2

(ix) Which quote best summarises the writer's description of the famous superstar Amitabh Bachchan as mentioned in the passage?

    (a) Everyone must accept that we will age and age is not always flattering—Amitabh Bachchan

    (b) You won't achieve success by nailing horseshoe outside your door, your feet need horseshoe to achieve success—Amitabh Bachchan

    (c) I've accepted that I was a failure in politics. I was not qualified for the job—Amitabh Bachchan

    (d) Donate and do not talk about it, they say you do nothing for the society; do and talk about it, they say you seek publicity— Amitabh Bachchan

(x) Select the option that clearly indicates the situation before and after 1987, in Amitabh's life.

(a)

Before 1987	After 1987
A superstar in the Indian Film Industry	An MP from Allahabad Lok Sabha

(b)

Before 1987	After 1987
A superstar and MP from Allahabad Lok Sabha	Resigned as an MP and moved away from politics

(c)

Before 1987	After 1987
An MP from Allahabad Lok Sabha	An MP from Rajya Sabha

(d)

Before 1987	After 1987
Won the Filmfare for Best supporting actor	Won the Filmfare for Best Actor

Passage 2

1. The art of living is learnt easily by those who are positive and optimistic. From humble and simple people to great leaders in history, science or literature, we can learn a lot about the art of living, by having a peep into their lives. The daily routines of these great men and women not only reveal their different, may be unique lifestyles but also help us learn certain habits and practices they followed. Here are some; read, enjoy and follow in their footsteps as it suits you.

2. A private workplace always helps. Jane Austen asked that a certain squeaky hinge should never be oiled so that she always had a warning whenever someone was approaching the room where she wrote. William Faulkner, lacking a lock on his study door, detached the doorknob and brought it into the room with him. Mark Twain's family knew better than to breach his study door-they would blow a horn to draw him out. Graham Green went even further, renting a secret office; only his wife knew the address and the telephone number. After all, everyone of us needs a workplace where we can work on our creation uninterruptedly. Equally we need our private space too!

3. A daily walk has always been a source of inspiration. For many artists, a regular stroll was essentially a creative inspiration. Charles Dickens famously took three hour walks every afternoon, and what he observed on them fed directly into his writing. Tchaikovsky made do with a two-hour jaunt but wouldn't return a moment early; convinced that doing so would make him ill. Ludwig van Beethoven took lengthy strolls after lunch, carrying a pencil and paper with him in case inspiration struck. Nineteenth century composer Erik Satie did the same on his long hikes from Paris to the working-class suburb where he lived, stopping under street lamps to jot down ideas that came on his journey; it's rumoured that when those lamps were turned off during the war years, his music declined too. Many great people had limited social life too. One of Simone de Beauvior's close friends puts it this way. "There were no receptions, parties. It was an uncluttered kind of life, a simplicity deliberately constructed so that she could do her work." To Pablo the idea of Sunday was an 'at home day'.

4. The routines of these thinkers are difficult. Perhaps it is because they are so unattainable. The very idea that you can organise your time as you like is out of reach for most of us, so I'll close with a toast to all those who worked with difficulties. Like Francine Prose, who began writing when the school bus picked up her children and stopped when it brought them back; or T.S. Eliot, who found it much easier to write once he had a day job in a bank than he had as a starving poet and even F. Scott Fitzgerald, whose early books were written in his strict schedule as a young military officer. Those days were not as interesting as the nights in Paris that came later, but they were much more productive–and no doubt easier on his liver.

5. Being forced to follow someone else's routine may irritate, but it makes it easier to stay on the path. Whenever we break that trail ourselves or take an easy path of least resistance, perhaps what's most important is that we keep walking.

Questions

Based on your understanding of the passage, answer **any eight** out of the **ten** questions by choosing the correct option.

(i) If the writer was forced to follow someone else's routine, they would feel.
   (a) furious   (b) annoyed
   (c) humered   (d) indifferent

(ii) Metaphor is a figure of speech in which a word or phrase is applied to an object or action to which it is not literally applicable.

   From the given options, choose a phrase from the above passage that can be an example of metaphor.
   (a) that we keep walking   (b) there were no receptions
   (c) close with a toast to   (d) All of these

(iii) Select the option that suitably completes the given dialogue as per the context of the passage.
   X. I don't think I can ever be a great writer like William Faulkner.
   Y. Why do you think like this ? …(1)… .
   X. No, I don't have weird habits and quirks like him.
   Y. …(2)… you just have to give it a try.
   (a) (1) Of course, you can be a good writer like him
       (2) That is true. But what can you do
   (b) (1) You can be better than him
       (2) Yeah, he was a special one
   (c) (1) But, I can see that you are right
       (2) Yeah, you don't have any special mannerism
   (d) (1) Sure, you can be a great writer like him.
       (2) That doesn't really matter

(iv) According to the passage, why did Erik Satie's music decline?
   (a) During the war years, singing and composing music was banned
   (b) His inspiration was lost when the lamps on his streets were turned off
   (c) He was overcome with grief due to the casaulties in war
   (d) He had isolated himself and as a result was driven mad

(v) During which time did Fitzgerald write the most productively?
   (a) when he would be walking during night in Paris
   (b) when he would be drinking
   (c) when he was in Paris
   (d) when he was in the army

(vi) What is the relationship between (1) and (2)?
   (1) The people who are hopeful and have a positive outlook in life can easily learn the art of living.
   (2) A lot can be learnt about a person by looking into their lives.
   (a) (2) is the cause for (1)
   (b) (1) and (2) are independent
   (c) (2) elaborates the problem described in (1)
   (d) (2) sets the stage for (1)

(vii) According to the passage, why did some artists resort to walking?
   (a) It is an exercise
   (b) It was a creative inspiration
   (c) It is essential for improving their health
   (d) It was helpful in interaction with others

(viii) Select the option that lists things that Beethoven carried with himself while walking after lunch.
   (a) pen and paper　　(b) pen and canvas
   (c) pencil and paper　　(d) pencil and canvas

(ix) Which quote best summarises the writer's feelings toward the artists mentioned in the passage?
   (a) Life beats down and crushes the soul and art reminds you that you have one – Stella Adler
   (b) There is no must in art because art is free–Wassily Kandinsky
   (c) Art washed away from the soul the dust of everyday life – Pablo Picasso
   (d) None of the above

(x) Select the option that lists what we can conclude from the text.
   1. All the artists have already learnt the art of living.
   2. If one is hopeful and sanguine, one can learn the art of living.
   3. One should never follow in anyone else's footsteps.
   4. By going on frequent walks, one can become a great artist.
   5. Forcing a person to follow someone else's routine can be irritating.
   (a) 2, 3 and 5　　(b) 2 and 5
   (c) 1, 2 and 4　　(d) 1, 3 and 5

Passage 3

1. Mentioning that "rights and duties are the two sides of the same coin" President Ram Nath Kovind in November, 2019 stressed on the need to perform our duties and create circumstances which would ensure effective protection of rights. Kovind's remark came during a joint sitting on the occasion of the 70th anniversary of the adoption of the Constitution of India organised here in the Central Hall of Parliament.

2. Rights and duties are two sides of the same coin. Our Constitution provides the fundamental right to freedom of speech and expression and it also enjoins upon citizens the duty to safeguard public property and to abjure violence. As per the President Kovind, if someone misconstrues the meaning of the freedom of speech and expression and is about to damage some public property, then another, who prevents him from indulging in such an act of violence and anarchy will be seen as a dutiful citizen.

3. Therefore, the President said, "we need to perform our duties and thereby create circumstances which would ensure effective protection of rights." Addressing Parliamentarians, Kovind said developing the spirit of humanism is also a fundamental duty of citizens and that to serve with compassion towards all, is also inherent in this duty. Mentioning one Muktaben Dagli of Gujarat, the President said: I had the honour of conferring 'Padma Shri' to Dagli at Rashtrapati Bhavan this year. Despite losing her eyesight in her childhood, she devoted her whole life to the welfare of others. She has brightened the lives of many visually impaired girls.

4. "Through her organisation, she has been instilling the light of hope in the lives of numerous blind women from many states of India. Citizens like her truly uphold the ideals of our Constitution. They deserve to be called nation-builders." Kovind suggested that parliamentarians be always 'mindful' of their 'oath and affirmation' and said that serving people should be our foremost priority.

5. "You (MPs) have taken an oath to bear true faith and allegiance to the Constitution of India as established by law and to uphold the sovereignty and integrity of the nation. As the President of India, I too have taken an oath to preserve, protect and defend the Constitution and the law to the best of my ability and devote myself to the service and well-being of the people of India." As citizens and voters expect their representatives to work to solve issues related to their welfare and most of them never get the chance to meet their own MP, he said they, however, have regard for you as the guardians of their hopes and aspirations.

Questions

Based on your understanding of the passage, answer **any eight** out of the **ten** questions by choosing the correct option.

(i) Which need is President Kovind stressed upon during his speech on the occasion of the 70th anniversary of the adoption of the Constitution of India as mentioned in the paragraph 1?
   (a) To perform our duties to uphold the unity and integrity of the nation
   (b) To perform our duties to ensure effective protection of rights
   (c) To perform our duties to ensure the fundamental right to freedom of speech and expression
   (d) To safeguard public property and to abjure violence

(ii) A phrase is a small group of words standing together as a conceptual unit.
   The writer mentions that 'Rights and duties are two sides of the same coin.'
   Select the words from the options that is a correct phrase using 'duty'.
   (a) Under the duty
   (b) Off the call of duty
   (c) Below the call of Duty
   (d) Above and beyond the call of duty

(iii) Select the option that suitably completes the given dialogue as per the context in paragraph 3.
   X: I feel honoured to award you the 'Padma Sri'.
   Y: I wish I could see you (1) ....
   X: You have inspired so many people.
   Y: (2) Today is ....
   (a) (1) with my own eyes giving me this award (2) a historic day in India's calendar
   (b) (1) but I am visually impaired (2) the most memorable day of my life
   (c) (1) so selfless and caring (2) the day when I lost the vision of my eyes
   (d) (1) so gracious and competitive (2) a special day as I have seen you

(iv) Which option represents the kind of audience President Kovind is addressing to on the occasion mentioned in the passage?
   1. Muktaben Pankaj Kumar Dagli
   2. MPs and Parliamentarians
   3. Engineering Students
   4. Medical Students

(a) Only 1 (b) Only 2
(c) Only 3 (d) Only 4

(v) Select the option that is correct with reference to the given passage.
   (a) Muktaben Dagli is a visually impaired social worker who hails from Mumbai.
   (b) Developing the spirit of humanism is also a fundamental duty of citizens.
   (c) Our Constitution provides the fundamental right to chose any religion and faith.
   (d) To protect women and children is also a fundamental duty of citizens.

(vi) What is the relationship between (1) and (2)?
   1. Someone misconstrues the meaning of the freedom of speech and expression and is about to damage some public property.
   2. Another person, who prevents him from indulging in such an act of violence and anarchy will be seen as a dutiful citizen.
   (a) (2) is the cause of (1)
   (b) (1) and (2) are independent of each other
   (c) (1) elaborates upon the premise of (2)
   (d) (1) sets the stage of (2)

(vii) "Citizens like her truly uphold the ideals of our Constitution." What does the Phrase 'uphold the ideals' mean in the context of the passage?
   (a) To give moral support or inspiration to something
   (b) To support an idea or principle
   (c) To support against an opponent
   (d) To be an exemplar or an idol to something

(viii) Which of the following options accurately describes the personality of a 'nation-builder' as described by President Kovind?
   1. Selfless and Benevolent
   2. Thoughtful and Helpful
   3. Kind and Philanthropic
   4. Humanitarian and Liberal
   (a) 1 and 3 (b) 2 and 4 (c) 3 and 4 (d) 1 and 2

(ix) Which quote best summarises the role and duty of our elected representatives as mentioned in the passage?
   (a) Bad officials are the ones elected by good citizens who do not vote —George Jean Nathan
   (b) We have a responsibility as elected officials to do good public policy in the best interest of all the people—Maxine Waters

(c) Voting is fundamental in our democracy. It has yielded enormous returns—Arlen Specter

(d) A politician is a fellow who will lay down your life for his country—Texas Guinan

(x) As mentioned in the passage, our Constitution always emphasises that-

(a) Rights and duties are closely related and cannot be separated from one another. Both go side by side

(b) It is committed to freedom, equality, social justice and some form of national unity

(c) Since state protects and enforces rights, it becomes a mandate for all citizens to be loyal to the state they belong to

(d) We all citizens have taken an oath to bear true faith and allegiance to the Constitution of India as established by law and to uphold the sovereignty and integrity of the nation

Passage 4

1. As a seasoned mountaineer who has been on over 100 expeditions, including seven summits of Mount Everest, I am no stranger to spending long periods of time confined to limited spaces, cut off from the rest of the world. In fact, most recently on my climb of Mount Vinson, the highest peak in Antarctica, what was supposed to be a 7-day expedition turned into a 21-day sojourn trapped in a tent, battling sub-zero temperatures and harsh winds.

2. My experiences have taught me several important skills and life lessons. I have learned to use the solitude and isolation to my advantage, by expanding my knowledge, learning new skills and cultivating hobbies that challenge me. A little over three months ago, our lives came to a sudden halt as we were driven indoors, largely unprepared, in a bid to survive the coronavirus. As the world rapidly defines a new normal, I take this opportunity to share with you some insights that I have gained on how to successfully combat lockdown anxiety and transition into this new way of living.

3. One of the biggest similarities of being on a summit and the current situation with coronavirus is accepting that there are various unknown variables which are not in our control. While it is important to take all precautions to ensure our safety, the most important is to prepare ourselves mentally.

4. When I am in the mountains, I must be willing to let the mountain have control, because we humans are small compared to it. Similarly, with this pandemic we must accept that we might not have all the answers right now, but if we continue to be patient and build mental toughness, we will, as Favre-Leuba aptly puts, conquer this frontier and emerge victorious.

5. Maintaining nutrition and health is of paramount importance, particularly in such times. I do not believe in living like a monk, so joining in on the baking trends and treating yourself occasionally is acceptable. However, we must stick to a healthy diet. Good nutrition not only helps to ensure that we stay fit, but it can also do wonders to energy levels and general psychological well-being.

6. Another important lesson that the mountains have taught me, is to engage in hobbies and keep your brain busy. On my summits, even when I am counting every single ounce that goes into my backpack, I make sure to carry books or a Kindle, in case I am confined to my tent for a while. I am a voracious reader, and this keeps my mind occupied.

Questions

Based on your understanding of the passage, answer **any eight** out of the **ten** questions by choosing the correct option.

(i) Why was the writer's most recent climb of Mount Vinson turned from a 7-day expedition to a 21-day sojourn?

(a) Because of the freezing sub-zero temperatures and severe winds

(b) Because of the avalanche in Antarctica

(c) Because of the sudden lockdown announced during the pandemic

(d) Because of the harsh winds and sudden rainfall

(ii) A phrase is a small group of words standing together as a conceptual unit.

The writer mentions that 'conquer this frontier and emerge victorious.'

Select the words from the options that is a correct phrase using 'victory'.

(a) Under the victory   (b) Pyrrhic victory

(c) Wingless victory   (d) Blue victory

(iii) Select the option that suitably completes the given dialogue as per the context in paragraph 2.

X: We are stuck during this coronavirus lockdown.

Y: We need to be positive (1) ....

X: The people need to focus on mental and physical health.

Y: (2) Let's use ……………… .

(a) (1) We should read good books (2) this lockdown as an opportunity to be healthy

(b) (1) We need to spend time with our family (2) some good sanitizers and masks

(c) (1) We need to fight like a warrior (2) this solitude and isolation to our advantage

(d) (1) and fight like a peacemaker (2) this seclusion to be closer to our nears and dears

(iv) Which option represents the kind of things the writer carries in his backpack during his summits?

1. Books only
2. Books and a Light
3. A torch and a Map
4. Books and compass

(a) Only 1
(b) Only 2
(c) Only 3
(d) Only 4

(v) Select the option that is correct with reference to the given passage.

(a) Maintaining nutrition and health is of trivial importance.

(b) Reading books and engaging in hobbies keeps our mind occupied and busy.

(c) Mount Vinson is the highest peak in Atlanta.

(d) As a seasoned mountaineer, the writer has been on over 100 expeditions, including eight summits of Mount Everest.

(vi) What is the relationship between (1) and (2)?

1. I make sure to carry books or a Kindle, in case I am confined to my tent for a while.
2. I am a voracious reader and this keeps my mind occupied.

(a) (2) is the cause of (1)

(b) (1) and (2) are independent of each other

(c) (2) elaborates upon the premise of (1)

(d) (2) sets the stage of (1)

(vii) "One of the biggest similarities of being on a summit." What does the word 'summit' mean in the context of the passage?

(a) Negotiation
(b) Mountaintop
(c) Conclave
(d) Foundation

(viii) Which of the following options accurately describes the personality of the writer of the passage?

1. Daring and Impudent   2. Adventurous and Gourmet
3. Insatiable and Devoted 4. Voracious and Keen

(a) 1 and 3
(b) 2 and 4
(c) 3 and 4
(d) 1 and 2

(ix) Which quote best summarises the role health and nutrition play in our lives as mentioned in the passage?

(a) Life is a tragedy of nutrition –Arnold Ehret

(b) Exercise is king, nutrition is Queen, put them together and you've got a kingdom–Jack Lalanne

(c) When diet is wrong, medicine is of no use. When diet is correct, medicine is of no need–Ayurvedic proverb

(d) To eat is a necessity, but to eat intelligently is an art –Francois de La Rohefoucould

(x) As mentioned in the passage, the writer says that during the pandemic

(a) It's important to take all precautions to ensure our safety, the most paramount of which is to prepare ourselves mentally

(b) We all need to unite and conquer this pandemic and emerge victorious

(c) We need to take care of all safety measures to protect ourselves from the virus

(d) We all need to focus on good mental and physical health to combat the stress of the lockdown

Passage 5

1. If you have grown up in the capital city which has been plagued by increasing levels of pollution, a breath of fresh air would be a welcome change any time. And if it is accompanied by lush green gardens overlooking your room, all the better. I reveled in this joyous change of scenery, sipping on a fresh filter kaapi, from the balcony of my King room at the Royal Orchid Brindavan Garden in Mysuru.

2. The journey had been arduous, with a change of flights and then, travel by road. And I had been up quite early. But the thought of the piping hot kaapi kept me going. When I finally reached the rather majestic palace, away from the bustle of the main city of Mysuru, I didn't think my weariness would wear off so easily after a refreshing welcome drink. Twelve hours of travel time is rather strenuous after all, and I was sure I'd want to snuggle under the covers for a bit, at least.

3. My fascination with the Southern part of India began during the one year I spent pursuing my higher education in Chennai. I don't say it lightly when I state that I fell in love with the city, the masala dosas, the beach, the people. I couldn't have been more delighted when I was assigned a trip to Mysuru. It was a chance to go back south, to a different location, but I could barely contain my excitement.

4. The Royal Orchid Brindavan Garden, located an hour away from the main city, is often the first choice for locals looking to escape the daily grind, albeit for a few days. Frequented equally by bird-watchers and photographers, the property provides an unmatched view of the gardens as well as the KRS (Krishna Raja Sagar) dam. All the rooms face the gardens, so you can cherish their stunning symmetry from the comfort of your room, with a cup of kaapi in your hands. The heritage property features 24 select spacious rooms with a private balcony. The canopy beds, wooden flooring and the colossal doors, all exude an old-world vintage charm. The property is also equipped with a spa, in case you want to unwind.

5. Mysuru's weather, much like close-by neighbour Bengaluru, is pleasant for most part of the day, the evenings are undeniably better. To further strengthen my belief, a quiet dinner at the open-air Elephant Bar was enough. Over a scrumptious meal, I was told of the many films that had been shot at the property, including massive hits like Linga and KGF.

Questions

Based on your understanding of the passage, answer **any eight** out of the **ten** questions by choosing the correct option.

(i) Which city does the writer originally belong to as mentioned in the passage?
(a) Bangalore   (b) Mumbai
(c) New Delhi   (d) Mysuru

(ii) A phrase is a small group of words standing together as a conceptual unit.

The writer mentions that 'I didn't think my weariness would wear off so easily.'

Select the words from the options that is a correct phrase using 'wear'.
(a) Wear your heart on your sleeves
(b) Wear up
(c) Wear down
(d) Wear too many bands

(iii) Select the option that suitably completes the given dialogue as per the context in paragraph 2.
X: How can I help you Sir?
Y: Please check my passport (1) ....
X: Which place are you visiting?
Y: (2) Going to (2)..................... .
(a) (1) I am excited to fly to South India (2) Mysuru in Bangalore
(b) (1) I am excited to fly to India (2) Visit my hometown
(c) (1) Could you assign me a window seat? (2) South India to my hometown
(d) (1) Hope I can check in easily now (2) visit my friends at Bangalore

(iv) Which option represents the features that attracted the writer towards 'The Royal Orchid Brindavan Garden'?
1. The heritage property features 24 select spacious rooms facing the garden.
2. The rooms overlook the beautiful Brindavan Gardens as well as the KRS dam.
3. The in-house spa offers rejuvenating treatments.
4. It offers indoor and outdoor games with an entertainment zone.
(a) 1 and 2   (b) 2 and 3
(c) 3 and 4   (d) Only 4

(v) Select the option that is correct with reference to the given passage.
(a) Bangalore and Mysore have a pleasant weather only at nights
(b) The writer did his higher education in Bangalore
(c) The writer travelled for less than ten hours to reach the Royal Orchid Brindavan Garden in Mysuru
(d) The writer is fond of drinking filter coffee

(vi) What is the relationship between (1) and (2)?
1. I couldn't have been more delighted when I was assigned a trip to Mysuru.
2. It was a chance to go back to south, to a different location, but I could barely contain my excitement.
(a) (2) is the cause of (1)
(b) (1) and (2) are independent of each other
(c) (1) elaborates upon the premise of (2)
(d) (1) sets the stage of (2)

(vii) "The first choice for locals looking to escape the daily grind, albeit for a few days." What does the word 'albeit' mean in the context of the passage?
(a) Unless   (b) Instead
(c) And   (d) Though

(viii) Which of the following reasons attract the people towards the Royal Orchid Brindavan Garden as described by the writer in the passage?
1. The hotel's courtyard-style coffee shop and Elephant Bar - both offer balcony-views of Brindavan Gardens.
2. It exudes charm and grandeur of the Maharajas era.
3. The hotel features a swimming pool engulfed in greens.
4. Royal Orchid Brindavan Garden and Spa is a 4-hour drive from Bangalore.
(a) Only 1
(b) Only 2
(c) Only 3
(d) Only 4

(ix) Which quote best summarises the writers' description about the love for the South Indian food?

    (a) The body becomes what the foods are, as the spirit becomes what the thoughts are –Kemetic Proverb

    (b) If you don't love South Indian cuisine, you are either an alien or your taste buds are spoiled –An Indian Citizen

    (c) The only thing I like better than talking about food is eating –John Walters

    (d) I've never been in love before. But I can imagine its similar to the feeling you get when you see your waiter arriving with your food –Zach Galifianakis

(x) "Twelve hours of travel time is rather strenuous after all." What does the writer mean to say in this statement?

    (a) His journey has been memorable and comfortable

    (b) His journey was quite hectic and exhausting

    (c) His travel route was very long and gruelling

    (d) His journey was like a marathon and required lots of energy

Passage 6

1. Amomon means 'fragrant spice plant' in Arabic and Hebrew and in Italian, canella means 'little tube'. These are a few of the many names given to the popular spice known as cinnamon. Dating back as far as 2800 BC, Chinese writings describe cinnamon as an important part of the culture, so much so that over the years this spice was traded right up there with silver. Now-a-days we find it in sweetened cereals, baked goods and sprinkled on various foods such as yogurt. Yet, many do not consider its wealth of healing capabilities including the potential as a weight loss remedy.

2. Cinnamon is derived from the inner bark of the cinnamon tree grown and harvested mostly in Sri Lanka but also found in Brazil, Indonesia, Vietnam, China and Burma. After a cinnamon tree grows for about six to eight years it is cut down leaving a stump to allow it to grow again making it a very sustainable practice. It is then stripped from the bark, dried and packaged as sticks for export.

3. Several studies have been published regarding the weight loss properties of cinnamon which include its unique ability to be used for type 2 diabetes which is a disease often resulting from obesity. When eaten, the spice seems to slow down glucose absorption within the intestines while stimulating insulin production. This normalises blood glucose levels which in turn can indirectly decrease weight gain.

4. "The results of a study demonstrate that intake of 1, 3 or 6 g of cinnamon per day reduces serum glucose, triglyceride, LDL cholesterol and total cholesterol in people with type 2 diabetes and suggest that the inclusion of cinnamon in the diet people with type 2 diabetes will reduce risk factors associated with diabetes and cardiovascular diseases."

5. A study from the Department of Family and Consumer Sciences, called "Effect of ground cinnamon on after meal blood glucose level in normal-weight and obese adults" found that cinnamon may be effective in moderating post meal glucose level in normal weight and obese adults.

6. Columbia University nutritionist Tara Ostrowe comments to Reader's Digest on the benefits of this spice : "Cinnamon really is the new skinny food … Scientists already credit cinnamon with helping lower blood sugar concentration and improving insulin sensitivity. When less sugar is stored as fat, this translate into more help for your body when it comes to weight loss".

7. Talk to your doctor about adding cinnamon daily into your healthy diet and exercise program. Add it to your tea, oatmeal, fruit, toast or anything else you can think of, as a small amount will go a long way and potentially assist in your weight loss mission.

Questions

Based on your understanding of the passage, answer **any eight** out of the **ten** questions by choosing the correct option.

(i) According to the passage, cinnamon is mostly grown in which country?

    (a) Brazil   (b) Sri Lanka

    (c) Indonesia   (d) Vietnam

(ii) A collocation is a group of words that often occur together.

The writer says that cinnamon helps in weight loss.

Select the word from the options that correctly collocates with loss.

    (a) Devastating

    (b) Gain

    (c) Problem

    (d) Fattening

(iii) Select the option that suitably completes the given dialogue as per the context of the passage.

X. I have to lose some weight. My weight has increased during this lockdown.

Y. You should ………… (1) …………

X. Why though?

Y. It ……… (2) ………

(a) (1) stop eating so much then (2) will kill you someday

(b) (1) see a nutritionist (2) will be good to get some professional advice

(c) (1) try to eat cinnamon every two-three weeks (2) is very flavourful and will work as a sugar substitute

(d) (1) try to include cinnamon in your food (2) helps in lowering the concentration of sugar in your blood

(iv) Which of the following signboards contains the most appropriate title for the above passage?

(a) Amomon Cures Diabetes

(b) Cinnamon is the Obesity

(c) Cinnamon : The Miracle Spic

(d) Amomon : The Magical Drug

(v) Cinnamon can help reduce the risk of which of the following ailments?

(a) Kidney infections   (b) Type 2 diabetes

(c) Cardiovascular diseases   (d) Both (b) and (c)

(vi) What is the relationship between (1) and (2)?

1. Cinnamon is the new skinny food.

2. Cinnamon reduces the level of sugar in blood.

(a) (2) is the cause for (1)

(b) (1) repeats the situation described in (2)

(c) (2) elaborates the problem described in (1)

(d) (2) sets the stage for (1)

(vii) The writer mentions that "cinnamon may be effective in moderating post meal glucose". By this, he means that

(a) Cinnamon increases the glucose created before eating one's food

(b) Cinnamon eradicates the glucose created after eating one's food

(c) Cinnamon controls the glucose created after eating one's food

(d) Cinnamon controls the glucose created before eating one's food

(viii) Select the option that mentions how long it takes for the cinnamon to be harvested.

(a) 6-18 years

(b) 16-18 years

(c) 6-8 years

(d) It is not grown anymore. It is non-renewable

(ix) Which quote best summarises the writer's feelings about cinnamon?

(a) Anyone who gives you a cinnamon roll fresh out of the oven is a friend for life - Daniel Handler

(b) I really don't think I need buns of steel. I'd be happy with buns of cinnamon - Ellen Degeneres

(c) For something warm, try adding cinnamon sticks and nutmeg to apple cider simmering on the stove - Clinton Kelly

(d) None of the above

(x) Select the option that lists what we can conclude from the text

1. Cinnamon helps in weight loss.

2. Cinnamon consumption can cure diabetes.

3. Cinnamon is described as an important part of culture in China.

4. Cinnamon can be consumed with tea, oatmeal, fruit and toast.

5. Cinnamon is not grown in Sri Lanka anymore.

(a) 1, 2 and 4   (b) 1, 3 and 4

(c) 2, 3 and 5   (d) 2, 3 and 4

Passage 7
May, Bistritz

1. Count Dracula had directed me to go to the Golden Krone Hotel, which I found, to my great delight, to be thoroughly old-fashioned, for, of course, I wanted to see all I could of the ways of the country.

2. I was evidently expected, for when I got near the door I faced a cheery-looking elderly woman in the usual peasant dress ... When I came close she bowed and said, 'The Herr Englishman?'

'Yes,' I said, 'Jonathan Harker.'

3. She smiled and gave some message to an elderly man in white shirtsleeves, who had followed her to the door. He went, but immediately returned with a letter:

4. "My friend - Welcome to the Carpathians. I am anxiously expecting you. Sleep well tonight. At three tomorrow, the diligence will start for Bukovina; a place on it is kept for you. At the Borgo Pass, my carriage will await you and will bring you to me. I trust that your journey from London has been a happy one and that you will enjoy your stay in my beautiful land-Your friend, Dracula." 4 May

5. I found that my landlord had got a letter from the Count, directing him to secure the best place on the coach for me; but on making inquiries as to details he seemed somewhat reticent and pretended that he could not understand my German.

6. This could not be true, because up to then he had understood it perfectly; at least, he answered my questions properly.

7. He and his wife, the old lady who had received me, looked at each other in a frightened sort of way. He mumbled out that the money had been sent in a letter, and that was all he knew. When I asked him if he knew Count Dracula, and could tell me anything of his castle, both he and his wife crossed themselves saying that they knew nothing at all and simply refused to speak further. It was all very mysterious and not by any means comforting. Just before I was leaving, the old lady came up to my room and said in a hysterical way: "Must you go? Oh! Young Herr, must you go?" She was in such an excited state that she seemed to have lost her grip of what German she knew, and mixed it all up with some other language which I did not know at all. I was just able to follow her by asking a number of questions. When I told her that I must go at once and that I was engaged on important business, she asked again:

8. "Do you know what day it is?" I answered that it was the fourth of May.   - *An excerpt from Dracula by Bram Stoke*

Questions

Based on your reading of the passage, answer **any eight** out of the **ten** questions by choosing the correct option.

(i) When the writer reached the Hotel, how did he feel?
(a) absurd
(b) enthusiastic
(c) exasperated
(d) enraged

(ii) Alliteration refers to the occurrence of the same letter or sound at the beginning of adjacent or closely connected words.

From the options given below, choose a phrase from the passage that can be example of alliteration.
(a) Do you know what day it is?
(b) Got a letter from the count
(c) Immediately returned with a letter
(d) None of the above

(iii) Select the option that suitably completes the given dialogue as per the passage.

X : Why are you visiting such a archaic hotel?

Y : ………
(a) Because new things are so corrupted
(b) Because I am also old
(c) Because I want to see the culture of the country
(d) Because you don't like it

(iv) Why did the old lady address the writer as 'Englishman'?
(a) He spoke english fluently
(b) He was from Britain
(c) He loved the United Kingdom
(d) She despised the United kingdom

(v) Did the old couple, especially the woman, want the writer to leave?
(a) Yes, she wanted him gone from her hotel
(b) No, she was stopping him from leaving
(c) yes, she didn't like him from the first day
(d) No, she hated his friend, Dracula

(vi) What is the relationship between (1) and (2)?
1. He went, but immediately returned with a letter.
2. I found that my landlord had got a letter from the count.
(a) (1) contradicts (2)
(b) (2) elaborates upon the premise in (1)
(c) (2) repeats the problem discussed in (1)
(d) (1) is the result of (2)

(vii) What is the social title of the writer's friend, as mentioned in the passage?
(a) Count
(b) Herr
(c) Duke
(d) Crone

(viii) Select the option that lists the language that the old woman was speaking in when she asked the writer if he was really going to leave.
(a) German
(b) English
(c) French
(d) Mixture of many languages

(ix) What did the old couple tell the writer when he asked them details about the count and his castle?
(a) That he and the castle were both scary
(b) That he was very wealthy and the castle was well kept
(c) Both (a) and (b)
(d) Nothing. They refused to speak about it

(x) Select the option that describes the ending of the passage.
(a) climatic
(b) happy
(c) abrupt
(d) enfuriating

Passage 8

1. The present turn of developments with the continuous discounting and dismissing of the opposition and farmer's struggle for justice through the repeal of the three farm laws only suggests that those who are standing in support of the ruling dispensation at the state and the centre are brazenly, and, at times, violently intolerant of the opposition that is being built up around the public's concerns.

2. The language of violence that was allegedly used by the protectors of constitutional rights and was enacted in the Lakhimpur Kheri road rage killing eight people—four of them being the farmers—only shows that those who are active in proposing violent means to crush the opposition and those who are passively endorsing such proposals by maintaining a rather stoic silence over the spate of -violent incidents see no relevance even for the language of pretension and hypocrisy. And what was perceived and what was expressed. Here, it is not necessary to repeat what was promised and what was not delivered by the ruling dispensation. In the local parlance, such discrepancy could be couched in the terminology called 'jumlebaazi'.

3. Arguably, atleast for the time being, this hypocrisy puts the violence on hold. As long as it works for the government, it eliminates the need to resort to more violent options. All those who have been making efforts to expose such 'jumlebazi' or hypocrisy are being accused of being antinational by supporters of the government, and the moral standards that are used for seeking condemnation of the dissenting voices are hardly applied to those who were levelling such accusations against their opponents. Hence, those who have Hypocrisy hinges on the discrepancy between what was promised and what was delivered been calling others as anti-national do not need to prove their nationalist credentials.

4. However, the use of hypocritical language cannot be accelerated beyond a point. The language of hypocrisy loses its relevance on the count that it becomes difficult for the defenders of the government to use such a language to hide something that is unrealistic. The inability to hide something, which is impossible to achieve, needs the mask of 'jumla'. Even the language of jumla becomes inadequate to offer any effective defence to the party in power. False promises given to the people, however, result in grave moral injury through disillusionment for the common people.

5. What, therefore, debunks hypocrisy is the experience of disillusionment that results from sensitive people's capacity to detect the gap between what was promised and what was delivered by the government. When the government finds it extremely difficult to use the language of jumla, then it is compelled to use the strategies that are deployed to deter the -aggrieved sections from expressing their legitimate dissent.

Questions

Based on your understanding of the passage, answer **any eight** out of the **ten** questions by choosing the correct option.

(i) Which hypocrisy is the writer discussing in the following line as mentioned in the paragraph 3.
"Arguably, atleast for the time being, this hypocrisy puts the violence on hold."
(a) To maintain a silence on the violent incidents
(b) To put the protest to an end using violent means
(c) The raged protect against the farm law
(d) To safeguard public property and to abjure violence

(ii) A phrase is a small group of words standing together as a conceptual unit.

The writer mentions 'Stoic silence over the violent incidents.'

Select the words from the options that is a correct phrase using 'silence'.
(a) Dead silence   (b) Silence is silver
(c) Broken silence   (d) Dumb silence

(iii) Select the option that suitably completes the given dialogue as per the context in paragraph 1.
X: We need to protest against the farm's laws.
Y: The protest should not have any violence ...(1)...... .
X: It's going to affect most of the farmers in the country.
Y: Today is ...(2)..... .
(a) (1) It affects the integrity of the nation (2) a historic day in India's calendar
(b) (1) But we all need to unite together (2) the most memorable day of my life
(c) (1) Try to keep the calm (2) the day we have finalized for the meeting betweenthe leaders and protestors
(d) (1) Be patient to wait for the decision (2) a special day the law is going to be amended

(iv) Which option represents the kind of protest the farmers are attempting against the farm laws?
1. Arbitrary and unpredictable
2. Peaceful and non-voilent
3. Tyrannical and hypocrite
4. Ceaseless and defin
(a) Only 1   (b) Only 2
(c) Only 3   (d) Only 4

(v) Select the option that is correct with reference to the given passage.

    (a) In the Lakhimpur Kheri road rage, eight people were killed and six injured

    (b) Most of the opposition parties try to give a helping hand to the aggrieved farmers

    (c) Our government is trying the best to repeal all of the three farm laws

    (d) The inability to hide something that is unachievable needs the mask of 'jumla'

(vi) What is the relationship between (1) and (2)?

    1. Arguably, at least for the time being, this hypocrisy puts the violence on hold.

    2. As long as it works for the government, it eliminates the need to resort to more violent options.

    (a) (2) is the cause of (1)

    (b) (1) and (2) are independent of each other

    (c) (1) elaborates upon the premise of (2)

    (d) (1) sets the stage of (2)

(vii) "False promises given to the people, however, result in grave moral injury through disillusionment for the common people." What does the phase 'grave moral injury' mean in the context of the passage?

    (a) Serious physical injury

    (b) Injury to an individual's moral conscience and values

    (c) To alleviate the confidence of a person

    (d) Fatal moral injury

(viii) Which of the following options accurately describes the Lakhimpur Kheri incident?

    1. Atrocious and Barbarous

    2. Thoughtful and Helpful

    3. Callous and Cold

    4. Sensitive and Complex

    (a) 1 and 3   (b) 2 and 4

    (c) 3 and 4   (d) 1 and 2

(ix) Which quote best summarises the role and notions of the opposition in the context of the protest of farmers as mentioned in the passage?

    (a) The greatest power is not money power, but political power –Walter Annenberg

    (b) Politics is war without bloodshed while war is politics with bloodshed –Mao Zedong

    (c) We live in a world in which politics has replaced philosophy–Martin L. Gross

    (d) Every time you work on a political campaign, half the people hate you. That's how it is –Brit any Kaisar

(x) As mentioned in the passage, "What… debunks hypocrisy is the experience of disillusionment that results from…" By this statement, the writer refers to

    (a) The people's callousness to detect the gap between what was promised and what was delivered by the government

    (b) The people's sensitiveness to detect the gap between what was promised and what was delivered by the government

    (c) The people's capacity to detect the gap between what was promised and what was delivered by the government

    (d) The people's response to detect the gap between what was promised and what was delivered by the government

Passage 9

1. Located in Eastern India along the Hoogly river, Kolkata (formerly known as Calcutta) is often referred to as the cultural capital of India. With the grand colonial architecture, rich traditions, beautiful music and art, this city has a unique character. As a home to esteemed artists like Rabindranath Tagore and Satyajit Ray, among others, the people of this city have a special appreciation for literature as well as cinema. The city also provides an unparalleled religious and cultural experience of Durga Puja each year.

2. 'Durga Durga' echo the united voices of all the ladies in the household as they move towards the pandals for Puja, wishing for a safe journey ahead in life. The sound of intense beats coming from the dhak mixed with the aroma of the dhunuchi lit in every house, park or corner fills the streets of Kolkata. Clad in the most beautiful attires, adorning the heaviest of jewels and thickest of bangles with sindoor and bindis on their temple, the women seem to walk a step ahead of the men today.

3. After all, Durga Puja is the day of the Devi. Nothing but colour and festivity flow through the lanes in the nine days that Maa Durga stays in her basha (house) with her four children, only to be united with her husband Shiva on the tenth day, (also known as Vijayadashami). But does it really end there? The massive grandeur and style of Durga Puja is not restricted to being just a nine-day festival. It houses itself in the hearts of the devotees who utter 'Maa Durga' at the smallest of hiccups in life. The resounding ullu (a high-pitched ululation sound created by striking both cheeks with the tongue, believed to be very auspicious and said to ward off any evil) echoes in the streets of the city long after the Puja is all wrapped up.

4. Celebrated in the month of Ashvin (September – October), Durga Puja (fondly referred to as Puja) is one of the most awaited festivals in India, especially in West Bengal. Even though the weather starts becoming cooler, the air is thick with the warmth radiated by the devotees.

5. The origins of the Devi as a deity are lost in the mists of time. Over time, we find mentions of the Goddess in various texts from the Vedic era and also in the Ramayana and Mahabharata. Even much later, Krittivasi's rendition of Ramayana, composed in the 15th century, speaks of Durga being worshipped with 108 blue lotuses and 108 sacred lamps by Lord Rama before his battle with Ravana. The day that Lord Rama defeated Ravana is celebrated as Dussehra which falls on the tenth day (Dashami) of the Durga Puja.

Questions

Based on your understanding of the passage, answer **any eight** out of the **ten** questions by choosing the correct option.

(i) Which month and festival is the writer discussing in these lines as mentioned in the passage: "Even though the weather starts becoming cooler, the air is thick with the warmth radiated by the devotees."
  (a) The festival of Kali Puja which comes after Kartika.
  (b) The festival of Navaratri which comes in the month of Chaitra.
  (c) The festival of Durga Puja which comes in the Ashvin.
  (d) The festival of Durga Puja which comes in the Vaisakha.

(ii) A phrase is a small group of words standing together as a conceptual unit.

  The writer mentions that 'echoes in the streets of the city long after the puja is all wrapped up.'

  Select the words from the options that is a correct phrase using 'wrap'.
  (a) To keep below wraps   (b) Wrap around
  (c) Wrap in   (d) To wrap the blindfolds

(iii) Select the option that suitably completes the given dialogue as per the context in paragraph II.

  X: Maa Durga has arrived.
  Y: It's our most awaited time of the year (1) ....
  X: I would perform a dhunuchi dance today.
  Y: (2) It ....
  (a) (1) It affects the integrity of the nation (2) would be so nice to watch you dancing
  (b) (1) When we should unite together (2) would be the memorable day of my life
  (c) (1) Try to keep the calm (2) I have practiced it the entire year
  (d) (1) When we eagerly wait to celebrate (2) spreads a nice aroma everywhere

(iv) Which option represents the kind of celebrations that are done during the Durga Puja in West Bengal as mentioned in the passage?
  1. Lighting of dhunuchi and playing of dhak
  2. Colourful sweets and bhog distribution
  3. Burning of the Ravana effigies
  4. Decoration of the idols

(a) Only 1   (b) Only 2
(c) Only 3   (d) Only 4

(v) Select the option that is correct with reference to the given passage.
  (a) Durga puja is a Ten-day festival celebrated across India in the month of Ashvin
  (b) Kolkata (formerly known as Calcutta) is often referred to as the cultural city of palaces India
  (c) Krittivasi's rendition of Ramayana, was composed in the 13th century
  (d) Lord Rama worshipped Durga with 108 blue lotuses and 108 sacred lamps before his battle with Ravana

(vi) What is the relationship between (1) and (2)?
  1. After all, Durga Puja is the day of the Devi.
  2. The origins of the Devi as a deity are lost in the mists of time.
  (a) (2) is the cause of (1)
  (b) (1) and (2) are independent of each other
  (c) (2) elaborates upon the premise of (1)
  (d) (1) sets the stage of (2)

(vii) "Echo the united voices of all the ladies in the household as they move towards the pandals for Puja, wishing for a safe journey ahead in life." What does the phrase 'echo the united voices' refer to the context of the passage?
  (a) To sing songs together in a group moving towards the pandals
  (b) The voices of the ladies that resonates as they chant 'Durga Durga' together
  (c) The sound of footsteps echoed around the hall near the Puja pandals
  (d) The sound of the resounding ullu while worshipping Durga during the Puja in the pandals

(viii) Which of the following options accurately describes the feelings of the people towards the Durga Puja festival?
  1. Love and Mortification
  2. Exuberance and Fervor
  3. Dilemma and Passion
  4. Gusto and Excitement
  (a) 1 and 3
  (b) 2 and 4
  (c) 3 and 4
  (d) 1 and 2

(ix) Select the option that lists what we can conclude from the text.

1. The women population in India is the largest in Kolkata.
2. Durga Puja is the most celebrated festival in Kolkata.
3. The people of Kolkata have a very strong faith and belief in Maa Durga.
4. The festival of Durga Puja coincides with the festival of Dusshera.
5. Maa Durga is the only deity the people of Kolkata believe in.

(a) 1, 2 and 4   (b) 2 and 3
(c) 1 and 5   (d) 3, 4 and 5

(x) What does the statement "The day that Lord Rama defeated Ravana is celebrated as Dussehra which falls on the tenth day (Dashami) of the Durga puja" mean?

(a) Dussehra coincides with the culmination of the nine-day Navratri festival and with the tenth day of the Durga Puja festival
(b) Dussehra marks the victory of good over evil as Lord Rama defeated Ravana on this day
(c) Dussehra marks the end of nine days of Navratri festivity also known as Durga Puja
(d) Dussehra is celebrated on the tenth day or dashami tithi of the shukla paksha of Ashwin month on Hindu calendar

Passage 10

1. Hand washing is as essential as eating food. It is the best way to be healthy and to stay away from various diseases. Soap plays an important role in removing dust, microbes and lubrication, maintaining good health every day. In comparison to the hand sanitizer, soap and water are more efficacious in removing certain microbes, pesticides and other chemical residues that dawdle on hands.

2. Hand sanitizers are more effective in hospitals when hands are in contact with germs, but not soiled or greasy. Other studies also reveal that hand sanitizers might be effective on lubricated hands with certain microbes. When hands are heavily soiled or greasy, for example, after playing outdoor games, gardening, fishing, travelling, executing extension activities such as campaigning and in certain cases, hand sanitizers may not be effective. In such circumstances, washing hands with soap and water is always preferable. Sanitizers cannot remove soil, dirt and grease rather they will make hands sticky, attracting more dirt.

3. According to the Center for Disease Control (CDC), hand hygiene encompasses the cleansing of hands by using soap and water, antiseptic hand washes, antiseptic hand rubs such as Alcohol-Based Hand Sanitizers (ABHS), foams or gels, or surgical hand antisepsis. Hand sanitizers as a disinfectant are in more use today because of its ease of availability, lack of water and time and their proven efficacy in lowering microbial load.

4. A review of research works states that limited literature is available in relation to hand sanitizers and washing hands. As COVID-19 has rapidly spread worldwide, panic buying of sanitizers over the coronavirus pandemic has led to stocking up of sanitizer sprays, gels, and so on, without knowing the effect of the sanitizer.

5. According to the World Health Organisation (WHO), an alcohol based hand sanitizaer is "an alcohol-containing preparation (liquid, gel, or foam) designed for application to the hands to inactivate microorganisms and/or temporarily suppress their growth. Such preparations may contain one or more types of alcohol, other active ingredients with excipients, and humectants." In 1966, hand sanitizers came into existence in healthcare facilities and were popularised significantly in early 1990s.

6. Hand sanitizers can be classified as alcohol-based or alcohol-free. Alcohol-based sanitizers comprise between 60 and 95 percent alcohol in the form of ethanol, isopropanol, or n-propanol. Alcohol have tendency to disseminate proteins and counteract certain micro-organisms at this concentration. Alcohol-free products have a property of disinfectants, such as Benzalkonium Chloride (BAC) or on antimicrobial agents, such as triclosan, which is immediate and purposeful. Several sanitizers comprise emollients (e.g. glycerin) that pacify the skin, thickening agents and provides aroma.

Questions

Based on your understanding of the passage, answer **any eight** out of the **ten** questions by choosing the correct option.

(i) "Such preparations may contain one or more types of alcohol ...." Which preparations is the writer discussing in these lines of the passage?

(a) Foams or gels, or surgical hand antisepsis that are only used in hospitals
(b) Glycerine that pacifies the skin, thickening agents, and provides aroma
(c) Non-Alcohol-based sanitizers used to clean dirt and germs from the hands
(d) An alcohol-containing preparation designed for application to the hands to inactivate microorganisms

(ii) A phrase is a small group of words standing together as a conceptual unit.

The writer mentions that 'coronavirus pandemic has led to stocking up of sanitizer sprays.'

Select the words from the options that is a correct phrase using 'stock'.
(a) Lock and stock
(b) A laughing stock
(c) Stock off
(d) Stock at

(iii) Select the option that suitably completes the given dialogue as per the context in paragraph I.

X: Wash your hands before you eat anything.

Y: But washing the hands only with water is not sufficient, (1)......... .

X: Could I use a sanitizer instead of the soap?

Y: No, (2) ....

(a) (1) As it would not properly clean your hands (2) the sanitizer is not so effective
(b) (1) You need a soap to remove germs and dirt (2) the soap is more effective
(c) (1) You need a sanitizer to remove dirt (2) the soap is not so effective
(d) (1) The plain water would harm your body (2) its not so effective

(iv) Which option best summarises the classification of the hand sanitizers as mentioned in the passage?
1. Aromatic and disinfecting
2. Alcohol-based and alcohol-free
3. Spray and gel-based
4. Ayurvedic and Herbal
(a) Only 1　　　　　(b) Only 2
(c) Only 3　　　　　(d) Only 4

(v) Select the option that is correct with reference to the given passage.
(a) Alcohol-based sanitizers comprise between 80 and 95 percent alcohol in the form of ethanol
(b) In 1986, hand sanitizers came into existence in healthcare facilities
(c) Alcohol-Based Hand sanitizers (ABHS) are better than foams and gels
(d) Hand sanitizers might be effective on lubricated hands with certain microbes

(vi) What is the relationship between (1) and (2)?
1. Sanitizers cannot remove soil, dirt, and grease rather they will make hands sticky, attracting more dirt.
2. Hand sanitizers are more effective in hospitals when hands are in contact with germs, but not soiled or greasy.
(a) (2) is the cause of (1)
(b) (1) and (2) are independent of each other
(c) (1) elaborates upon the premise of (2)
(d) (1) sets the stage of (2)

(vii) "In comparison to the hand sanitizer, soap and water are more efficacious in removing certain microbes, pesticides." What does the term 'efficacious' mean in the context of the passage?
(a) Skillful and valid　　　(b) Dynamic and versed
(c) Productive and effective　(d) Futile and vain

(viii) Which of the following options can accurately describes the hand sanitizers?
1. Fumigant and germicide
2. Decontaminant and sterilizer
3. Germicide and musty
4. Cleanser and antihistamine
(a) 1 and 3　　　　　(b) 2 and 4
(c) 3 and 4　　　　　(d) 1 and 2

(ix) Which quote best summarises the importance of hand sanitization and cleanliness?
(a) One hand washes the other … both hands wash the face –Proverb
(b) Practice good personal hygiene. Wash your hands before you eat. Be aware of good clean water and food sources –James wright
(c) Dirty water does not wash clean –Proverb
(d) We dream of having a clean house–but who actually dreams of doing the cleaning? –Markus Buckingham

(x) As mentioned in the passage, World Health Organisation (WHO) emphasises that
(a) alcohol has tendency to disseminate proteins and counteract certain micro-organisms at this concentration
(b) several sanitizers comprise emollients (e.g., glycerin) that infuriate the skin
(c) hand sanitizers can be classified as alcohol-based or ethynol-free
(d) sanitizers were significantly popularized in the healthcare facilities in the early 1980s

Answers

Passage 1

(i) (a) Amitabh's 'steadfastness' helped him in leaving an indealible mark on the Indian cinema.

(ii) (a) 'Within walking distance' is the correct phrase using 'distance'.

(iii) (b) The phrases in option (b) are appropriate to complete the dialogue.

(iv) (b) Amitabh Bachchan was awarded Dada Saheb Phalke award by the President in 2019.

(v) (d) The sentence in option (d) is correct in reference to the passage.

(vi) (d) Because Amitabh entered the television with 'Kaun Banega Crorepati', he gained financial strength and fame and success. Hence, option (a) is the correct answer.

(vii) (a) He played a role in the movie 'zanjeer' which is being referred to in the given line.

(viii) (a) His versatility, skillfulness, grace and painstaking attributes describes Amitabh as 'the Pride of India'.

(ix) (b) The quote in option (b) best summarises the writer's description of Amitabh Bachchan.

(x) (b) Before 1987, Amitabh was a superstar and an MP from Allahabad Lok Sabha and after 1987, he resigned and moved away from politics.

Passage 2

(i) (b) On being forced to follow someone else' routine, the writer would feel irritated and annoyed.

(ii) (a) The phrase 'that we keep walking' is an example of metaphor.

(iii) (d) The phrase in option (d) are appropriate to complete the dialogue.

(iv) (b) Grik Satie's music declined because his inspiration was lost when the street lamps were turned off during the war.

(v) (d) Fitzgerald wrote the most productively when he was in the army.

(vi) (b) Both the statements listed as (1) and (2) are true but unrelated and independent of each other.

(vii) (b) Some artists resorted to walking as it was a creative inspiration.

(viii) (c) Beethoven carried pen and paper with himself while walking post lunch.

(ix) (d) None of the given quotes is correct.

(x) (b) It can be concluded from the passage that if someone is hopeful and optimistic, they can learn the art of living and forcing someone to follow other's routine can be irritating.

Passage 3

(i) (b) President Kovind stressed upon the need to perform our duties to ensure effective protection of rights.

(ii) (d) The phrase "above and beyond the call of duty" is correct using 'duty'.

(iii) (b) The phrases in option (b) are appropriate to complete the dialogue.

(iv) (b) MPs and Parliamentarians were the audience President Kovind is addressing to on the occasion mentioned in the passage.

(v) (b) The sentence in option (b) is correct in reference to the passage.

(vi) (d) The sentence listed as (1) set the stage for the sentence listed as (2).

(vii) (b) The Phrase 'uphold the ideals' means to support an idea or principle.

(viii) (a) President Kovind described a 'nation-builder' as being selfless, benevolent, kind and philanthropic, according to the passage.

(ix) (b) The quote in option (b) best summarises the role and duty of elected representatives.

(x) (d) Our constitution always emphasise that rights and duties are closely related and cannot be separated from one another.

Passage 4

(i) (a) The writer's most recent climb of Mount Vinson was turned from a 7-day expedition to a 21-day Sojourn because of the freezing sub-zero temperatures and server winds.

(ii) (b) 'Pyrrhic Victory' is the correct phrase using 'victory'.

(iii) (c) The phrases in option (c) are appropriate to complete the dialogue.

(iv) (b) The writer carries books and a light in his backpack during his summits.

(v) (b) The sentence in option (b) is correct in reference to the passage.

(vi) (c) The sentence listed as (2) tells more about that in (1) and thus, elaborates upon the premise of the sentence in (1).

(vii) (b) The word 'summit' means mountaintop.

(viii) (b) Adventurous, gourmet, voracious and keen describes the writer's personality, in the passage.

(ix) (c) The quote in option (c) best summarises the role health and nutrition play in our lives.

(x) (a) The writer says that during the pandemic, it's important to take precautions to ensure safety, most important of which is to prepare ourselves mentally.

Passage 5

(i) (a) The writer originally belonged from New Delhi.

(ii) (a) 'Wear your heart on your sleeves' is the correct phrase using 'wear'.

(iii) (a) The phrases in option (a) is are appropriate to complete the dialogue.

(iv) (a) The property features 24 select spacious rooms facing the garden and the rooms overlook the beautiful Brindavan Gardens as well as the KRS dam. These features attracted the writer towards 'The Royal Orchid Brindavan Garden'.

(v) (d) The sentence in option (d) is correct in reference to the given passage.

(vi) (d) The sentence listed as (1) introduces and sets the stage for that listed as (2).

(vii) (d) The word 'albeit' means through.

(viii) (a) The hotel's courtyard-style coffee shop and elephant Bar attracted the people towards the hotel.

(ix) (b) The quote in option (b) best summarises the writer's description of the love of for South Indian food.

(x) (b) In the given statement, the writer means that his journey was hectic and exhausting.

Passage 6

(i) (b) According to the passage, cinnamon is mostly grown in Sri Lanka.

(ii) (a) The Phrase 'devastating loss' is the correct collocation.

(iii) (d) The Phrases in option (d) are appropriate to complete the dialogue.

(iv) (c) The signboard listed as option (3) contains the most appropriate title for the given passage. The title is 'Cinnamon : the miracle spice'.

(v) (d) Cinnamon can help reduce the risk of type 2 diabetes and cardiovascular disease.

(vi) (a) Cinnamon reduces the level of sugar in blood, which is why, it is called as the new skinny food. Hence, option (a) is the correct answer.

(vii) (c) By the given phrase, the writer means that glucose created after eating food can be controlled by cinnamon.

(viii) (c) It takes around 6-8 years for cinnamon to be harvested, according to the given passage.

(ix) (d) None of the quotes is correct.

(x) (b) The sentence listed as (1), (3) and (4) can be concluded from the given passage.

Passage 7

(i) (b) The writer felt excited and enthusiastic when he reached the hotel.

(ii) (a) The sentence "Do you know what day it is?" is an example of alliteration.

(iii) (c) The phrase given in option (c) is appropriate to complete the dialogue.

(iv) (b) The old woman addressed the writer as 'Englishman' because he was from Britain.

(v) (b) The old woman didn't want him to leave and hence, stopped him too.

(vi) (b) The sentence (1) mentions that the old man went and got the letter which, as mentioned in sentence (2) was sent by the Count. Hence, the sentence (2) elaborates upon the premise in (1).

(vii) (a) The writer's friend, Dracula, has the title 'Count'.

(viii) (b) The woman spoke a mix of German with other languages when she visited the writer to question him.

(ix) (d) Neither of the old couple talked about the count and his castle.

(x) (c) The passage ended abruptly, in the middle of a conversation.

Passage 8

(i) (a) The given line discusses the hypocrisy of maintaining silence in violent incidents.

(ii) (a) 'Dead silence' is the correct phrase with 'silence'.

(iii) (c) The phrases given in option (c) are appropriate to complete the dialogue.

(iv) (a) The protest of the farmers was arbitary and upredictable.

(v) (d) The sentence given in option (d) is correct in reference to the passage.

(vi) (d) The sentence listed as (1) introduces what hypocrisy does the one listed as (2) elaborates upon it. Hence, (1) sets the state of (2) is the correct answer.

(vii) (b) The phrase 'grave' moral injury' means injury to an individual's moral conscience and values.

(viii) (a) The Lakhimpur Kheri incident can be described as atrocious, barbarous, cold and callous.

(ix) (b) The quote given in option (b) best summarises the role and notion of opposition in context of the protests of farmers.

(x) (c) According to the passage, hypocrisy results from the people's capacity to detect the gap between what was promised and what ws delivered.

Passage 9

(i) (c) In the given lines, the writer is discussing the festival of Durga Puja which comes in the month of Ashvin.

(ii) (a) 'Wrap around' is the correct phrase using 'wrap'.

(iii) (a) The phrases given in option (a) are appropriate to complete the dialogue.

(iv) (a) The people of West Bengal light dhunuchi and play dhak during the Durga Puja, according to the passage.

(v) (d) The sentence given in option (d) is correct in reference to the passage.

(vi) (b) Both the statements are true according to the passage but they are not dependent on each other. Hence, option (b) is the correct answer.

(vii) (b) The phrase 'echo the united voices' means that the ladies' voices resonates as they all chant together.

(viii) (b) The people feel exuberance, fervour, gusto and excitement for the festival of Durga Puja.

(ix) (b) It can be concluded from the passage that Durga Puja is the most celebrated festival in Kolkata and that the people there share a strong faith in Maa Durga.

(x) (a) The given sentence means that Dusshera coincides with the tenth day of the Durga Puja festival and the culmination of the nine-day Navratri festival.

Passage 10

(i) (d) The writer is discussing the alchol-containing preparation designed for application to the hands to inactivate microorganisms, in the given line.

(ii) (b) 'A laughing stock' is the correct phrase using 'stock'.

(iii) (b) The phrases given in option (b) are appropriate to complete the dialogue.

(iv) (b) Hand-sanitizers can be classified as alcohol-based and alcohol-free.

(v) (d) The sentence given in option (d) is correct in reference to the passage.

(vi) (c) The sentence listed as (1) elaborates upon the premise of (2).

(vii) (c) The term 'effacious' means productive and effective.

(viii) (d) The hand sanitizers can be described as fumigant, germicide, decontaminant and steritizer.

(ix) (b) The quote given in option (b) best summarises the importance of hand sanitizers and cleanliness.

(x) (a) Who emphasises that alcohol has tendency to disseminate proteins and counteract certain micro-organisms.

Chapter Test (Reading)

1. Read the passage given below.

1. The term 'child labour' is often defined as work that deprives children of their childhood, their potential and their dignity, and that is harmful to physical-mental development. It refers to work that is mentally, physically, socially or morally dangerous and harmful to children, and interferes with their schooling by depriving them of the opportunity to attend school, obliging them to leave school prematurely or requiring them to attempt to combine school attendance with excessively long and heavy work. The statistical figures about child workers in the world have variation because of the differences in defining categories of age group and engagement of children in formal and informal sector.

2. Child labour continues to be a great concern in many parts of the world. In 2008, some 60% of the 215 million boys and girls were estimated to be child labourers worldwide. Major engagement was in agriculture sector, followed by fisheries, aquaculture, livestock and forestry. In addition to work that interferes with schooling and is harmful to personal development, many of these children work in hazardous occupations or activities that are harmful.

   Incidentally, 96% of the child workers are in the developing countries of Africa, Asia and South America. With respect to the child workers between the ages of 5 and 14, Asia makes up 61% of child workers in developing countries, while Africa has 32% and Latin America 7%. Further, while Asia has the highest number of child workers, Africa has the highest prevalence of child labour (40%).

3. The latest global estimates indicate that the number of children in child labour has risen to 160 million worldwide – an increase of 8.4 million children in the last four years. 63 million girls and 97 million boys were in child labour globally at the beginning of 2020, accounting for almost 1 in 10 of all children worldwide.

4. This report warns that global progress to end child labour has stalled for the first time in 20 years. The number of children aged 5 to 17 years in hazardous work – defined as work that is likely to harm their health, safety or morals – has risen by 6.5 million to 79 million since 2016. In sub-Saharan Africa, population growth, extreme poverty, and inadequate social protection measures have led to an additional 16.6 million children in child labour over the past four years.

5. Additional economic shocks and school closures caused by COVID-19 mean that children already in child labour may be working longer hours or under worsening conditions, while many more may be forced into the worst forms of child labour due to job and income losses among vulnerable families. The report warns that globally 9 million additional children are at risk of being pushed into child labour by the end of 2022 as a result of the pandemic.

Based on your understanding of the passage, answer any eight out of the ten questions by choosing the correct answer.

(i) Select the correct inference with reference to the following, 'This report warns that global progress to end child labour has stalled for the first time in 20 years.'
   (a) Due to the efforts of the countries child labour has been controlled to a greater extent.
   (b) Globally the child labour cases have risen due to the delay by the action taken by different governments.
   (c) Globally the child labour cases have fallen due to the strict course of action taken by different governments.
   (d) A majority of children involved in the child labour globally have been rehabilitated to ensure their safety and growth.

(ii) According to the data given in the passage
   (a) Since 2016, around 79 million children aged between 5 to 17 years have been involved more in works dangerous for their health.
   (b) Africa has the highest prevalence of around 50% child labour.
   (c) In sub-Saharan Africa, population growth, extreme poverty, and inadequate social protection measures have pushed around 156 lakh children in child labour.
   (d) India has majority of around 80 lakh children who have been pushed in child labour since 2018.

(iii) Pick the option that lists statements that are NOT TRUE according to the passage.
   1. Due to COVID-19 the children who are already in child labour need to work now under more worsening conditions.
   2. The latest global estimates indicate that the number of children in child labour has risen to 1600 lakh worldwide.
   3. In 2008, some 60% of the 2180 lakh boys and girls were estimated to be child labourers worldwide.
   4. Around 86% of the child workers are in the developing countries of Africa, Asia and South America.
   (a) 1 and 2   (b) 3 and 4
   (c) 2 and 4   (d) 1 and 4

(iv) Based on your reading of the passage, select the counter-argument to the given argument.

   Argument: I am an Indian and belong to a poor family. I have to work for more than 8 hours in a Dhabha to earn money for our family.

(a) India is a secular nation and all religions are equal in the eyes of law.

(b) Data shows that most of the Indian people equally respect all religions.

(c) I do have freedom to choose between my studies and work as my parents are not so rich.

(d) Child labour is strictly prohibited in India.

(v) Select option that displays the correct cause-effect relationship.

Options	Cause	Effect
A	Africa and India have more case of child labour.	Government has taken preventive measures to elevate education.
B	The number of children aged 5 to 17 years work in hazardous conditions.	The health of the children below 17 years is being affected severely.
C	COVID 19 has affected most of the families worldwide.	The families are taking care of their children's education.
D	Child labour is not prohibited in most of the countries.	It's causing more harm to the health of the underprivileged children

(vi) According to passage, which of the statements is one of the reasons why in 2008, some 60% of the 215 million boys and girls were estimated to be child labourers worldwide?

(a) Majority of the children from different countries come from families having uneducated parents.

(b) Additional children were risked into child labour by the end of 2010 due to poverty.

(c) Children already in child labour are working longer hours or under worsening conditions due to the pandemic.

(d) Major engagement of the children was in agriculture sector, followed by fisheries, aquaculture, livestock and forestry.

(vii) As mentioned in the paragraph 1 of the passage, the phrase 'depriving them of the opportunity to attend school' means that

(a) COVID-19 has pushed the children into child labour as most of the heads of the families have lost their jobs.

(b) The lack of good education and teachers is preventing the children from going to schools.

(c) The children are being prevented to go to schools due to demand to work because of poverty.

(d) Children are unable to go to attend schools due to the virtual education after the pandemic.

(viii) Read the two statements given below and select the option that suitably explains them.

1. While Africa has 32% and Latin America 7%.

2. With respect to the child workers between the ages of 5 and 14, Asia makes up 61% of child workers in developing countries.

(a) (1) is the problem and (2) is its solution

(b) (1) is false but (2) correctly explains it

(c) (2) elaborates on (1)

(d) (1) is true and (2) is the reason for (1)

(ix) Find the word similar in meaning to 'deprive' in paragraph 1.

(a) Enrich

(b) Abundance

(c) Impoverish

(d) Indulge

(x) Find the word opposite in meaning to 'vulnerable' in paragraph 5.

(a) Immunity

(b) Feebleness

(c) Perilous

(d) Risky

2. Read the passage given below.

1. You've probably heard the following statistic: Men apply for a job when they meet only 60% of the qualifications, but women apply only if they meet 100% of them. The finding comes from a Hewlett Packard internal report, and has been quoted in Lean In, The Confidence Code and dozens of articles.

It's usually invoked as evidence that women need more confidence. As one Forbes article put it, "Men are confident about their ability at 60%, but women don't feel confident until they've checked off each item on the list." The advice: women need to have more faith in themselves.

2. I was skeptical, because the times I had decided not to apply for a job because I didn't meet all the qualifications, faith in myself wasn't exactly the issue. I suspected I wasn't alone. So, I surveyed over a thousand men and women, predominantly American professionals, and asked them, "If you decided not to apply for a job because you didn't meet all the qualifications, why didn't you apply?"

3. According to the self-report of the respondents, the barrier to applying was not lack of confidence. In fact, for both men and women, "I didn't think I could do the job well" was the least common of all the responses. Only about 10% of women and 12% of men indicated that this was their top reason for not applying.

WHY DIDN'T YOU APPLY FOR THAT JOB? Men and women give their reasons.		
I didn't think they would hire me since I didn't meet the qualifications and I didn't want to waste my time and energy.	Man	46.4%
	Woman	40.6%
I was being respectful of the time and preferences of the person reviewing applications — they had already made clear who they were looking for.	Man	20.0%
	Woman	13.1%
I didn't think they would hire me since I didn't meet the qualifications and I didn't want to put myself out there if I was likely to fail.	Man	12.7%
	Woman	21.6%
I didn't think I could do the job well.	Man	12.4%
	Woman	9.7%
I was following the guidelines about who should apply.	Man	8.5%
	Woman	15.0%

SOURCE TARA SOPHIA MOHR   HOR.ORG

4. Men and women also gave the same most common reason for not applying, and it was by far the most popular, twice as common as any of the others, with 41% of women and 46% of men indicating it was their top reason: "I didn't think they would hire me since I didn't meet the qualifications, and I didn't want to waste my time and energy."

5. In other words, people who weren't applying believed they needed the qualifications not to do the job well, but to be hired in the first place. They thought that the required qualifications were...well, required qualifications. They didn't see the hiring process as one where advocacy, relationships, or a creative approach to framing one's expertise could overcome not having the skills and experiences outlined in the job qualifications.

6. What held them back from applying was not a mistaken perception about themselves, but a mistaken perception about the hiring process. This is critical, because it suggests that if the HP finding speaks to a larger trend, women don't need to try and find that elusive quality, 'confidence,' they just need better information about how hiring processes really work.

Based on your understanding of the passage, answer **any eight** out of the **ten** questions by choosing the correct answer.

(i) Select the correct inference with reference to the following, 'Men apply for a job when they meet only 60% of the qualifications, but women apply only if they meet 100% of the them."

(a) Women are more qualified than men so they are shortlisted easily after applying for any job.

(b) Men are more qualified than women so they are shortlisted easily after applying for any job.

(c) Men are more confident than women while applying for jobs.

(d) Women are more confident than men while applying for jobs.

(ii) According to the figure 1 of the passage, it can be concluded that-

(a) Women are more apprehensive to work on the professional front due to the fear of failure.

(b) Men are more apprehensive to work on the professional front due to the fear of rejection.

(c) Women are more concerned about being qualified before applying for any job.

(d) Men are more concerned about following the guidelines about applying for any job.

(iii) Pick the option that lists statements that are TRUE according to the passage.

1. Hewlett Packard internal report highlights that men need to be more confident than women.

2. HP report indicates that 46% of men do not apply for a job once they know they are not meeting the required qualifications for the same.

3. HP report indicates that 55% of women do not apply for a job once they know they are not meeting the required qualifications for the same.

4. Most of the women lack rich professional background that is very important to boost their confidence.

    (a) 1 and 2   (b) 3 and 4

    (c) 2 and 4   (d) 1 and 4

(iv) Based on your reading of the passage, select the counter-argument to the given argument.
Argument: Only about 10% of women and 12% of men indicated that the lack of confidence was their top reason for not applying for any job.

(a) Women are more qualified and skilled as compared to men.

(b) Most of the women are confident about getting any job as compared to men.

(c) Men always feel hesitant about getting success when they apply for any job.

(d) Men reach to the pinnacle of their professional career very quickly as they are more skilled and confident.

(v) Select option that displays the correct cause-effect relationship.

Options	Cause	Effect
A	I am a housewife and do not wish to apply for a job.	I need to focus more on my strengths and weaknesses.
B	I do not wish to apply for any job which does not match my qualifications.	I may miss the opportunity which matches my other skills.
C	I am working as a manager in my company.	I feel that I am apt for getting good increment this year.
D	My wife is more qualified than me.	I still need to encourage her to do any work with confidence and dedication.

(vi) According to passage, which of the statements is one of the reasons why men and women hold back from applying for any job?

(a) Majority of the men and women believe that good references are necessary before applying.

(b) They believed they needed the qualifications not to do the job well, but to be hired in the first place.

(c) They believed that young and experienced candidates are given more chances.

(d) They do not feel so confident if they lack any skill mentioned in the job description.

(vii) The phrase 'What held them back from applying for the jobs' means

(a) the means and ways that fostered the chances of getting a good job.

(b) what eased their applying processes for getting a job.

(c) what facilitated them in applying for the jobs.

(d) what hampered their ideas to apply for the jobs.

(viii) Read the two statements given below and select the option that suitably explains them.

1. According to the self-report of the respondents, the barrier to applying was lack of confidence.

2. Men and women also gave the same most common reason for not applying for a job which requires good qualifications.

(a) (1) is the problem and (2) is its solution

(b) (1) is false but (2) correctly explains it

(c) (2) elaborates on (1)

(d) (1) is true and (2) is the reason for (1)

(ix) Find the word similar in meaning to 'elusive' in paragraph 6.

(a) Evanescent   (b) Enticing

(c) Inviting   (d) Respecting

(x) Find the word opposite in meaning to 'creative' in paragraph 5.

(a) Imaginative   (b) Imitative

(c) Talented   (d) Fertile

Answers

Passage 1

(i) (b) (ii) (a) (iii) (b) (iv) (d) (v) (b) (vi) (d) (vii) (c) (viii) (c) (ix) (c) (x) (a)

Passage 2

(i) (c) (ii) (a) (iii) (c) (iv) (c) (v) (b) (vi) (b) (vii) (d) (viii) (b) (ix) (a) (x) (b)

Note-Making and Summarisation

In this Chapter...

- Note-Making and Summarisation
- Solved Example
- Chapter Practice

Note-Making and Summarisation

Note making and summarising are crucial skills that helps us not only in academics but also at our work place. Note making essentially involves taking record or noting down the main points of whatever is read or heard.

The purpose of making notes is to filter important information so that they can be referred back to, whenever needed. It is useful as it saves time and energy, and accelerates the process of recalling.

The note making passage is of **5 marks** and consists of two parts

(i) **Making notes of the given passage** This part requires the students to make notes with proper headings, sub headings, abbreviations and symbols indenting and the title. In this part, marks are given for the title, indentation key of abbreviations and the notes.

(ii) **Writing a summary of the passage** This part requires the students to write a summary on the basis of the notes. It should not include any abbreviations. Marks are given for content and expression.

How to make good notes and summary

The following tips will help you in making good notes

1. Keep the notes short and compact so that they are easy to understand.

2. Read the passage carefully and mark the keywords as you read.

3. Organise your notes into heading and sub-heading.

4. The heading must reflect the main theme and sub-heading should point out how the theme is developed.

5. Give a suitable title to the notes and summary.

6. Do not write complete sentences in notes.

7. Follow the proper numbering and indentation while making notes.

8. While making the summary, remember to keep it under the word limit. It should not exceed 1/3rd of the length of the passage.

9. The summary should contain only the main ideas and the supporting details.

10. Remember to make a key of abbreviations and enclose it in a box.

Uses of Abbreviations in Note-Making

Abbreviation helps in writing the information briefly. Following are some of the ways in which you can use abbreviations.

- Use common symbols
- Use acronyms, contractions and short forms wherever possible

Some Common Abbreviations

Abbreviations	Words	Abbreviations	Words
+	Positive, Plus	e.g.	for example
−	Minus, Negative	i.e.	that is
=	equals, is the same as,	w/o	without
≠	does not equal, is not the same as	etc.	etcetera
≈	is approximately equal to	♂♀	male / female
<	is less than, is smaller than	Viz	namely
>	is greater than, is larger than	Asap	as soon as possible
↑	increase, rise, growth	Mr.	Mister
↓	decrease, fall, shrinkage	Mrs.	Mistress
&	and	Dr.	Doctor
*	special, important, notable	Govt.	Government
/	per, each		

A student can also create his/her our abbreviations by using the following method

- First few letters of the word are, sometimes, enough to remember what the abbreviation stands for.

For example
- imp for 'important'
- info for 'information'

- Remove all (or most of) the vowels from the word and use just the key consonants bunched together.

For example
- mngmt for 'management'
- mkt for 'market'
- mktng for 'marketing'
- dvpt for 'development'

Format of Note Making and Summarising

Title :
1. Heading
  1.1 (Sub-heading)
  1.2
  1.3
    1.3.1 (Sub-sub heading)
    1.3.2
2. Heading
  2.1 (Sub-heading)
    2.1.1 (Sub-sub-heading
    2.1.2
  2.2
  2.3
3. Heading
  3.1 (Sub-heading)
    3.1.1 (Sub-sub-heading
    3.1.2
  3.2
  3.3

4. Heading
  4.1 (Sub-heading)
    3.1.1 (Sub-sub-heading
    3.1.2
  4.2
  4.3

Key to Abbreviation here, Full form or meaning of the abbreviation used in notes are written

(1)	—	(6)
(2)	—	(7)
(3)	—	(8)
(4)	—	(9)
(5)	—	(10)

Solved Examples

Read the passages carefully and answer the questions that follow.

Passage

1. The Earth is the fifth largest of the planets in the solar system. It is smaller than the four giant planets i.e., Jupiter, Saturn, Uranus and Neptune, but larger than the three other rocky planets, i.e., Mercury, Mars and Venus. Almost 71 percent of the Earth's surface is covered with water, and most of that is in the oceans. About a fifth of the Earth's atmosphere consists of oxygen, produced by plants.

2. While the Earth orbits the Sun, the planet is simultaneously spinning on an imaginary line called an axis that runs from the North Pole to the South Pole. It takes the Earth 23.934 hours to complete a rotation on its axis and 365.26 days to complete an orbit around the Sun.

3. The Earth's axis of rotation is tilted in relation to the ecliptic plane, an imaginary surface through the planet's orbit around the Sun. This means the Northern and Southern hemispheres will sometimes point toward or away from the Sun depending on the time of year, and this changes the amount of light the hemispheres receive, resulting in different seasons.

4. The Earth's orbit is not a perfect circle, but rather an ellipse, similar to the orbits of all the other planets. Our planet is a bit closer to the Sun in early January and farther away in July, although this variation has a much smaller effect than the heating and cooling caused by the tilt of the Earth's axis.

5. According to scientists, the Earth was formed at the same time as the Sun and other planets, some 4.6 billion years ago, when the solar system coalesced from a giant, rotating cloud of gas and dust known as the 'solar nebula'.

   As the nebula collapsed because of its gravity, it spun faster and flattened into a disk. Most of the material was pulled towards the centre to form the Sun. Other particles within the disk collided and stuck together to form other bodies, including the Earth.

6. The Earth's magnetic field is generated by currents flowing in the Earth's outer core. The magnetic poles are always on the move, with the magnetic North Pole accelerating its northward motion to 40 km annually since tracking began in the 1830s. It will likely exit North America and reach Siberia in a matter of decades.

Questions

(a) On the basis of your reading of the above passage, make notes on it using headings and subheadings. Use recognisable abbreviations (minimum four) and a format you consider suitable. Supply a suitable title to it.

(b) Make a summary of the above passage in about 80 words.

ANSWERS

(a) **Title:** Solar System & The Earth

   1. The Earth – position
      1.1. 5th largest planet
      1.2. size
         1.2.1. < Jupiter, Saturn, Uranus, Neptune
         1.2.2. > Mercury, Mars, Venus
      1.3. 71% water
      1.4. O_2 in 1/5th of atmosphere
   2. Movement on axis
      2.1. runs from NP to SP
      2.2. takes 23.934 hours to rotate
      2.3. 365.26 days to revolve

   3. Elliptical plane
      3.1. imaginary surface
      3.2. results in
         3.2.1. change in amt of light received
         3.2.2. diff seasons
   4. Earth's orbit
      4.1. not a perfect circle
      4.2. ellipse
   5. Solar nebula form
      5.1. formed 4.6 billion yrs ago
      5.2. solar system coalesced
      5.3. collapsed
      5.4. formation of the Sun and the Earth

6. Earth's magnetic poles
   6.1. always on move
   6.2. north pole
      6.2.1. accelerating northward
   6.3. changes in decade
      6.3.1. exit North America
      6.3.2. reach Siberia

Key to Abbreviations		
&	—	and
5th	—	Fifth
O_2	—	Oxygen
NP	—	North Pole
SP	—	South Pole
amt	—	amount

diff	—	different
<	—	less than
>	—	greater than
form	—	formation
yrs	—	years

(b) The Earth is the 5th largest planet in the solar system. 71% of the Earth's surface is covered in water found in the oceans and one fifth of its atmosphere consists of oxygen. It revolves around the Sun in 365.26 days and rotates on its axis in about 23.934 hours. Its rotation in elliptical plane ensures that there are different seasons. As per scientists, earth was formed along with the Sun about 4.6 billion years ago, with the collision of particles. The Earth has a magnetic field because of the two poles which are on constant move.

Chapter Practice

Read the passages carefully and answer the questions that follow.

Passage 1

1. How does television affect our lives? It can be very helpful to people who carefully choose the shows that they watch. Television can increase our knowledge of the outside world, there are high quality programmes that help us understand many fields of study, science, medicine, the different arts and so on. Moreover, television benefits very old people, who can't leave the house, as well as patients in hospitals. It also offers non-native speakers the advantages of daily informal language practice. They can increase their vocabulary and practice listening.

2. On the other hand, there are several serious disadvantages of television. Of course, it provides us with a pleasant way to relax and spend our free time, but in some countries people watch television for an average of six hours or more a day. Many children stare at the TV screen for more hours a day than they spend on anything else, including studying and sleeping. Its clear that TV has a powerful influence on their lives and that its influence is often negative.

3. Recent studies show that after only thirty seconds of television viewing, a person's brain 'relaxes' the same way that it does just before the person falls asleep. Another effect of television on the human brain is that it seems to cause poor concentration. Children who view a lot of television can often concentrate on a subject for only fifteen to twenty minutes. They can pay attention only for the amount of time between commercials.

4. Another disadvantage is that television often causes people to become dissatisfied with their own lives. Real life does not seem so exciting to these people. To many people, television becomes more real than reality and their own lives seem boring. Also many people get upset or depressed when they can't solve problems in real life as quickly as television actors seem to do.

5. Before a child is fourteen years old, he or she views eleven thousand murders on the TV. He or she begins to believe that there is nothing strange about fights, killings and other kinds of violence. Many studies show that people become more violent after viewing certain programmes. They may even do the things that they see in a violent show.

Questions

(a) On the basis of your reading of the above passage, make notes on it using headings and sub-headings. Use recognisable abbreviations (minimum four) and a format you consider suitable. Supply a suitable title to it.

(b) Make a summary of the above passage.

Passage 2

1. Getting enough sleep is as important as taking time out to relax. A good night's sleep is essential for preserving the health of your brain and gives you the best chance to meet the coming day with a razor sharp mind. An average person needs about six to eight hour sleep a night–although it is also true that you need slightly less than this as you grow older-another advantage of aging.

   Stress and sleep deprivation often feed on each other, since stress tends to make it harder for you to fall asleep at night and sleep deprivation in itself causes stress.

2. Eventually, too little sleep can dramatically interfere with the performance of your memory–something you obviously want to prevent. If you are not getting enough sleep, try going to bed 30 to 60 minutes earlier than your normal bed time for a few days. Lie down on the bed and try to relax by dissociating yourself from your daily routine work. This is normally enough to catch up on any sleep deprivation.

3. If, however, you suffer from insomnia, you should seek the advice of your doctor. The chances are it is already affecting your ability to remember and recall information–and if you are struggling to improve your memory scores, this could be at the root of your problem. Prolonged periods of insufficient sleep can deplete your immune system, make you more accident prone and even cause depression–this can also reinforce a more negative outlook on life, which can contribute to your stress burden. The good news is that your memory and mood should automatically improve once you improve your sleep patterns. Tackle your sleep issues and everything else should fall into place.

4. Because stress management is so essential to maximise your brain power, if you are not in the habit of setting aside time to relax. Make it a priority to do so. Even a minute or two of deep breathing can start to work wonders. Often the best ideas and memories can come to you when you are in a state of relaxation, as it is during these moments that your brain stores, processes and plays with the information it has received.

5. Meditation has long been part of religious and spiritual life, specially in Asia. Today, more and more people are adopting it in Western countries too, for its value in developing peace of mind and lowering stress. There is some evidence that regular meditation can have real sleep gain and health benefits, particularly in terms of protecting your brain against aging.

Questions

(a) On the basis of your understanding of the above passage, make notes on it using headings and subheadings. Use recognisable abbreviations (wherever necessary-minimum four) and a format you consider suitable. Also supply an appropriate title to it.

(b) Write a summary of the passage.

Passage 3

1. To live in harmony with oneself and the environment is the wish of every human. However, in modern times greater physical and emotional demands are constantly placed upon many areas of life. More and more people suffer from physical and mental tension such as stress, anxiety, insomnia, and there is an imbalance in physical activity and proper exercise. This is why methods and techniques for the attainment and improvement of health, as well as physical, mental and spiritual harmony, are of great importance, and Yoga meets this requirement.

2. The word 'Yoga' originates from Sanskrit and means "to join, to unite". Yoga exercises have a holistic effect and bring body, mind, consciousness and soul into a balance. In this way, Yoga assists us in coping with everyday demands, problems and worries. Yoga helps to develop a greater understanding of our self, the purpose of life and our relationship with God.

3. On the spiritual path, Yoga leads us to supreme knowledge and eternal bliss in the union of the individual Self with the universal Self. Yoga is that supreme, cosmic principle. It is the light of life, the universal creative consciousness that is always awake and never sleeps; that always was, always is, and always will be.

4. Many thousands of years ago in India, Rishis (wise men and saints) explored nature and the cosmos in their meditations. They discovered the laws of the material and spiritual realms and gained an insight into the connections within the universe. They investigated the cosmic laws, the laws of nature and the elements, life on earth and the powers and energies at work in the universe both in the external world and on a spiritual level. The unity of matter and energy, the origin of the universe and the effects of the elementary powers have been described and explained in the Vedas. Much of this knowledge has been rediscovered and confirmed by modern science.

5. From these experiences and insights a far-reaching and comprehensive system known as 'Yoga' originated and gave us valuable, practical instructions for the body, breathing, concentration, relaxation and meditation. The system "Yoga in Daily Life" is taught worldwide in Yoga Centres, Adult Education Centres, Health Institutions, Fitness and Sports Clubs, Rehabilitation Centres and Health Resorts. It is suitable for all age groups – the name itself indicates that Yoga can be and should be used 'in Daily Life'.

6. The exercise levels have been worked out in consultation with doctors and physiotherapists and can therefore–with observation of the stated rules and precautions–be practised independently at home by anyone. "Yoga in Daily Life" is a holistic system, which means it takes into consideration not only the physical, but also the mental and spiritual aspects. Positive thinking, perseverance, discipline, orientation towards the Supreme, prayer as well as kindness and understanding, form the way to Self-Knowledge and Self-Realisation.

Questions

(a) On the basis of your understanding of the above passage, make notes on it using headings and subheadings. Use recognisable abbreviations (wherever necessary-minimum four) and a format you consider suitable. Also supply an appropriate title to it.

(b) Write a summary of the above passage.

Passage 4

1. Physical education which is commonly part of the curriculum at school level includes training in the development and care of the human body and maintaining physical fitness. Physical education is also about sharpening overall cognitive abilities and motor skills via athletics, exercise and various other physical activities like martial arts and dance.

2. Physical education promotes the importance of inclusion of a regular fitness activity in the routine. This helps the students to maintain their fitness, develop their muscular strength, increase their stamina and thus, stretch their physical abilities to an optimum level. Physical fitness helps them to inculcate the importance of maintaining a healthy body, which in turn keeps them happy and energised.

3. Participating in sports, be it team sports or dual and individual sports, leads to a major boost in self-confidence. The ability to go on the field and perform instills a sense of self-confidence, which is very important for the development of a person's character. Every victory achieved on the field, helps to boost a person's self-confidence. Moreover, the ability to accept defeat on the field and yet believe in your capabilities brings a sense of positive attitude as well.

4. Physical education classes are about participating in the physical fitness and recreation activities, but they are also about learning the overall aspects of physical health. For example, in today's world the problem of obesity, or anaemia and bulimia are common amongst teenagers. Physical education provides an excellent opportunity for teachers to promote the benefits of healthy and nutritious food and warn against the ill effects of junk food. Promoting sound eating practices and guidelines for nutrition are some of the most valuable lessons that can be taught through physical education classes at school level.

5. Participation in team sports and even dual sports helps to imbibe a sense of team spirit amongst the students. While participating in team sports, the children have to function as an entire team, and hence they learn how to organise themselves and function together. This process of team building hones a person's overall communication skills and the ability to get along with different people.

6. Participation in sports and physical education activities help to sharpen the reflexes of the students. It also brings order and discipline to the body movements and helps in development of a sound body posture. The hand-eye coordination improves as well.

7. Physical education classes also include lessons about the importance of personal hygiene and importance of cleanliness. Thus, these classes help the students to know the important hygiene practices that must be practised in order to maintain health and wellness throughout life.

8. Physical education classes help to enhance the overall cognitive abilities of the students, since they get a knowledge of the different kinds of sports and physical activities that they participate in. For example, a person who is participating in a specific type of martial arts class, will also gain knowledge of the origins of the martial arts, and the other practices and historical significance associated with it.

Questions

(a) On the basis of your understanding of the above passage, make notes on it using headings and subheadings. Use recognisable abbreviation (wherever necessary – minimum four) and a format you consider suitable. Also supply an appropriate title to it.

(b) Write a summary of the above passage.

Passage 5

1. Occasional self-medication has always been part of normal behaviour in India. Only during the last hundred years or so has the development of scientific techniques made diagnosis possible. The doctor is now able to follow up the correct diagnosis of many illnesses — with specific treatment of their causes. In many other illnesses of which the cause remains unknown, he is still limited to the treatment of symptoms. The doctor is trained to decide when to treat symptoms only and when to attack the cause. This is the essential difference between medical prescribing and self-medication.

2. The advance of technology has brought about much progress in some fields of medicine, including the development of scientific drug therapy. In many countries public health organisation is improving and people's nutritional standards have risen. Parallel with such beneficial trends are two trends which have an adverse effect: one is the use of high pressure advertising by the pharmaceutical industry which has tended to influence both patients and doctors and has led to the overuse of drugs generally. The other is the emergence of the sedentary society with its faulty ways of life : lack of exercise, overeating, unsuitable eating, insufficient sleep, smoking and drinking. People with disorders arising from faulty habits such as these, as well as from unhappy human relationships, often resort to self-medication and so add the taking of medicines to the list. Advertisers go to great lengths to catch the market.

3. Clever advertising, aimed at chronic sufferers who will try anything because doctors have not been able to cure them, can induce such faith in a preparation, particularly if steeply priced, that it will produce — by suggestion though — a very real effect in some people. Advertisements are also aimed at people suffering from mild complaints such as simple cold and cough which clear up by themselves within a short time.

4. These are the main reasons why laxatives, indigestion-remedies, painkillers, cough mixtures, tonics, vitamins and iron tablets, etc., are found in many households. It is doubtful if taking these things ever improves a person's health, it may even make it worse. Worse, because the preparation may contain unsuitable ingredients; worse because the taker may become dependent on them; worse because they might be taken in excess; worse because they may cause food poisoning and worst of all because symptoms of some serious underlying cause may be masked and therefore medical help may not be sought. Self-diagnosis is a greater danger than self-medication.

Questions

(a) On the basis of your understanding of the above passage, make notes on it using headings and subheadings. Use recognisable abbreviations (wherever necessary – minimum four) and a format you consider suitable. Also supply an appropriate title to it.

(b) Write a summary of the above passage.

Passage 6

Fasting is said to bring a host of benefits, provided it is done under medical supervision. Doctors explain how to go about it. Food is to the body what fuel is to a motor vehicle. It provides energy, helps repair and rejuvenates and confers many other benefits. A lot of research has been done and is being done on fasting. When one fasts, the digestive organs get rest and all body mechanisms are cleansed.

While fasting, the natural process of toxin removal continues, while the entry of new toxins is reduced. The energy usually used for digestion is redirected to immune system and cell growth. Fasting helps you lose excess weight and water, flushes out toxins, helps you heal at greater speed, cleanses your liver, kidney and colon, purifies your blood, clears the eyes and tongue and cleanses the breath.

Another research says fasting, even occasionally, helps in de-toxification. Through fasting we restrict digestive activity and so energy is utilised to cleanse different systems. Fasting improves metabolism, sharpens the senses, calms the mind, improves general immunity, improves concentration and mental clarity. Fasting has tremendous benefits and impacts one at various planes: mental, emotional, physical and spiritual. Specifically it helps in de-toxification, repair and rejuvenation, gives rest to the gastro-intestinal system and promotes mobilisation of excess fat. The crucial point to note is the difference between fasting and starvation. Research suggests there are other benefits of fasting. It slows down the aging process, stress resistance, increased insulin sensitivity and increases lifespan. On the other hand, starvation occurs when the body begins to use protein for fuel and may lead to death in some cases.

Questions

(a) On the basis of your reading of the above passage, make notes on it in points only, using abbreviations wherever necessary (minimum four). Supply a suitable title.

(b) Write a summary of the above passage.

Passage 7

Keeping cities clean is essential for keeping their residents healthy. Our health depends not just on personal hygiene and nutrition, but critically also on how clean we keep our cities and surroundings. The spread of dengue and chikungunya are intimately linked to the deteriorating state of public health conditions in our cities.

The good news is that waste management to keep cities clean is now getting attention through the 'Swachh Bharat Mission'. However, much of the attention begins and stops with the brooms and the dustbins, extending at most to the collection and transportation of the mixed waste to some distant or not so distant place, preferably out of sight. The challenge of processing and treating the different streams of solid waste, and safe disposal of the residuals in scientific landfills, has received much less attention in municipal solid waste management than is expected from a health point of view.

One of the problems is that instead of focusing on waste management for health, we have got sidetracked into "waste for energy". If only we were to begin by not mixing the biodegradable component of solid waste (close to 60 percent of the total) in our cities with the dry waste, and instead use this stream of waste for composting and producing a gas called methane.

City compost from biodegradable waste provides an alternative to farmyard manure (like cow-dung). It provides an opportunity to simultaneously clean up our cities and help improve agricultural productivity and quality of the soil. Organic manure or compost plays a very important role as a supplement to chemical fertilisers in enriching the nutrient-deficient soils. City compost can be the new player in the field.

Benefits of compost on the farm are well-known. The water holding capacity of the soil which uses compost helps with drought-proofing, and the requirement of less water per crop is a welcome feature for a water-stressed future. By making the soil porous, use of compost also makes roots stronger and resistant to pests and decay. Farmers using compost, therefore, need less quantity of pesticides. There is also evidence to suggest that horticulture crops grown with compost have better flavour, size, colour and shelf-life.

City compost has the additional advantage of being weed-free unlike farmyard manure which brings with it the seeds of undigested grasses and requires a substantial additional labour cost for weeding as the crops grow. City compost is also rich in organic carbon, and our soils are short in this. Farmers clearly recognise the value of city compost. If city waste was composted before making it available to the farmers for applying to the soil, cities would be cleaned up and the fields around them would be much more productive.

Quite apart from cleaning up the cities of biodegradable waste, this would be a major and sustainable contribution to improving the health of our soil without further damage by excessive chemical inputs. What a marvellous change from waste to health!

The good news is that some states are regularly laying plastic roads. Plastic roads will not only withstand future monsoon damage but will also solve a city's problem of disposing of non-recyclable plastic. It is clear that if the mountains of waste from our cities were to be recycled into road construction material, it would tackle the problem of managing waste while freeing up scarce land.

Questions

(a) On the basis of your understanding of the above passage, make notes on it using headings and sub-headings. Use recognisable abbreviations wherever necessary (minimum four) and a format you consider suitable. Also supply an appropriate title to it.

(b) Write a summary of the above passage.

Passage 8

1. There are two types of diabetes, insulin dependent and non-insulin dependent. 90-95% of the estimated 13-14 million people in the United States with diabetes have non-insulin dependent, or type II diabetes. Because this type of diabetes usually begins in adults over the age of 40 and is most common after the age of 55, it used to be called 'adult onset diabetes', its symptoms often develop gradually and are hard to identify at first; therefore nearly half of all the people with diabetes do not know it. So, someone who has developed Type II diabetes may feel tired or ill without knowing why. This can be particularly dangerous because untreated diabetes can cause damage to the heart, blood vessels, eyes, kidneys and nerves. While the causes, short term effects, and treatments of the two types of diabetes differ, both types can cause long term health problems.

2. Most importantly, both types affect the body's ability to use digested food for energy. Diabetes does not interfere with digestion, but it does prevent the body from using an important product of digestion, 'glucose', for energy. After a meal, the normal digestive system breaks some food down into glucose. The blood carries the glucose or sugar throughout the body, causing blood glucose levels to rise. In response to this, insulin is released into the blood stream and signals the body tissues to metabolise or burn the glucose for fuel, which causes blood glucose levels to return to normal. The glucose that the body does not use is stored in the liver, muscle or fat.

3. In both types of diabetes, the normal function of glands is affected. A gland called pancreas makes insulin. In people with insulin-dependent diabetes, the pancreas does not produce insulin at all. People with non-insulin dependent diabetes usually produce some insulin in their pancreas but their body tissues do not metabolise the glucose property, a condition known as insulin resistance.

4. There's no cure for diabetes yet. However, there are ways to get relief from its symptoms. Foods that are rich in carbohydrates break down into glucose during digestion, causing blood glucose to rise. Also studies have shown that cooked foods raise blood glucose higher than raw, unpeeled foods. So, we should eat such uncooked whole grain foods.

Questions

(a) On the basis of your reading of the above passage, make notes on it using headings and sub-headings. Use recognisable abbreviations wherever necessary (minimum four). Also supply an appropriate title to it.

(b) Write a summary of the above passage.

Passage 9

The most alarming of man's assaults upon the environment is the contamination of air, earth, rivers and sea with lethal materials. This pollution is for the most part irrevocable; the chain of evil it initiates is for the most part irreversible. In this contamination of the environment, chemicals are the sinister partners of radiation in changing the very nature of the world; radiation released through nuclear explosions into the air comes to the earth in rain, lodges into the soil, enters the grass, or corn or wheat grown there, and reaches the bones of a human being, there to remain until his death. Similarly, chemicals sprayed on crops lie long in soil, entering living organisms, passing from one to another in a chain of poisoning and death. Or they pass by underground streams until they emerge and combine into new forms that kill vegetation, sicken cattle, and harm those who drink from once pure wells.

It took hundreds of millions of years to produce the life that now inhabits the earth and reached a state of adjustment and balance with its surroundings. The environment contains elements that were hostile as well as supporting. Even within the light of the sun there are short-wave radiations with power to injure. Given time, life has adjusted and a balance reached. For time is the essential ingredient, but in the modern world there is no time. The rapidity of change and the speed with which new situations are created follow the heedless pace of man rather than the deliberate pace of nature. Radiation is no longer the bombardment of cosmic rays; it is now the unnatural creation of man's tampering with the atom.

The chemicals to which life is asked to make adjustments are no longer merely calcium and silica and copper and all the rest of the minerals washed out of the rocks and carried in the rivers to the sea; they are the synthetic creations of man's inventive mind, brewed in his laboratories, and having no counterparts in nature.

Questions

(a) On the basis of your understanding of the above passage make notes on it using headings and sub-headings. Use recognisable abbreviations (wherever necessary-minimum four) and a format you consider suitable. Also supply an appropriate title to it.

(b) Write a summary of the above passage.

Passage 10

The Great Wall of China was built to link existing fortifications into a united defense system and better keep invading Mongol tribes out of China. It is the largest man-made monument ever to have been built and it is said that it is the only one visible from space. Thousands of people must have given their lives to build this huge construction.

The Great Wall of China is a series of towers made of stone, brick, earth, wood and other materials, generally built along an East-to-West line across the historical Northern borders of China to protect the Chinese states and empires against the raids and invasions of the various nomadic groups of the Eurasian Steppe. Several walls were being built as early as the 7th century BCE; these, later joined together and made bigger and stronger, are now collectively referred to as the Great Wall. Especially famous is the wall built (220-206 BCE) by Qin Shi Huang, the first Emperor of China. Little of that wall remains. Since then, the Great Wall has on and off been rebuilt, maintained and enhanced; the majority of the existing wall is from the Ming Dynasty (1368-1644).

Other purposes of the Great Wall have included border controls, allowing the imposition of duties on goods transported along the Silk Road, regulation or encouragement of trade and the control of immigration and emigration. Furthermore, the defensive characteristics of the Great Wall were enhanced by the construction of watch towers, troop barracks, garrison stations, signaling capabilities through the means of smoke or fire and the fact that the path of the Great Wall also served as a transportation corridor.

The Great Wall stretches from Dandong in the East to Lop Lake in the West, along an arc that roughly delineates the Southern edge of Inner Mongolia. A comprehensive archaeological survey, using advanced technologies, has concluded that the Ming walls measure 8,850 km. This is made up of 6,259 km sections of actual wall, 359 km of trenches and 2,232 km of natural defensive barriers such as hills and rivers. Another archaeological survey found that the entire wall with all of its branches measures out to be 21,196 km.

King Zheng of Qin conquered the last of his opponents and unified China as the First Emperor of the Qin dynasty ("Qin Shi Huang") in 221 BCE. Intending to impose centralised rule and prevent the resurgence of feudal lords, he ordered the destruction of some sections of the walls, however, he ordered building of new walls to connect the remaining fortifications along the empire's Northern frontier. Transporting the large quantity of materials required for construction was difficult, so builders always tried to use local resources. Stones from the mountains were used over mountain ranges, while earth was used for construction in the plains. The Great Wall concept was revived under the Ming dynasty in the 14th century, to gain a clear upper hand over the Mongolian tribes.

Questions

(a) On the basis of your reading of the above passage, make notes on it, using headings and subheadings. Use recognisable abbreviations (wherever necessary, minimum four) and a format you consider suitable. Also supply an appropriate title to it.

(b) Write a summary of the passage.

Passage 11

People tend to amass possessions, sometimes without being aware of doing so. They can have a delightful surprise when they find something useful which they did not know they owned. Those who never have to change houses become indiscriminate collectors of what can only be described as clutter. They leave unwanted objects in drawers, cupboards and attics for years in the belief that they may one day need them. Old people also accumulate belongings for two other reasons, lack of physical and mental energy, and sentiment. Things owned for a long time are full of associations with the past, perhaps with the relatives who are dead, and so they gradually acquire a sentimental value.

Some things are collected deliberately in an attempt to avoid wastage. Among these are string and brown paper, kept by thrifty people when a parcel has been opened. Collecting small items can be a mania. A lady cuts out from newspapers sketches of model clothes that she would like to buy if she had money. As she is not rich, the chances are that she will never be able to afford such purchases. It is a harmless habit, but it litters up her desk.

Collecting as a serious hobby is quite different and has many advantages. It provides relaxation for leisure hours, as just looking at one's treasure is always a joy. One doesn't have to go out for amusement as the collection is housed at home. Whatever it consists of-stamps, records, first editions of books, China–there is always something to do in connection with it, from finding the right place for the latest addition to verifying facts in reference books. This hobby educates one not only in the chosen subject, but also in general matters which have some bearing on it. There are other benefits also. One gets to meet like-minded collectors to get advice, compare notes, exchange articles, to show off one's latest find. So one's circle of friends grows- Soon the hobby leads to travelling, perhaps a meeting in another town, possibly a trip abroad in search of a rare specimen, for collectors are not confined to one country.

Over the years one may well become an authority on one's hobby and will probably be asked to give informal talks to little gatherings and then, if successful, to larger audiences.

Questions

(a) On the basis of your understanding of the above passage, make notes on it using headings and sub-headings. Use recognisable abbreviations (wherever necessary-minimum four) and a format you consider suitable. Also supply an appropriate title to it.

(b) Write a summary of the passage.

Passage 12

It is surprising that sometimes we don't listen to what people say to us. We hear them, but we don't listen to them. I was curious to know how hearing is different from listening. I had thought both were synonyms, but gradually, I realised there is a big difference between the two words.

Hearing is a physical phenomenon. Whenever somebody speaks, the sound waves generated reach you, and you definitely hear whatever is said to you. However, even if you hear something, it doesn't always mean that you actually understand whatever is being said. Paying attention to whatever you hear means you are really listening. Consciously using your mind to understand whatever is being said is listening.

Diving deeper, I found that listening is not only hearing with attention, but is much more than that. Listening is hearing with full attention, and applying our mind. Most of the time, we listen to someone, but our minds are full of needless chatter and there doesn't seem to be enough space to accommodate what is being spoken. We come up with a lot of prejudices and preconceived notions about the speaker or the subject on which he is talking. We pretend to listen to the speaker, but deep inside, we sit in judgement and are dying to pronounce right or wrong, true or false, yes or no. Sometimes, we even come prepared with a negative mindset of proving the speaker wrong. Even if the speaker says nothing harmful, we are ready to pounce on him with our own version of things.

What we should ideally do is listen first with full awareness. Once, we have done that, we can decide whether we want to make a judgement or not. Once we do that, communication will be perfect and our interpersonal relationship will become so much better. Listening well doesn't mean one has to say the right thing at the right moment. In fact, sometimes if words are left unspoken, there is a feeling of tension and negativity. Therefore, it is better to speak out your mind, but do so with awareness after listening to the speaker with full concentration.

Let's look at this in another way. When you really listen, you imbibe not only what is being spoken, but you also understand what is not spoken as well. Most of the time we don't really listen even to people who really matter to us. That's how misunderstandings grow among families, husbands and wives, brothers and sisters.

Questions

(a) On the basis of your reading of the above passage, make notes on it, using headings and sub-headings. Use recognisable abbreviations (wherever necessary—minimum four) and a format you consider suitable. Also supply an appropriate title to it.

(b) Write a summary of the passage.

Passage 13

Although stupidity is commonly defined as 'a lack of normal intelligence', stupid behaviour is not the behaviour of a person lacking in intelligence but the behaviour of a person not using good judgement or sense. In fact, stupidity comes from the Latin word that means 'senseless'. Therefore, stupidity can be defined as the behaviour of a person of normal intelligence who acts in a particular situation as if he or she isn't very bright. Stupidity exists at three levels of seriousness.

First is the simple, relatively harmless level. Behaviour at this level is often amusing.

It is humorous when someone places the food from a fast food restaurant on the roof of the car while unlocking the door and then drives away with the food still on the roof. We call this absent-minded. The person's good sense or intelligence was temporarily absent. At this level, other than passing inconvenience or embarrassment, no one is injured by the stupid behaviour.

The second type-serious stupidity-is more dangerous. Practical jokes such as putting sugar in the salt shakers are at this level.

The intention is humorous, but there is a chance of harm. Irresponsible advice given to others is also serious stupidity. An example is the person who plays psychiatrist on the basis of an introductory psychology course or doing a TV program on psychiatry. The intention may be to help, but if the victim really needs psychiatric help, an amateur will only worsen the situation.

Even worse is the third kind of stupidity. Kind people, who would never injure another living being, stupidly throw away a box of six-week-old kittens along a country road. Lacking the heart to kill the poor things, they sentence them to almost certain death from wild animals, infections, exposure or the wheels of a passing vehicle.

Yet, they are able to tell themselves that 'they will find nice homes' or 'animals can get along in the wild'. Another example of this kind of stupidity is the successful local businessman who tries to have as many office affairs as he can get away with. He risks the loss of his business and his home. He fails to see that what he is doing is wrong. His is the true moral stupidity of a person not willing to think about the results of his actions or take responsibility for them. The common defence of a person guilty of stupidity is – 'But I didn't think.....''! 'This, however, is not a proper excuse, especially when serious or harmful stupidity is involved.

Questions

(a) On the basis of your reading of the above passage, make notes on it using headings and sub-headings. Use recognisable abbreviations, wherever necessary. Also supply an appropriate title to it.

(b) Write a summary of the above passage.

ANSWERS

PASSAGE 1

(a) **Title** How Television Affects Lives

  1. Positive impacts of television
    1.1 increase our knowledge
    1.2 entrtnmnt for old people and patients who cannot leave house
    1.3 daily lang practice for non-native speakers
  2. Negative impacts of television
    2.1 people spend more than reqd time on tv
    2.2 affects studying and sleeping of children
    2.3 decreases concntrtn in children
  3. Impact on Real life
    3.1 exciting reel life causes dissatisfaction in real life
    3.2 results in deprsn
    3.3 real life seems boring
  4. Promotes violence
    4.1 fights, killings look to be a part of everyday life
    4.2 before turng fourteen, a child has viewed thousands of murders on TV
    4.3 violent tendencies increase
    4.4 imitation of violent show may cause problm

Key to Abbreviations		
entrtnmnt	—	entertainment
lang	—	language
reqd	—	required
concntrtn	—	concentration
deprsn	—	depression
turng	—	turning
problm	—	problem

(b) Television can be both beneficial and harmful for us. If we choose wisely it helps in increasing knowledge, entertains old people and patients and provides language practice to non-native speakers. But it has its own disadvantages too.

People, especially children, spend more time on TV than required. Thus, they lose concentration power. People start believing in reel life making their real life look boring. This increases depression. TV also promotes violence. People often end up imitating violence they see on TV.

PASSAGE 2

(a) **Title** Sleep is essential

1. Importance of Slp
   - 1.1. preserves health
   - 1.2. sharpens brain & mind
   - 1.3. six to eight hrs slp–a must
2. Impact of Slp Deprivation
   - 2.1. stress
   - 2.2. memory loss
3. Insomnia
   - 3.1. affects ability to recall / remember
   - 3.2. depletes immune sys
   - 3.3. makes one accident prone
   - 3.4. causes depression
     - 3.4.1 dev –ve outlook
     - 3.4.2 increases stress burden
4. Stress management works wonders
   - 4.1. essential for brain power
   - 4.2. uplifts mood, sharpens mmry
   - 4.3. brain relaxes, stores info
5. Meditation
   - 5.1 devs peace of mind
   - 5.2 lowers stress
   - 5.3 protects brain against aging

Key to Abbreviations		
slp	—	sleep
hrs	—	hours
–ve	—	negative
sys	—	system
dev/devs	—	develops
mmry	—	memory
info	—	information

(b) A good night's sleep is essential to preserve brain health. Six to eight hours of sleep is required at night. Sleep deprivation causes stress and affects memory. To prevent this, go to bed 30 to 60 minutes earlier than normal with no thoughts in mind. If you have insomnia, you will struggle to sleep. Make stress management your priority, as it is essential for maximising brain power. Regain sleep through meditation, as it helps sleep gain and protects the brain against aging.

PASSAGE 3

(a) **Title** Yoga

1. Wish of every human
   - 1.1. harmony of oneself with envnmt
   - 1.2. phy and emo demand
   - 1.3. free from phy & mental tension
   - 1.4. an imbalance in phy act & prop exer
2. Yoga
   - 2.1. its meaning – to join & unite
   - 2.2. its impact–holistically on mind, body and soul
   - 2.3. its practice–at home following rules
   - 2.4. worldwide & for all age gps
3. Meditation by Rishis 1000s of yrs ago
   - 3.1. elements, nature & cosmos
   - 3.2. laws of nature & souls
   - 3.3. life on earth, power of energy
4. Ways for self knldg
   - 4.1. +ve thinking
   - 4.2. discipline
   - 4.3. prayer & kindness
5. Yoga in daily life
   - 5.1. yoga centres
   - 5.2. adult education clubs
   - 5.3. fitness & sports clubs
   - 5.4. a holistic system

Key to Abbreviations		
envnmt	—	environment
phy	—	physical
emo	—	emotional
act	—	activity
&	—	and
exer	—	exercise
gps	—	groups
yrs	—	years
knldg	—	knowledge
+ve	—	positive
prop	—	proper

(b) Today, people face greater physical and mental problems in their daily lives. These problems are related to lack of physical, mental and spiritual harmony. Yoga helps bridge this gap. 'Yoga' originated from Sanskrit and means 'to join' or 'to unite'. Yoga exercises brings body, mind, consciousness and soul into a balance. This, in a way, helps us to tackle various problems that afflict us in our day-to-day life. The practice of Yoga has been prevalent since ancient times as prescribed in the Vedas. "Yoga in daily life" provides practical instructions for the body, breathing, concentration, relaxation and meditation. Yoga paves the way from self-knowledge to self-realisation.

PASSAGE 4

(a) **Title Importance of Physical Education**

1. Phy Ed-part of crclm
   - 1.1. dvlpt & care of human body
   - 1.2. sharpens cgntv abilities & motor skills
   - 1.3. maintains physical fitness
2. Benefits
   - 2.1. enhances physical abilities
     - 2.1.1. maintains personal hygiene & cleanliness
     - 2.1.2. dvlps muscular strengths
     - 2.1.3. increases stamina
   - 2.2. Character Building
     - 2.2.1. boost in self-confidence
     - 2.2.2. ability to accept defeat
     - 2.2.3. positive attitude
     - 2.2.4. belief in one's capabilities

2.3. Other Benefits
    2.3.1. overcomes obesity, anaemia, bulimia
    2.3.2. warns against ill effects of junk food
    2.3.3. promotes sound eating habits
    2.3.4. hones comm skills
    2.3.5. sharpens reflexes
3. Participation in team spirits
    3.1. inculcates team spirit
    3.2. learn to work together, to be organised & cooperative
4. Other lessons learnt
    4.1. imp of personal hygiene
    4.2. maintaining health and wellness
    4.3. knowledge of diff sports
    4.4. Origin and hist significance of games

Key to Abbreviations		
crclm	—	curriculum
dvlpt	—	development
cgntv	—	cognitive
&	—	and
dvlps	—	develops
hist	—	historical
comm	—	communication
imp	—	importance
diff	—	different

(b) Physical education is part of the curriculum in school. It gives training in development and care of the human body and maintaining physical fitness. It is important for a child because it benefits the child in physical aspects as well as in improving mental fitness and social well-being. It develops team skills, a sportsman's spirit and soft skills such as good communication.

It promotes healthy eating and living and discourages consumption of junk food. It also helps in improving cognitive skills and hand-body coordination. It helps us to know the origin and history of different art forms and skills, thus improving our knowledge.

PASSAGE 5

(a) **Title** Self-Medication
1. Self-medication
    1.1. Part of normal living—last 100 yrs
    1.2. Advance in diagnostic technology
    1.3. Doc required – diagnosis & treatment of disease
2. Self-medication differs from medical prescription
    2.1. Technological Advmnt in medicine
    2.2. Drug therapy
    2.3. Improvement in public health organisations
    2.4. Increase in nutritional standards
3. Emrgng trends with advrs effects
    3.1. Advertising
        3.1.1. Influences patients and doctors
        3.1.2. Led to overuse of drugs
    3.2. Sedentary lifestyle
        3.2.1. lack of exercise

        3.2.2. overeating
        3.2.3. unsuitable eating
        3.2.4. insufficient sleep
        3.2.5. smoking & drinking
    3.3. Clever advertising by pharmaceutical companies
4. Take advantage of people's need
    4.1. Chronic sufferers
    4.2. Ppl will try anything
5. Dangers of self-medication
    5.1. Preparation of some drugs contains unsuitable ingredients
    5.2. Taker becomes dependent
    5.3. Taker consumes medicine in excess
    5.4. Preparations may cause food poisoning
    5.5. Real cause of illness gets suppressed or untreated

Key to Abbreviations		
Yrs	—	Years
Advmnt	—	Advancement
Doc	—	Doctor
Emrgng	—	Emerging
Advrs	—	adverse
Ppl	—	People

(b) Self-medication is part of normal living. Medicinal experts are required for diagnosis and treatment of diseases according to symptoms and causes. The development of drug therapy and improvement in public health organisations as well as nutritional standards have helped progress in medicinal science. Excessive advertising by pharmaceutical companies and emergence of the sedentary society are two counter trends. Self-medication is dangerous as the preparation may be toxic or contain unsuitable ingredients; the user becomes dependent and consumes medicine in excess. Self-diagnosis is worse than self-medication.

PASSAGE 6

(a) **Title** Fasting
1. Benefits
    1.1. provides energy
    1.2. helps repair/ rejuvenates
    1.3. digestive organs get rest
    1.4. all body mech cleansed
    1.5. entry of new toxins is redcd
    1.6. energy redirected to immune systm & cell growth
    1.7. helps lose excess wt & H_2O
    1.8. flushes out toxins
    1.9. helps heal at greater speed
    1.10. cleanses
        1.10.1. liver
        1.10.2. kidney
        1.10.3. colon
        1.10.4. blood
        1.10.5. eyes
        1.10.6. tongue
        1.10.7. breath

2. Other benefits
   2.1. helps in de-toxification
   2.2. improves metabolism
   2.3. sharpens
      2.3.1. senses
      2.3.2. mind
      2.3.3. cncntrtn
      2.3.4. mental faculties
3. Difference b/w fasting & starvation
   3.1. Fasting
      3.1.1. slows down aging process
      3.1.2. slow down stress resistance
      3.1.3. increased insulin sensitivity
      3.1.4. increases life span
   3.2. Starvation
      3.2.1. begins when body uses protein as fuel

Key to Abbreviations		
wt	—	weight
H_2O	—	water
/	—	or
b/w	—	between
&	—	and
Cncntrtn	—	concentration
Redcd	—	reduced
systm	—	system

(b) Fasting has various benefits if it is done under medical supervision. According to research, it detoxifies the body, cleanses different systems, improves metabolism and general immunity and provides benefits at the mental, emotional, physical and spiritual planes. It is wrong to mistake fasting for starvation. If starvation continues, the body consumes glucose from the liver, muscles and the protein content of the body and ultimately, death can occur.

PASSAGE 7

(a) **Title** Some Facts on Waste Management
1. Reasons for keeping cities clean
   1.1. to keep the residents healthy
   1.2. health depends on
      1.2.1. personal cleanliness
      1.2.2. cleanliness of city
   1.3. to prevent spread of dengue and chikun
   1.4. to prevent deterioration of public health conditions in cities
2. Reasons for waste management
   2.1 helps keep cities clean
   2.2 being promoted through SBM
   2.3 earlier began and stopped with brooms and dustbin
   2.4 to sensitize imp of waste separation
3. Challenges of waste management
   3.1 has received less attn
   3.2 focus only on waste management for energy
   3.3 no focus on W.M. for health
   3.4 biodegradable being mixed with solid waste
   3.5 processing & treatment of solid waste
   3.6 safe disposal of residuals in scientific landfills

4. Benefits of org manure
   4.1 supplement of chem fertilisers
   4.2 drought-proofing
   4.3 makes roots stronger
   4.4 free
   4.5 rich in org Carbon
   4.6 requires less water
5. Benefits of city compost
   5.1 weed-free
   5.2 more productive fields
   5.3 chemical inputs avoided
   5.4 less labour cost
6. Benefits of plastic roads
   6.1 withstand monsoon damage
   6.2 solve city problem of plastic disposal
   6.3 free lands from dumping waste

Key to Abbreviations		
Chikun	—	chikungunya
SBM	—	Swachh Bharat Mission
attn	—	attention
imp	—	importance
&	—	and
Chem	—	chemical
Org	—	organic
W.M.	—	waste management

(b) Keeping cities clean is important for keeping their residents healthy. Spread of diseases like dengue and chikungunya is linked to unclean surroundings. Swachh Bharat Mission is a waste management initiative by the government. But, the attention begins and stops with the brooms and the dustbins. Solid waste management has not been given much attention.

The policy of 'waste for energy' should be adopted. It means that biodegradable waste should not be mixed with dry waste. City compost from biodegradable waste is an alternative to farmyard manure. It does a dual job of cleaning the cities and improving the productivity of the soil. Compost has a great water-holding capacity.

By making the soil porous, the roots will become stronger and will need less quantity of pesticides. It is also weed free and is rich in carbon content, which our soil lacks. But the good news is, some states are regularly laying plastic roads. These will withstand future monsoons and solve the problem of non-recyclable plastic. Also, the problem of managing waste will be tackled and scarce land will be freed.

PASSAGE 8

(a) **Title** Facts about Diabetes
1. Types of diabetes
   1.1. insulin dpndnt
   1.2. non-insulin dpndnt
2. Non-insulin dpndnt–facts
   2.1. also clld Type II diabetes
   2.2. begins by 40 years
   2.3. cmmn after 55 years

2.4. earlier clld adult onset diabetes
2.5. smptms
    2.5.1. dvlps gradually
    2.5.2. hard to identify at 1st
    2.5.3. 1/2 affected unaware
    2.5.4. feeling of tiredness/illness
2.6. results: damage to
    2.6.1. heart
    2.6.2. blood vessels
    2.6.3. eyes
    2.6.4. kidneys
    2.6.5. nerves
    2.6.6. health
3. Process of food digestion in body
  3.1. food broken into glucose
  3.2. glucose carried thru body-by-blood
  3.3. causes blood glucose levels to rise
  3.4. insulin released into blood stream
  3.5. signals body tissues to metabolise glucose for fuel
  3.6. blood glucose levels return to normal
  3.7. excess glucose stored in liver/muscle/fat
4. Function of Pancreas
  4.1. produces insulin
  4.2. insulin not produced in insulin-dependent diabetes
  4.3. some insulin produced in non-insulin dependent diabetes
    4.3.1. body tissues do not metabolise glucose
    4.3.2. known as insulin resistance
5. Remedies
  5.1. no cure yet
  5.2. only relief possible
    5.2.1. avoid food rich in carbohydrates
    5.2.2. avoid cooked food
    5.2.3. eat raw, unpeeled food
    5.2.4. eat uncooked, whole grain food

Key to Abbreviations		
Dpndnt	—	dependent
Clld	—	called
cmmn	—	common
Smptms	—	symptoms
dvlps	—	develops
ll	—	two
Yrs	—	years
1st	—	first
1/2	—	half
thru	—	through

(b) There are two types of diabetes- insulin dependent and non-insulin dependent. The non-insulin dependent is also called type II diabetes and most common after 55 years. It develops gradually and is hard to identify. People who suffer have a feeling of tiredness. It damages the heart, blood vessels, eyes, kidneys, nerves   and overall health. Both type of diabetes affect the process of food digestion in body wherein excess glucose stored in liver.

Pancreas produces insulin but it is not produced in insulin-dependent diabetes while some insulin is produced in non-insulin dependent diabetes. There is no cure for this disease yet. One can get only relief possible like avoiding food rich in carbohydrates, eating raw and unpeeled food etc.

PASSAGE 9

(a) **Title** Man's Assault on Environment
1. Contaminants of Envn
  1.1. Where
    1.1.1. air
    1.1.2. earth
    1.1.3. rivers & seas
  1.2. Features
    1.2.1. irreversible
    1.2.2. irrevocable
2. Role of Man
  2.1. tampering atoms- creating radiation
  2.2. creating synthetic material causing chemical pollution
3. Nuclear Pollutants
  3.1. rad released through nuc explosions
  3.2. enter earth thru rain
  3.3. enter grass and crops
  3.4. reach human bones
4. Chemicals Pollutants
  4.1. sprayed on crops
  4.2. enter liv org
  4.3. kill vegetation
  4.4. sicken cattle
  4.5. harm those drinking from wells

Key to Abbreviations		
Envn	—	environment
rad	—	radiation
nuc	—	nuclear
thru	—	through
liv	—	Living
org	—	organism

(b) Our Environment is slowly being destroyed by human as they are contaminating their surroundings with lethal materials. This contamination brings irrevocable and irreversible changes in the environment. The main culprit of this is the chemicals along with the harmful nuclear radiations. We are exposed to them through a 'poison and death chain'. The chemicals enter the soil through rain or repeated sprinkling on crops and enter our body. The environment has been exposed to these difficulties always.

PASSAGE 10

(a) **Title** The Great Wall of China
1. Introduction
  1.1. lgst man made monument
  1.2. only one visible from outer space
  1.3. many gave their lives for its cnstrtn
2. Physical description
  2.1. series of towers
  2.2. made of local materials like

      2.2.1 stones
      2.2.2 bricks
      2.2.3 Earth
      2.2.4 wood
   2.3. blt from Dandong in East to Lop Lake in West
   2.4. svrl walls being built in 7th century BC
3. Purpose of Great Wall
   3.1. prtcd Chinese states and empire against raids
   3.2. rgltn and encrgmt of trade
   3.3. cntrld
      3.3.1. immigration
      3.3.2. emigration

Key to Abbreviations		
lgst	—	largest
encrgmt	—	encouragement
cnstrtn	—	construction
blt	—	built
svrl	—	several
prtcd	—	protected
cntrld	—	controlled
rgltn	—	regulation

(b) The Great Wall of China is the largest man-made monument ever built and is the only one visible from outer space. It was constructed with a series of towers using local materials like stones, bricks, earth and wood. It was built from Dandong in the East to Lop Lake in the West. Its purpose was to protect the Chinese states and empire against raids, control the border and immigration as well as emigration, enable imposition of duties on goods as well as regulating and encouraging trade.

PASSAGE 11

(a) **Title** Collecting : A Hobby
   1. Rsns
      1.1. a delightful surprise
      1.2. old people lack energy
         1.2.1. phy
         1.2.2. mental
      1.3. stmtl values
      1.4. mania
   2. Advtgs
      2.1. avoid wstg
      2.2. saves money
      2.3. provides
         2.3.1. rlxtn
         2.3.2. joy
         2.3.3. amsmt
      2.4. educational value
   3. Other Benefits
      3.1. meet like-minded collectors to
         3.1.1. advise
         3.1.2. compare notes
         3.1.3. exch articles
         3.1.4. show off latest find
      3.2. socialise / make friends

   3.3. become an authority

Key to Abbreviations		
rsns	—	reasons
stmtl	—	sentimental
wstg	—	wastage
advtgs	—	advantages
rlxtn	—	relaxation
amsmt	—	amusement
phy	—	physical
exch	—	exchange
/	—	or

(b) People have various reasons for collecting things. Some do it for sentimental reasons, while others are simply lacking energy. People who don't change houses become collectors of unwanted objects, leading to a clutter. However, collecting as a hobby has many benefits. It helps in getting educated about the subject, avoids wastage and saves money. It also provides relaxation, joy and amusement. Because of this hobby we meet like minded people who advise, compare, exchange and show off. It is a great way of making friends and socialising.

PASSAGE 12

(a) **Title** Hearing v/s Listening
   1. Hrg and lstg are different
      (a) Hrg
         (i) Phscl phenomenon   (ii) Undstdg not necessary
      (b) Lstg
         (i) Paying attention   (ii) Aplg mind to undsd
         (iii) Avoiding distractions
   2. Undstdg marred due to
      (a)   prejudices & preconceived notions
      (b)   judging lstd words
      (c)   –ve mindset
      (d)   having own version
   3. Ideal lstr
      (a)   fully aware
      (b)   proper communication
      (c)   better interpersonal relationship
      (d)   speaks out their mind
   4. What is real lstg
      (a)   Imbibe & undsd unspoken words also
      (b)   misunderstandings in family if not lstg

Key to Abbreviations		
hrg	—	Hearing
phscl	—	Physical
undstdg	—	Understanding
lstg	—	Listening
aplg	—	Applying
undsd	—	Understand
&	—	and
lstd	—	Listened
–ve	—	Negative
lstr	—	Listener
undstdg	—	Understanding

(b) Hearing is just a physical phenomenon, while listening is much more. Effective listening means paying attention, consciously applying one's mind to what is said and avoiding distractions. Prejudices and preconceived notions mar understanding. One may be judging the words spoken, having a negative mindset or have one's own version of what is said. The ideal listener communicates effectively by being fully aware and speaking his mind. They imbibe and understand even what is left unspoken. Not listening causes misunderstandings in families.

PASSAGE 13

(a) **Title** Facts about Stupidity

1. Def. of Stupidity
   1.1. common def
       1.1.1 lack of nrml int
       1.1.2 bhvr without good judgement
   1.2. author def
       1.2.1 bhvr of nrml int
       1.2.2 has three levels
2. Level of stupidity
   2.1 1st level
   2.1.1 simple
       2.1.2 relatively harmless
       2.1.3 often amusing
       2.1.4 abset minded
       2.1.5 no one injured
   2.2 2nd level
       2.2.1 more dangerous
       2.2.2 practical Jokes
       2.2.3 int hmrs but chance of harm
   2.3 3rd level
       2.3.1 worst
       2.3.2 moral stupidity
       2.3.3 unwilling to take resp

Key to Abbreviations		
def	—	Definition
nrml	—	normal
int	—	intention
bhvr	—	behaviour
hmrs	—	humorous
resp	—	responsibility
1st	—	first
2nd	—	second
3rd	—	third

(b) Stupidity is not a behaviour of a person without intelligence, but behaviour not using good judgement or sense. Stupidity exists at three levels of seriousness. The first level is simple and relatively harmless. It is called as absent-minded behaviour. It only causes inconvenience or embarrassment. The second level of stupidity can cause harm. Practical jokes and irresponsible advice are at this level. The third level is moral stupidity, which is harmful. At this level, one does not take responsibility for one's actions.

Read the passages carefully and answer the questions that follows.

Passage 1

Smoking is the major cause of mortality, with bronchogenic carcinoma of the lung, and is one of the factors causing death due to malignancies of larynx, oral cavity, oesophagus, bladder, kidney, pancreas, stomach and uterine cervix, as well as coronary heart diseases. Nicotine is the major substance present in the smoke that causes physical dependence. The additives do produce damage to the body. For instance, ammonia can result in a hundred-fold increase in the ability of nicotine to enter into the smoke.

Levulinic acid, added to cigarettes to mask the harsh taste of the nicotine, can increase the binding of nicotine to brain receptors, which increases the 'kick' of nicotine. Smoke from the burning end of a cigarette contains over 4000 chemicals and 40 cancer-causing chemicals, also known as carcinogens. It has long been known that tobacco smoke is cancer-causing.

The lungs of smokers collect an annual deposit of one to one-and-a-half pounds of the gooey black material. The invisible gas phase of cigarette smoke contains nitrogen, oxygen and toxic gases like carbon monoxide, formaldehyde, hydrogen cyanide and nitrogen oxides. These gases are poisonous and in many cases interfere with the body's ability to transport oxygen. Like many carcinogenic compounds, these gases can act as tumour promoters or tumour initiators by acting directly on the genetic make-up of cells of the body, leading to the development of cancer. During smoking, within the first 8 - 10 seconds, nicotine is absorbed through the lungs and quickly moved into the bloodstream and circulated throughout the brain. Nicotine can also enter the bloodstream through the mucous membranes that line the mouth (if tobacco is chewed) or nose (if snuff is used) and even through the skin.

Our brain is made up of billions of nerve cells. They communicate with each other by chemical messengers called neuro-transmitters. Nicotine is one of the most powerful nerve poisons and binds stereo-selectively to nicotinic receptors located in the brain, autonomic ganglia, the medulla and neuro-muscular junctions. Located throughout the brain, they play a critical role in cognitive processes and memory.

The nicotine molecule is shaped like a neuro-transmitter called acetylcholine which is involved in many functions including muscle movement, breathing, heart-rate, learning and memory. Nicotine, because of the similar structure with acetylcholine when it gets into the brain, attaches itself to acetylcholine sites and produces a toxic effect. In high concentrations, nicotine is more deadly. In fact one drop of purified nicotine on the tongue will kill a person. It has been used as a pesticide for centuries.

Recent research studies suggest that acute nicotine administration would result in increased dopamine release from the brain, producing perceptions of pleasure and happiness, increased energy and motivation, increased alertness, as well as an increased feeling of vigour during the early phase of smoking.

However, notwithstanding these superficial effects, research shows that the relationship between smoking and memory loss is strongest in people who smoke more than 20 cigarettes each day and this is not specific to the socio-economic status, gender or a range of associated medical conditions. Smoking may speed up age-related memory loss, but the details are not yet clear. Some studies suggest that repeated exposure to high nicotinic smoke related to the 'brain-wiring' is nothing but neuron-biochemistry that deals with complex interaction among genetic experience and bio-chemistry of brain-cells.

Questions

(a) On the basis of your reading of the given passage make notes on it using headings and sub-headings. Use recognisable abbreviations wherever necessary. Supply an appropriate title to it.

(b) Write a summary of the given passage.

Passage 2

Here are some questions to ponder. Do you know why a certain film star received an arsenal of weapons from a gangster terrorist? Do you know why witnesses who turn hostile do not get prosecuted for either perjury or wasting police time, or both? Do you know why it takes a decade or longer to try a criminal case in India? Have you ever thought through any solutions to these problems? If you haven't, it might be because of the type of education you received!

Most of us reluctantly accept the way things are because we have been educated to be accepting. We are not educated to be openly critical. We are not educated to argue, protest or confront. The British made no bones about it: in their schools we were educated to accept given values and ways of doing things. We were trained to be loyal servants to the status quo.

Most of us oldies were subjected to the traditional approach to learning that focused on mastery of content, with little emphasis on the development of analytical skills and the nurturing of inquiring attitudes. We were the receivers of information and the teacher was the dispenser. The passivity encouraged by teachers was typified by one of my principals who implored all the girls to be like 'limpid water in a crystal vase'.

These days I am kept very busy by schools that are running teacher-training courses to introduce the 'inquiry approach' to learning. Unlike traditional learning, this approach is focused on using and learning content as a means to develop information-processing and problem-solving skills. This system is more student-centred, with the teacher as a facilitator of learning. There is more emphasis on 'how we come to know' and less on 'what we know'. Students are more involved in the construction of knowledge through active analysis and investigation. They are encouraged to ask questions, and give opinions and share what they know. They are encouraged to criticise and argue and confront conventional wisdom.

At the moment, this new approach is restricted to only a few schools. However, this year the ability to critically analyse has been introduced as part of the CBSE school syllabus. It is a small start, but it is a move towards introducing thinking skills into all of our schools. It is the start of a big change. Our government and bureaucracy are full of old, well-educated people of a traditionalist background, who also see, read and hear the news reports about hostile witnesses, gangsters and film stars and murders by politician's sons. Like us, they find them outrageous, but they don't know how to change things.

Critical analysis, change management and innovation were not part of their schooling, and in adult life they have not become freely critical, outspoken analysts capable of applying the fruits of their analysis to increasingly complex problems.

We often come across the shortcomings of our government, judiciary and media. With very little effort, these shortcomings will become a thing of the past. But they will be a long time coming. Not because our 'leaders' and societal managers are unfeeling, immoral, self-seekers; but because they were educated and excelled in consulting a textbook and regurgitating someone else's opinion and knowledge. As the newly educated might say, we can expect the same for a long time to come.

Questions

(a) On the basis of your reading of the above passage make notes on it using headings and sub-headings. Use recognisable abbreviations wherever necessary. Supply an appropriate title to it.

(b) Write a summary of the above passage.

Passage 3

A republic is essentially a nation-state in which supreme political power vests in the people and in elected representatives given a mandate to govern by those people. Most importantly, this is the principal point of difference from a monarchy-republics have an elected or nominated head of state, usually a President, not a hereditary monarch. In effect, all sovereignty, power and authority in a republic are vested in the people.

The word 'republic' is derived from the Latin phrase 'res publica', meaning 'a public thing'. Ancient Romans used this to describe the wellspring of their governance system for their city-state by about 500 BC. Inspired by notions of Athenian democracy, Rome's republic was a noble experiment. The inscription 'SPQR', emblazoned on all Roman standards and public buildings, expanded to 'The Senate and People of Rome'. It touted to the world that Roman political power was vested in a great many, not concentrated in one ruler or family.

Rome's republican tryst, sustained by public elections and classical debate, lasted until Julius Caesar seized control in 44 BC. Being succeeded by his wily nephew, Augustus, who founded a famous empire that lasted a while longer, consigned the republican ideal to the dustbin of the world. Rome took much of its republican template from Greece. In particular, from Athens, most luminous of ancient Greece's many city-states. The notion of moving political power away from an individual to the masses sprang from the need to safeguard the new notion of personal and individual freedom. It meant citizens would willingly join any battle to safeguard this freedom from any aggressor. But it was a troubled ideal.

Athens ran on slave labour and democracy became limited to narrower sections as time went by. Tyranny and mob rule reared their ugly heads; Athenian imperialism overstretched the city-state so much so that even Plato and Aristotle, in effect, argued for enlightened oligarchies in their political philosophy.

Besides the many obvious fruits of the Renaissance and Reformation, Europe's two most epochal events in the second millennium, the republican ideal owes much to Niccolo Machiavelli and John Locke. Machiavelli, a 15th century Italian statesman-writer, located sovereignty in a collective exercise of power.

The governed would guide actions of their ideal governor, he argued forcefully. Little wonder that Rousseau later referred to Machiavelli's 'The Prince' as a handbook for Republicans.

The rise of England's parliament soon after injected a strong republican element into its body politic. Modern liberalism, which sprang from Locke's work, did the same in most of the western world.

Two revolutions, one decade and two continents apart, brought forth two republican models the world still looks to: the American in 1776 and the French in 1789. The first saw England lose its earliest colony. Monarchy was sternly repudiated and the ideas behind the Declaration of Independence exploded onto the Western world as a serious alternative whose time had come.

The declaration laid the basis for much republican-democratic ideation. The US's new Constitution firmly located power with the people by stating that government derived their just powers from the consent of the governed.

The French Revolution brought French monarchy, and all its attendant power structures, to a violent end, sending shockwaves through European kingdoms. The new republic's bloody convulsions and military campaigns for liberty, equality, and national self-aggrandisement spread the spirit of revolution. Even under Napoleon Bonaparte, France would flirt with monarchy again but remained firmly democratic and republican in spirit ever after.

Questions

(a) On the basis of your reading of the above passage make notes on it using headings and sub-headings. Use recognisable abbreviations wherever necessary. Supply an appropriate title to it.

(b) Write a summary of the above passage..

CHAPTER 01

Posters

In this Chapter...

- Types of Posters
- Sample Posters
- Chapter Practice

A poster is a very useful means of making an announcement or appeal, issuing a notice, advertising a product or bringing about awareness on any issue of public interest. Essentially a very brief communication with a powerful visual and message, a poster is always prepared with a particular target audience in mind. It very clearly mentions the theme or the topic, the schedule of an event and the occasion for it. The poster should be clear in communicating the intended message in an easily readable manner. It has to be captivating, attractive and persuasive so as to influence a large number of people.

They are extensively used by NGO's, political parties, government departments, etc.

Types of Posters

There are two types of posters

A. For Awareness of a Social Problem

- Details associated with the theme
- Solution to the problem
- Effect of the problem
- Any additional useful information

B. For an Event

- Name of the event
- Date/ time/ venue
- Highlights of the event
- Purpose
- Entry tickets/ passes
- Any other relevant information

Points to be Kept in Mind

- A poster is designed to be put up at a public place, so it should be designed in such a way that it **catches the attention** of the passers by.
- A poster should have **bigger/ bold/ capital letters** because it is read by the public from a distance.
- A poster should not have any **extra** or **irrelevant matter**.
- A poster can be made more catchy by using **phrases**, **slogans** and **attractive language**.
- Always put a poster in a box.
- Remember not to use any short forms or slangs.
- Always fit the poster on one page.

Sample Posters

1. You are the Director of National Agriculture Organisation, Jaipur. You have to make the people all over Rajasthan state aware of the necessity of conserving water and also how to do it. Design a suitable poster to be inserted in the newspapers as well as to be put up at prominent places in the towns of Rajasthan.

SAVE WATER - SAVE LIFE!

Water is the Essence of Life

Water Level Going Low
Dangerously Year by Year

Apply

Rain-Water Harvesting

- Don't let rain-water run waste.
- Preserve it in tanks and ponds.
- Save this gift of nature for the coming generation.

Issued by : National Agriculture Organisation, Rajasthan

2. You are the Marketing Manager of Starbucks Coffee Products Company. To promote the sales of 'Starbucks Coffee', you have to planned an event for three days giving offers on several varieties of coffee. To Design a suitable poster detailing the vast variety of Starbucks coffee available in restaurants all over India.

3. Incidents of Road- rage are increasing day by day. Draft a poster on behalf of Delhi Traffic Police on Road Safety tips.

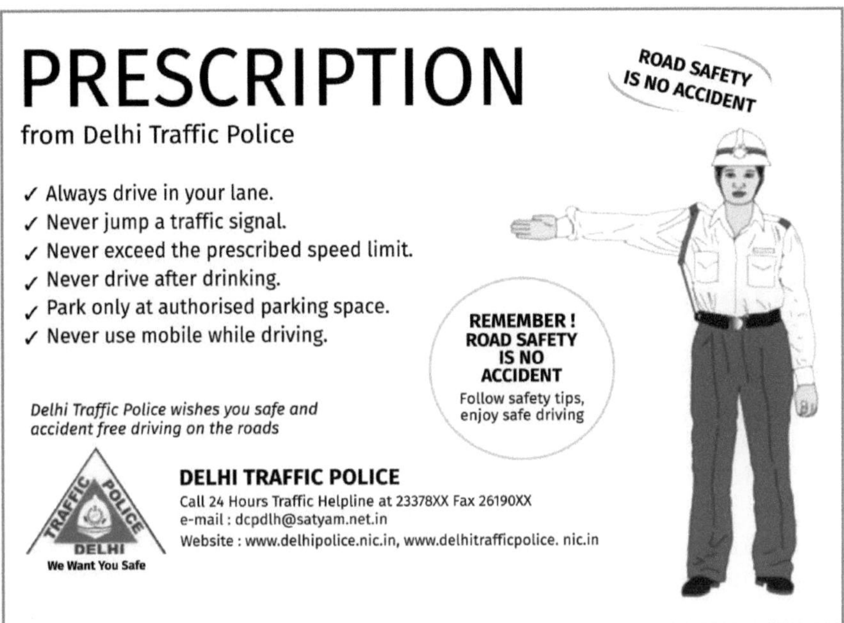

4. Ministry of Social Justice and Empowerment needs a poster for its 'Prevention of Drug Abuse' campaign on the occasion of International Day against Drug Abuse (26th June every year). Draft a poster to raise public awareness against drug abuse.

Chapter Practice

Objective Questions

• Multiple Choice Questions

Directions (Q. Nos. 1-5) Keeping in mind that the incidents of road rage are increasing day by day, the Delhi traffic police wants you to draft a poster for them on road safety tips.

On the basis of the letter you drafted, choose the correct option to answer the following questions.

1. Select the most appropriate title for the poster.
(a) Road Safety Prescription
(b) Attention all the drivers
(c) Drive legally
(d) Against road rage

Ans. (*a*) The poster is about road safety tips hence, 'Road Safety Prescription' is the most appropriate title.

2. Select the option that mentions the issuing authority of the poster.
(a) Transport department, Delhi
(b) Delhi Government
(c) Delhi Traffic Police
(d) There will no mention of the issuing authority.

Ans. (*c*)

3. Would this poster contain any image?
(a) Yes, it would make it eye-catching
(b) No, it would make it informal
(c) Yes, it would reflect the seriousness of the issue
(d) No, it would make it costly

Ans. (*a*)

4. Which of the following can be added to make the poster more attractive?
(a) Contact information of the issuing authority
(b) Slogans and jingles related to the theme
(c) Pledge towards the cause
(d) Both (b) and (c)

Ans. (*d*) Slogans and jingles can be added to the poster to make it more attractive along with a pledge towards the cause. Hence, option (d) is the correct answer.

5. Select the option that lists the most accurate points that will be included in the poster.

(i) Don't drive   (ii) Drive under guidance
(iii) Follow traffic rules   (iv) Do not bribe
(v) Give way to emergency services
(vi) Use authorised parking
(a) (i), (ii) and (iii)   (b) (i), (iii) and (vi)
(c) (ii), (iii) and (iv)   (d) All of these

Ans. (*c*) The notice requires safety tips including 'drive under guidance', 'following of traffic rules' and 'not bribing anyone', as it aims to provide road safety tips.

Directions (Q. Nos. 6-10) You are the Director General of Health Services. You want to invite people to come forward for eye donation and have to draft a poster for the same.

One the basis of the letter you drafted, choose the correct option to answer the following questions.

6. Select the most appropriate title for the poster.
(a) Donate your eyes
(b) Bring light in the dark world of the blind
(c) Help with corneal blindness
(d) Both (a) and (b)

Ans. (*d*) The poster aims to invite people for eye donation hence, 'donate your eyes' and 'bring light in the dark world of the blind' and both appropriate titles for the poster.

7. Select the option that mentions issuing authority for the poster.
(a) General Health Services
(b) Rotary Club
(c) National Programme for Control of Blindness
(d) Ministry of Health and Family Welfare

Ans. (*c*)

8. Select the option that lists the ways in which the poster can be made attractive.
(i) Images   (ii) Slogans
(iii) Jingles   (iv) Awareness information
(v) Use of different fonts
(a) (i), (ii) and (iii)   (b) (ii), (iii) and (iv)
(c) (iii), (iv) and (v)   (d) All of these

Ans. (*d*)

9. Would this poster include event details?
(a) Yes, it would include day, date, time and venue
(b) No, it would make the poster an invitation
(c) Yes, it would include the day and time along with contact information
(d) No, it would take unnecessary details.

Ans. (*a*)

10. Select the information that can be included in the poster.
   (a) Need to donate eyes
   (b) How it reflects on your personality
   (c) Nearest eye bank
   (d) Privileges associated with eye donation

Ans. (a)

Directions (Q. Nos. 11-15) *As a part of a competition on the occasion of World Environment Day in your school, you have to draft a poster on the ill-effects of plastic on the environment.*

On the basis of the letter you drafted, choose the correct option to answer the following questions.

11. Select the most appropriate title for the poster.
   (a) Giving up on plastics
   (b) Be Fantastic, Do Drastic, Cut Plastic
   (c) Plastic free world
   (d) Free the world of plastic

Ans. (b) 'Be Fantastic, Do Drastic, Cut Plastic' is a very catchy and appropriate title for the poster on ill-effects of plastic on the environment.

12. Will the poster reflect the issuing body?
   (a) Yes, it would reflect the maker's name
   (b) No, it has been made as a part of a competition
   (c) Yes, it would include the name of the school
   (d) No, it is not required

Ans. (c)

13. Which of the following would the poster include as a negative impact of plastic?
   (a) Pollution
   (b) Health problems like lung cancer
   (c) Extinction of aquatic species
   (d) All of the above

Ans. (d) As the poster is talking about ill-effects of plastic, the health problems, pollution and aquatic species extinction which are its key negative impacts should be included in the poster. Hence, option (d) is the correct answer.

14. Select the option that lists the correct alternative for maintaining the environment.
   (a) Reusable biodegradable materials
   (b) Proper disposal of plastics
   (c) Banning plastic production
   (d) All of these

Ans. (a) The correct alternative for maintaining a healthy environment is to reuse biodegradable materials.

15. Which of the following slogans can be used in the poster?
   (a) Go Green, Plastic is Obscene!
   (b) Preserve the environment
   (c) Think before you trash it
   (d) Plastic is laminating the earth

Ans. (a)

PART 2
Subjective Questions

1. Fireworks and crackers are known to create pollution during festivals. As an environmentalist, design a poster to create awareness of their ill effects.

Ans.

2. Design a poster in about 50 words to create awareness among the people of your city on the importance of following traffic rules.

Ans.

BE A GOOD CITIZEN-OBEY TRAFFIC RULES
KEEP SAFETY-YOUR PRIMARY GOAL

Do's and Dont's

- Do not jump red lights
- Do not cross the speed limits
- Do not drink and drive
- Do not use mobile phones while driving
- Always wear helmets and seat belt

Issued in Public Interest by : National Road Federation

3. Publicly we proclaim that dowry is an evil. Privately we want our sons to fetch good dowries. Right from our school days we should be taught that demanding and even giving dowry is not only illegal but also immoral. Draw a poster in about 50 words highlighting dowry as a curse.

Ans.

DOWRY IS A CURSE
It is not only illegal but also immoral !!!

As an evil, it causes:

- Unnecessary mental pressure on the bride and her family.
- Death of bride, in some cases.
- Ill treatment of bride and her family at the hands of the groom and his family.

Raise your voice against Dowry

4. Prepare a poster advising people not to take alcoholic drinks, illustrating the dangers of consuming alcohol. Invent details. You are Rajan/Rajani.

Ans.

SAY NO TO ALCOHOL
SAY IT NOW!

Addiction leads to:

- Ruined Health
- Ruined Family Life
- Ruined Self
- Finally .... painful death

Join De-addiction Camp Today and Regain
Health Control and Happiness

Call at Helpline 'Saathi' 18001800XX or Call us 252525XX

5. You are Vinayak/Revati from the Green School, Thoothukudi. You read an article about the proposed garbage segregation programme in the neighbourhood, which is set to begin from next week. You decide to make a poster telling your neighbourhood about the programme and the value of garbage segregation. Draft the poster to be put in your neighbourhood.

Ans.

Garbage Segregation Drive

Learn all about your garbage type and put it in the correct bin to keep the environment safe and recycle wet waste properly on 5th November at district park.

WET WASTE

Hello, I am green. Put in me biodegradable kitchen waste like fruit/vegetable peels, tea leaves, coffee powder, egg shells, meat and bones, food scraps; also leaves and flowers.

DRY WASTE

Hello, I am blue. Put in me paper, plastics, metal, glass, rubber, thermocol, fabric, leather, rexine, wood, etc.

ISSUED IN PUBLIC INTEREST

6. Water is precious and each one of us must stop its wastage to avoid its scarcity in the near future. Prepare a poster requesting people of your colony to adopt means to save water, prevent its wastage, etc. You are Rama/Rohan of Ahimsa Vihar, Saket, Ahmedabad.

Ans.

Conserve Water and Consume it Wisely

Every Drop Counts, Reduce Your Use!

- Wasting water is bad
- All living things need water
- Together we should save it
- Everyone can help
- Reuse water please

Water is precious and each one of us must stop its wastage to avoid its scarcity in the near future.

Issued by : Rama, President of Ahimsa Vihar Colony, Saket (Ahmedabad)

7. Prepare a poster highlighting the dangers of drunk driving advising motorists to abstain from alcohol before taking the wheel.

Ans.

8. You are Secretary, Social Service League of your school. Design a poster to be displayed in your colony and in a local hospital premises inspiring people to make a pledge to donate eyes and other organs of their bodies.

Ans.

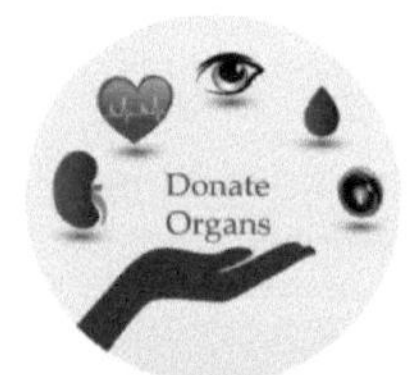

9. You are a professional poster designer who has been asked to design a poster for recruitment of soldiers in the Indian Army, to be put up at prominent places in a district where a recruitment camp is to be held. Draft a poster giving details of the recruitment camp.

Ans.

10. You are the Director of Health Services, Mizoram. You have to educate the public about the necessity of oral polio vaccine for small children. Design a simple and catchy poster to be put up at prominent locations in the whole state.

Ans.

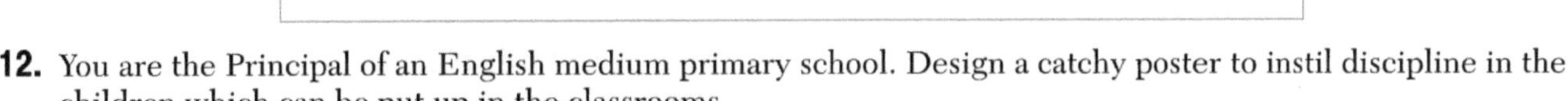

11. Draft an attractive poster for 'Save Trees, Save Earth' Campaign.

Ans.

12. You are the Principal of an English medium primary school. Design a catchy poster to instil discipline in the children which can be put up in the classrooms.

Ans.

13. Draft a poster to be issued by the Delhi Police cautioning people not to touch any unclaimed object.

Ans.

14. You are the Sports Instructor at Sadbhavna Primary School. You are arranging the Annual Sports Day of the school. Design an attractive poster to inform the parents of the students about it.

Ans.

15. You are the Director of Disaster Management Authority. You want to make the people aware about earthquakes. Draft a poster for the same.

Ans.

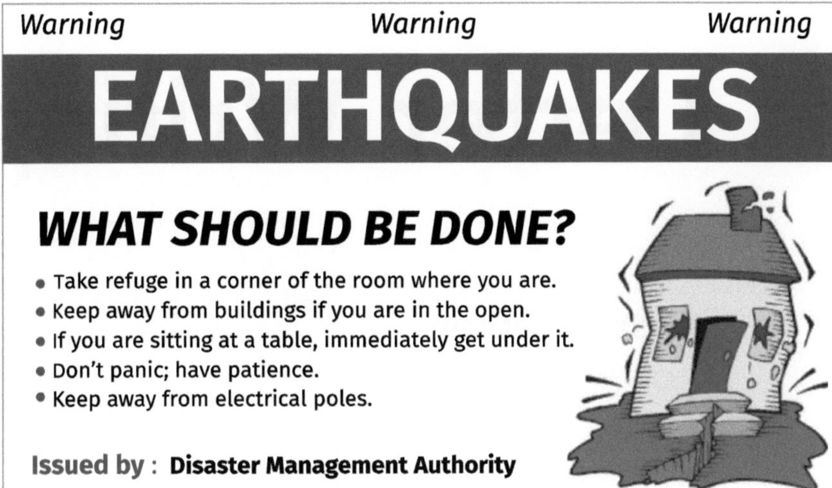

Letter Writing
(Official Letters)

In this Chapter...

- Official Letters
- Format of Official Letters
- Chapter Practice

Letter writing is an essential skill. In spite of the prevalence of e-mail and text messages, letters are still one of the most important and popular means of communication. Trade, official correspondence, public representation, complaints and other dealings, transactions and communication with people are still conducted through letters.

In Class XI term II examination, only official letters, which fall into the category of formal letters, are given in the syllabus. So, here we have covered only the category of official letters.

Official Letters

An official letter is a kind of written communication which demands the most formal and matter-of-fact treatment. Such letters are generally written to commercial firms or enterprises as well as academic institutions, so they must be simple and systematic, brief and to the point in content. We write official letters for the following purposes

- Making enquiries/asking for information
- Replying to enquiries/ giving information
- Sending quotations in response to enquiries
- Placing orders
- Registering complaints
- Cancelling orders
- Making request/ appeals

Note Letters to principal/school or college authorities regarding admissions, school issues and suitability of courses are given in CBSE Class 12 Term II Syllabus.

Steps to Write an Official Letter

To write an effective letter, one must follow the correct format and the steps given below

- **Sender's Address** Make sure that the sender's address is clear and precise. Specify the house number first, followed by the street, town/ state and pin code.

  Example 2334/31, Mangal Pandey Nagar
  Ekta Park
  Meerut-250002

  This portion includes the sender's full address. While writing the address, one must **NOT** use a comma at the end of each line. Further, if a student is writing a letter to the principal of his/her own school, writing sender's address is not mandatory.

- **Date and Receiver's Address** Next comes the date on which the letter is written, followed by the receiver's address which comprises the receiver's designation and address.

  Example 12th December, 20XX
  The Editor
  The Times of India
  Daryaganj
  New Delhi-110002

- **Subject** One of the most important parts of a letter is the subject. One must ensure that the subject expresses the main theme or crux of the letter clearly.

- **Salutation** The salutation used in formal letters is a greeting to the person to whom the letter is addressed. For official letter, we stick to Sir/Ma'am.

- **Body of the Letter** The body of the letter is a complex part which contains all the information the writer (you) wants to convey. For this, start with introducing the purpose of writing. Then, build up the topic to develop the interest of the reader by stating the causes, effects and solutions to the problem being discussed.

The body includes three main parts

  (i) **Introductory Paragraph/ Sentence** States the purpose of writing.

 (ii) **Informative Paragraph** Gives details of the problem, cause, effect, possible solution, etc.

(iii) **Concluding Paragraph/ Sentence** States your hope, comment, request, suggestion, etc.

- **Complimentary Close/Subscription** This is a courteous way of ending a letter. For this, we write Yours sincerely/ Yours faithfully/Yours truly, in official letters. The first letter of the second word (here 's', 'f', 't') should always start with a small letter.

- **Sender's name** Just below the complimentary close, sender's name is written as a mark of signing off. If applicable, the sender's designation may be added.

Points to be Kept in Mind

- Keep your letter to the point.
- Be brief, clear, polite and formal at all times.
- Strictly avoid short forms or slang and use refined language.
- Use simple and direct language.
- Use proper format.

Format of Official Letter

You are Rohan Sharma, monitor of class XI in Hariram Sr Secondary School, Dev Nagar, Sonipat. Write a letter to your Principal asking him to arrange for special coaching in Maths for your class. Give reasons why you need this.

The Principal
Hariram Sr Secondary School, Dev Nagar
Sonipat

Receiver's name/ rank and his/ her address
The head of the Institute or the Principal and the name of the School is written here.

15th November, 20XX

Date
After giving the space of a line, date is written.

Subject Arranging Special Coaching in Maths

Theme of formal letter
It indicates the subject of the letter.

Sir,

Salutation
The formal address to the addressee.

I am the monitor of class XI - A. On behalf of my class, I am making a special request. Our teacher of Maths was ill with typhoid and was on leave for more than one month. Our pre-board exams are approaching and our syllabus has not yet been covered completely. If he now covers the balance topics of the course in a hurry, we shall not understand the lessons fully.

This will not only impact our performance in the Board exams as well as in the pre-boards, but will erode our confidence severely. It will also affect the reputation of our wonderful school.

Body of the letter
The theme or subject of the letter in detail forms the body of the letter.

Thus, we shall be highly obliged and thankful to you if you can arrange extra coaching classes in Maths so that we get enough time to practise .

Thanking you
Yours obediently
Rohan Sharma

Subscription and Signature
Name and designation of the sender, if applicable.

Chapter Practice

Objective Questions

• Multiple Choice Questions

Directions (Q. Nos. 1-5) As the sports in-charge of the school, you wrote a letter to Lightways School placing an order for sports articles (minimum 4) for the school.

On the basis of the letter, choose the correct option to answer the following questions.

1. Select the subject of the letter.
   (a) Sports goods
   (b) Order of sports goods
   (c) Sports articles for school
   (d) Need of sports articles

Ans. (*b*)

2. Which of the following will be the correct introduction for the letter?
   (a) With reference to our previous correspondence …
   (b) As the school is preparing for sports day….
   (c) This is to notify the placing of order….
   (d) Through the medium of this letter I would like to…..

Ans. (*a*)

3. Select the option that lists the things that can be a part of the letter.
   (i) Expected delivery
   (ii) Payment details
   (iii) Discounts to be availed
   (iv) List of items with specific details
   (v) Quality of goods
   (a) (i) and (ii)   (b) (iii) and (iv)
   (c) (iv) and (v)   (d) All of these

Ans. (*d*)

Directions (Q. Nos. 4-7) You are Sumit Saxena of Class XI in Hariram Sr. Secondary School, Dev Nagar, Sonipat. Write a letter to your Principal asking him for special coaching in Maths for your class.

On the basis of the letter, choose the correct option to answer the following questions.

4. Select the most appropriate subject for the letter.
   (a) Special coaching in Maths
   (b) Need of Special coaching in Maths
   (c) Request for Special coaching in Maths
   (d) All of the above

Ans. (*d*)

5. Would this letter include the sender's address?
   (a) Yes, it makes the letter genuine
   (b) No, it is not necessary in such letters
   (c) Yes, it is an official letter
   (d) No, it is addressed to the principal of the same school

Ans. (*b*)

6. Which of the following is the most appropriate complimentary close for the letter?
   (a) Yours only   (b) Yours dearly
   (c) Yours sincerely   (d) Yours

Ans. (*c*)

7. Given below is a sentence from the letter draft. Complete it by selecting the most appropriate option.

   Therefore, on the behalf of Class XI, I ……………. .
   (a) will be kindly obliged if you can arrange special classes for Maths.
   (b) Request you to arrange special classes for Maths.
   (c) Wish to get special classes for Maths.
   (d) Hope to avail special classes for Maths.

Ans. (*b*)

Subjective Questions

1. You are interested in doing a course in fashion design. For this you want to join NIFT. NIFT holds a competitive examination for admission. Sapphire Academy, Dadar, Mumbai gives coaching for the admission test. Write a letter to the Director, Sapphire Academy requesting him to provide you with all the necessary information. You are Karan / Kirti, 48 Fort Apartments, Pune.

Ans. 48, Fort Apartments
Pune
18th March, 20XX
The Director
Sapphire Academy
Dadar, Mumbai

Subject Information about coaching for admission to NIFT.

Sir/Ma'am,

With reference to your advertisement in 'The Hindu dated 16th March, I would like to enquire about a course. I have just appeared for my Class XII CBSE Examination after which I want to join NIFT to pursue fashion designing. I would like to join the coaching classes offered by your academy for the same to clear admission entrance. I would be grateful if you could provide me with the following information for admission:
(a) Courses offered for NIFT
(b) Procedure for admission and the eligibility criteria
(c) Duration of coaching classes offered by your academy
(d) Course fee (both for NIFT and your academy)
(e) Any other relevant information regarding NIFT

I am extremely keen to join NIFT and would appreciate if you could forward me all the necessary information related to the courses available in your academy as soon as possible.

Thanking you
Yours sincerely
Kirti Kulkarni

2. You are R. Kanta of 92 BPL Colony, Kochi. You want to do a course in nursing. Write a letter to the Registrar, College of Nursing, Thiruvanantha-puram, describing your present qualification, percentage of marks, age, etc. Ask for the courses you are eligible to pursue, procedure for admission, fee structure, any scholarship available, hostel facilities, etc.

Ans. 92 BPL Colony,
Kochi

14th February, 20XX

The Registrar
College of Nursing
Thiruvananthapuram

Subject Enquiring about course in Nursing

Sir/Ma'am,

This is in reference to your advertisement about the Nursing course taught in your college. I wish to pursue a career in nursing and have completed my graduation with first honors degree in B. Com. I request you to please send me the details, such as choice of courses offered and their eligibility criteria, fee structure, admission

procedure, hostel facility, prospects of placement, any scholarship available, etc., for the session starting in April.

I will appreciate if you forward me the details at the earliest. I am enclosing a self-addressed envelope.

Thank you
Yours faithfully
R. Kanta

3. You are Mahesh/ Manju Patwardhan, the class monitor of Class XI-B in Shradhanand Public School, Kanpur. Write a letter to your school Principal in 120-150 words asking him to arrange for special classes in English. Also give reasons why you need this.

Ans. Shradhanand Public School

Kanpur

14th December, 20XX

The Principal
Shradhanand Public School, Kanpur

Subject _Arranging Special Classes in English_

Respected Sir

I am writing this letter on the behalf of my class. You are aware that our English teacher, Mr Ratneshwar Rathore, had been bedridden due to typhoid and had been on leave for nearly a month. As a result, the coverage of our English Core syllabus is lagging behind. The major problem confronting us at the moment is that our Pre-board Exams are going to be held in four weeks' and the time and our syllabus of the subject may not get completed by that time. If Mr Rathore now tries to finish the course quickly, we would not be able to fully understand the lessons and our performance in the Pre-boards will suffer.

Therefore, all the students of our class request you to kindly arrange for special English classes after the school hours. A two hour class at least four days a week for the next four weeks would be enough to help us cover the syllabus properly.

We shall be highly obliged if you could arrange these extra classes so that we get enough time to practise and complete our syllabus.

Yours obediently

Mahesh Patwardhan

Class Monitor, Class XI – B

4. Mountview Public School, Kalka is run by an NGO to give quality education to the children of the deprived sections of society. The Principal of the school feels that blackboards in the classrooms need to be replaced. She decides to ask the chairperson of the NGO 'Education for All' for funds. Write her letter. Her name is Shweta Pandit.

Ans. Mountview Public School
Kalka, New Delhi

16th March, 20XX

The Chairperson
Education for All
New Delhi

Subject Funds required for Replacement of Blackboards

Sir/Ma'am,

Your NGO is taking good care of the children of deprived sections of society by providing them education. Now that the school is completing almost ten years of its existence, some of the fixtures need to be replaced. The most urgent need at present is of replacement of the blackboards in the classrooms, as they are either damaged, worn out or totally unusable.

I suggest that we should replace them with permanent whiteboards, as these are more durable and can also be used to project slides as well as for using audio-visual teaching equipment, necessary in today's education scenario. The school has around 50 blackboard which needs replacement.

Therefore, I request you to release funds for this purpose at the earliest. I am enclosing a quotation for the whiteboards from a local supplier to help you understand the amount of funds required.

Thanking you
Yours sincerely
Shweta Pandit
(Encl. Quotation)

5. As the Head Boy of your school, write a letter to the Principal requesting him/her to arrange programmes of career counselling for the students of classes XI and XII. Request him to invite experts from several professions to speak to the students to give insights and information.

Ans. The Principal
National High School
Model Town, Amritsar-143001

15th November, 20XX

Subject Request to arrange Career Counselling Programmes

Sir/Ma'am,

I shall deem it a great favour if you kindly arrange programmes of career counselling for the students of classes XI and XII as soon as possible. As the Head Boy of your esteemed institution, I consider it a great opportunity for the higher secondary section. We, the students, will be highly obliged if you kindly arrange such programmes.

I therefore earnestly request you to invite professionals and scholars from different fields to interact with the students to give insights and share information. They can spend an hour or two with the concerned students so that students can decide on which career to pursue.

Thanking you
Yours obediently
Suresh Banerjee
Head Boy

6. You have just passed your CBSE examination of Class X and wish to seek admission to Class XI in another school. Write an application to the Principal of St. James school, 29, Saket Road, New Delhi. Indicate the subjects that you would like to choose and mention the achievements that you consider will help you to gain admission.

You can take help from the clues given below.
- Details of past schooling
- Necessary criteria for admission
- Choice of stream
- Academic accomplishments, if any

Ans. 63, B-Block
Greater Kailash II
New Delhi-110048

19th December, 20XX

The Principal
St James School
29, Saket Road
New Delhi-110017

Subject Application for Admission to Class XI

Sir/Ma'am,

This is to inform you that I, Surendra Singh, have passed the CBSE examination with a First Division from Don Bosco High School, Lajpat Nagar. I wish to seek admission to Class XI in your esteemed institution. To study in your esteemed institution has been like a dream to me and so I will be highly obliged if you will like kindly acquaint me with the necessary criteria for admission.

I would like to choose the subjects of the Science stream with Computer Science as the additional subject. In this regard, I have received the award for the best student in Mathematics in Class X and also the second prize for the research scholar in a science workshop. I feel that these honours will be helpful for admission into your school.

I therefore earnestly request you to kindly consider my case. I am enclosing a copy of my Board exam marksheet for your pursual.

Yours faithfully
Amit Sheel
(Encl : Marksheet copy)

7. You have borrowed some books from your school library. Unfortunately you have to go away to visit a sick relative and cannot return the books in time. Then you find that you cannot even locate them. Write a letter to the library incharge. Explain what has happened and propose what you can do in this regard.

Clues

- Details of books
- Issue date and due dates
- Reason for not returning
- Pardon for inconvenience
- Way for compensation

Ans. The Library Incharge

St Thomas School

Rajouri Garden

New Delhi-110027

17th January, 20XX

Subject Failure to Return Library Books

Respected Sir,

This is to inform you that I, Suresh Roy, a student of class XI, have failed to return the two books of Science borrowed by me on 27th December, 20XX in time. My library card number is RL110012. The due date for the books was 15th January, 20XX. Unfortunately the books have been misplaced by me at home. Now, I have been forced to stay away from home for a few days to tend to my sick relative who has been hospitalised. I will be able to search for the missing books at my home only after my relative gets well enough to be discharged from hospital.

I am really sorry for the inconvenience caused. Kindly inform me what action I should take in this regard. I can buy the copies of the lost books from the market if you kindly allow me.

Thanking you

Yours faithfully

Suresh Roy, Class XI

8. Write a letter to the Principal of your school, asking for long leave due to severe illness.

Ans. The Principal

National High School

Model Town

Delhi-110007

15th January, 20XX

Subject Application for Long Leave due to Illness

Respected Sir,

This is to inform you that I, Seema Sen of class XI of your school, have been suffering from acute jaundice and diarrhoea since last week. So, I am unable to attend the school. I have consulted a doctor and he has advised me to take fifteen days bed rest and further rest a few days at home without any exertion after that.

I understand that this enforced absence from school will impact my attendance record and may affect my performance in the exams. However, I will make up for the time I am away from school by studying longer hours after I recover.

I therefore earnestly request you to kindly grant me permission for leave from 12th of January to 31st of January, 20XX. I will submit a medical certificate at the time of joining the school.

Thanking you

Yours obediently

Seema Sen

9. You plan to join an advanced course in English Speaking offered by the Vocational Training College, New Delhi. You are Anil/ Shobha Gupta of Dhruva Apartments, Patparganj. Write a letter to the Director, English Language Teaching Division of the college, requesting to send you the information on the courses offered, fees and duration of the courses etc.

Ans. 65-A Block

Dhruva Apartments, 9, Patparganj

New Delhi-110092

14th December, 20XX

The Director

English Language Teaching Division

Vocational Training College

New Delhi-110001

Subject Request for Information Regarding Admission to English Speaking Course

Respected Sir

This is to inform you that I, Shobha Gupta, wish to join the advanced course in English Speaking in your esteemed institution. I would prefer to join the classes from the month of February. I therefore earnestly request you to send me the prospectus for this course and criteria for admission to the course. I would also like to know whether you are planning to start a batch in February, as I am currently busy in some other work.

Further, I want to know what kind of employment I can expect after completing this course successfully. In addition, I will be highly obliged to you if you acquaint me with the details of the other courses offered by you and also the corresponding fees and duration of the courses. I hope to receive a positive response from your end.

Yours sincerely

Shobha Gupta

10. You are Anuj Dixit of Chitra Senior Secondary School, Pandav Puram, Delhi. You are captain of the Hockey team of your school. You have no playground in your school. Write a letter to the Principal, requesting him to arrange playground facility from a neighbouring school for practice of your team.

Ans. The Principal
Chitra Senior Secondary School
Pandav Puram, Delhi

10th September, 20XX

Subject *Arrange Playground Facility*

Respected Sir,

With due regards I would like to bring your kind notice towards our difficulties and feelings. We all know that we have no playground in our school, but we have a bunch of students who are very good hockey players.

Due to non-availability of playground all the players cannot practice as a team. The zonal school tournaments are to commence within a fortnight. As the captain of our school hockey team, I feel morally bound that our players have proper co-ordination and play as a team and not as a bunch of players grouped together.

For this purpose, we need playground facilities. I, therefore, earnestly request you to arrange playground facilities from a neighbouring school in the morning/evening for an hour or two so that we may practice together under the guidance of our coach.

I hope to have a favourable consideration.

Yours obediently

Anuj Dixit
(Captain of Hockey Team)

Debate

Debate is a contest between two speakers or two groups of speakers to show their skills and abilities in an argument over a topic. It is a kind of formal discussion before a public assembly or legislature in a persuasive manner of speaking with the aim of converting the view of another person, or of the audience, to your own point of view. A speaker either speaks for or against the issue being discussed.

Points to be Kept in Mind

- Debate should always have a good introduction to grab the audience's attention and garner interest in the topic.
- Prepare the debate properly by considering both positive and negative aspects of the topic.
- Address the jury and the audience properly.
- Make your stand clear from the very beginning.
- Highlight the main points of your argument.
- While developing points, substantiate them with relevant examples, statistics, etc.
- Use argumentative style and logical reasoning.
- State your own opinion or view in the concluding lines with a powerful statement to emphasise your stand on the issue.
- Throughout the debate, stick to your viewpoint whether it is in favour or against.
- Include rhetorical questions, which make your opponents consider the validity of your point while it undermines their point.

Format of A Debate

Write a debate in 120-150 words either for or against the motion on the topic 'The Right to Education Act is a Realistic and Achievable Goal that will change the Face of Education in India'. You are Harshita/ Rahul.

Against the Motion

Worthy Chairperson, Secretary and Dear Students

Today I, Harshita, stand before you to speak against the motion 'The Right to Education is a realistic and achievable goal that will change the face of education in India.'

There is no denying the fact that our country has taken some very bold steps towards spreading education to the remotest areas of the country and to all the deprived sections of our society. One of these steps is the passing and implementation of the Right to Education (RTE) Act. However, we still have a long way to go to fully change the face of education in the country. What is the use of the act if parents simply do not send their children to school? In rural areas and in many urban slums, this is a stark reality due to the necessity of making children work for meeting the family budget.

I would also like to draw your attention to the wide gap between what is shown to us through various media as well as data publicised by the government and what is the ground reality. We still see dropouts from schools searching for trinkets in heaps of garbage. There are villages where there are no schools, no teachers and nothing worth the name called 'a school'. The lack of a realistic picture of the state of education and improper awareness strategies and law enforcement stand in the way of making The RTE an achievable goal.

I don't think RTE will succeed in its mission unless we change our work culture and recognise the reality behind facts and figures. I, therefore, oppose the motion.

Thank you!

Formal address

A debate begins with a formal address to the chief guest, other eminent people and the audience.

Content

Expression

(a) Grammatical accuracy, appropriate words and spelling

(b) Coherence and relevance of ideas and style

Formal thanks

At the end of the debate, the speaker formally thanks the audience for their cooperation and listening to him/her.

For the Motion

Worthy Chairperson, Secretary and Dear Students

Today I, Rahul, stand before you to speak for the motion, 'The Right to Education Act (RTE) is a realistic and achievable goal that will change the face of education in India'.

I would like to say that the RTE makes it obligatory for the state to guarantee the right to education and ensure compulsory admission, attendance and completion of elementary education by every child of 6 to 14 years. I feel very strongly that the three basic goals of RTE will greatly benefit the children coming from poor and marginalised families, provided that they are implemented with due seriousness.

The benefits of properly implementing RTE are three. First, it brings poor children to school. Second, it ensures that all schools meet the norms specified by the government. And, third it ensures that all children receive quality schooling. In my opinion, education and literacy are the keys to many problems that the people face. I would like to draw your attention to the fact that today the condition of India on the education front is not like what it was when the nation achieved independence. Successive governments have helped to increase the literacy of the population significantly, particularly that of females.

Thus, if the RTE Act is effectively implemented, it is a realistic and achievable goal. So, I strongly feel that, with the passage of time, RTE will change the face of education in India.

Thank you!

Formal address

A debate begins with a formal address to the chief guest, other eminent people and the audience.

Content

Expression

(a) Grammatical accuracy appropriate words and spelling

(b) Coherence and relevance of ideas and style

Formal thanks

At the end of the debate, the speaker formally thanks the audience for their cooperation and listening to him/her.

Chapter Practice

Directions (Q. Nos. 1-5) Your school's debate group has participated in a inter-school debate competition and you have to speak for the motion 'Are old age homes necessary today'.

On the basis of the stand you taook, choose the correct option to answer the following questions.

1. Select the most appropriate introduction for the debate.
(a) Today, I am here to present my views….
(b) A very good morning to honourable judges, teachers and my dear friends.
(c) In today's world, old age homes are necessary…
(d) The question regarding old age homes is becoming central…

Ans. (*b*)

2. While elaborating upon the benefits of old age homes, which option should not be concerned?
(a) Security   (b) Medical assistance
(c) Love and care   (d) Overall welfare

Ans. (*c*)

3. Which of the following reasons can be elucidated to validate your opinion?
(a) Travelling jobs
(b) Inability to provide proper medical care
(c) Lack of time
(d) All of the above

Ans. (*d*)

4. Given below are a few statements that can be used in the debate. Choose the correct option to complete it.

Whatever be the case, old age is ………… . It is a safe place where elders can have proper medical care. They can relax and interact while their children can work without any stress.
(a) the only proper refuge
(b) the backup plan
(c) a place of importance
(d) an ideal place for elders

Ans. (*a*)

5. How would you conclude the debate?
(a) With an appeal for action
(b) With a note of thanks
(c) With a question that prompts the other side of the debate
(d) Both (a) and (b)

Ans. (*b*)

Directions (Q. Nos. 6-10) You have participated in a debate on 'It is cruel to put stray dogs to sleep' and have been asked to speak against the motion.

On the basis of the stand you taook, choose the correct option to answer the following questions.

6. Which of the following lists the reason for your opinion?
(a) Health risks   (b) Accidents
(c) Violent nature   (d) All of these

Ans. (*d*)

7. Supposing you are asked to speak after the person who spoke for the motion, how will you address their concerns?
(a) While I agree that dogs are loyal creature, one cannot also deny the nuisance they create
(b) While I do not deny the loyal nature of dogs, I also cannot deny that they can rapidly rising in numbers
(c) While I agree with my opponent that dogs are man's best friends, I also agree that dogs pose a number of risks that cannot be ignored
(d) While my opponent is correct in pointing out the Animal Protection laws, I would like to point that they also do not promote stray dogs

Ans. (*b*)

8. Select the option that would assert your opinion.
(a) I believe that all stray dogs need to be put to sleep
(b) I consider it necessary to kill stray dogs to control their rising population
(c) I do not consider it cruel to kill the stray dogs as and when necessary
(d) I accept that killing dogs is not cruel but a rising necessity

Ans. (*c*)

9. Your opponent has suggested adoption as an alternative. Select a suitable reply to this point.
(a) Not everyone prefers keeping pets
(b) Not all dogs can be kept as pets
(c) Even pet dogs are known to create nuisance
(d) All of the above

Ans. (*a*)

10. Given below are a few statements that can be used in the debate. Choose the correct option to complete it.

The increasing population of stray dogs creates a lot of nuisance to everyone alike. These dogs display a lot of violence, fighting each other in the middle of the road, ………. . Not just that, these dogs are the carriers of many diseases which can even be fatal.

(a) biting people and barking non-stop
(b) scaring people and spreading diseases
(c) scaring children and even adults and littering all across the roads
(d) holding traffic and even causing accidents

Ans. (*c*)

PART 2
Subjective Questions

1. The government has banned the use of animals in the laboratories for the purpose of dissection.Write a debate either for or against this decision.

Ans. **For the Motion**

Honourable Judges, my worthy opponents and dear students. Today I, Meena of Class XI, will speak in favour of the motion 'Government's ban on dissection of animals in laboratories is justified'.

We all are aware that animals are creatures with feelings, just like human beings. Many of you have pets in your homes. Do they not respond to feelings of affection or even when they are reprimanded for some wrong action on their part?

Then why do we want to kill and abuse animals for no fault of theirs? For furthering the cause of research, my opponents will say. Well, this research can be carried out otherwise also, by using modern technology and without dissecting animals. If my honourable opponents say that this is part of education, for science students to practically observe what they have been taught in theory, I say that this can be done by providing models of suitable cross-sections of the insides of the animals to be studied. Such models can be made by commercial organisations for sale to educational institutions. This will also prevent repetition of such killing and dissection in future, which not only promotes education and research but also maintains ecological balance and biodiversity. The relentless killing of animals is enough unpleasant as well as unethical.

Hence, it is my earnest appeal to ban the use of animals in laboratories for the purpose of dissection.

Thank you!

Against The Motion

Good morning everyone. Today I am going to express my views against the motion 'Banning the use of animals for dissection'.

Dissection of animals in the school laboratories provides a practical experience of the theoretical knowledge that students learn from books. They get an opportunity to actually put their learning into practice. Looking at this act of education as unjust is flawed because the sole purpose of such an activity is to develop the student's knowledge of the elements and functions of the living being. The dissection of animals has a scientific purpose; it is a mode of hands-on education for students wherein they actually look at what they are being taught.

Now, my worthy opponent will say that there are many other ways to do so through models. But I would like to point here that even then, the real understanding will be lost. The purpose of dissection will be lost as the entire process will become similar to theoretical knowledge.

Further, we should give more credit to the sensitivity and intelligence of our students so as not to believe that a dissection class will make them more prone to animal violence. Students understand the value of animal life and how an animal has the same kind of organs as human beings that perform similar functions. The governing philosophy behind teaching students to dissect animals should be that life, whether human or animal, is the same; each living being is tied to each other by their inner similarity. Thus, a ban on dissection of animals in school laboratories would not be the best course of action. I hope my views on this topic were substantial enough to throw light on this topic.

Thank you!

2. Some people feel that electronic media (TV news) will bring about the end of print media (newspapers). What are your views on the issue? Write a debate either for or against this view.

Ans. **For The Motion**

Respected Principal, members of the Jury, teachers and my dear opponents. Good morning to you all. Today I, Faisal, take the opportunity to express my views for the motion 'Electronic media (TV news) will bring about the end print media (newspapers)'.

We are living in a rapidly developing and modernised era where technology is taking charge in every walks of our life. Thus, it comes as no surprise that the electronic media is taking over print media rapidly. Let us take an example of news. Earlier people depended on daily newspapers as there was no other source of news and information. Today, in comparison to the one day wait, we get all new information we need almost instantly. With the 24-hour format, we have access to better and fast flowing news and information.

Further, newspapers cater to only the urban educated sections of the society while the electronic media caters to every individual making the world an inclusive society. The best part of Electronics media is that it gives picture and the scenes of the places of incidents which makes the information much more relatable and authentic. In addition, e-media is also environment friendly. Therefore, electronic media is preferred by all and thus, will soon take over print media.

Thank you!

Against The Motion

Some people believe that electronic media (TV news) will bring about the end of the print media (newspaper). But is it really so? Respected Principal, members of the Jury, teachers and my dear opponents. Good morning to you all.

Today I, Ruchi, take the opportunity to express my disagreement with this view. The print media is a tried and tested medium which has been functioning over centuries and still its popularity has not diminished. Infact, it has managed to hold its ground despite the fact that TV news channels telecast news 24 x 7. News in the print media are analysed and verified and are not repetitive like TV news. Moreover, newspapers cater to the varied interests of different people who eagerly await their morning newspaper.

The 24-hour news channels have revolutionised the world which now appears closer and smaller. Though news conveyed by TV news channels is quicker and faster, these, many times, tend to omit facts and details about an incident and sometimes even sensationalise news without a reason. There are times when due to lack of sufficient news, news either becomes repetitive and dull or sometimes stories are fabricated in a manner that they become news. Here, the newspaper comes in handy as it gives not only vital details but also contains more reliable news.

Besides, the newspaper is easy to carry and can be read at any time. The permanence of the printed word helps in refreshing one's memory about certain facts and incidents reported in the past. Newspapers also contain many columns dedicated to advertisements like vacant situations, buying or selling of goods, information about missing persons, obituary news, editorial comments, etc. All this and much more information is contained only in the newspaper. Thus, I would like to conclude by saying that newspapers have been and will remain the mouthpiece of the nation and the unseen advisers of the common people.

Thank you!

3. Consumerism is increasing day-by-day. Luxuries of yesterday have become necessities of today. The result is that the more we want the more miserable we become. Write a debate on 'The only way to minimize human suffering and pain is to control our needs'. You are Navtej/Navita.

Ans. For The Motion

Honourable Judges, my worthy opponents and dear students. Today I, Navtej of Class XI, will speak in favour of the motion 'The only way to minimize human suffering and pain is to control our needs.'

I am sure all of you watch TV programmes regularly, particularly entertainment programmes, serials and telecasts of cricket matches on various TV channels. You will find it hard to believe that just 25 years ago there was only one TV channel to watch, i.e., Doordarshan. Even then, having a TV set was a luxury and not a necessity, like it is nowadays. If we are prevented from watching TV by our parents even for a few days, like during exam time, most of us become miserable.

However, our ancestors did not face any such misery. Their needs were minimum and items like a TV, fridge, etc., were just considered as luxury. This clearly points to the fact that we must learn to control our needs. Our need becomes greed which then becomes an obstacle in our lives. In greed, the material world controls us and we join a rat-race which puts us through immense physical and mental stresses. We all know that excessive desires and needs have always been considered immoral and a violation of divine law.

Thus, we all must control our needs and desires to live our life without any suffering and pain.

Thank you!

Against The Motion

Respected Principal, members of the Jury, teachers and my dear opponents. Good morning to you all. Today I, Shant, take the opportunity to express my disagreement with this view. Scientifically stating, all human beings are born with defined needs which are different for each and every individual. These needs grow and develop with time and age. A small child always has small and meager needs but a grownup has a much larger and different set of needs.

With this knowledge, the concept of controlling our needs and desires seem to be flawed. Fulfillment is the key here. Pain and suffering that human faces is because of the lack of satisfaction and fulfillment. If we focus on fulfillment, we can easily remove the obstacle that hurt us. Finding joy in simple things, and happiness and peace is the main aim of human life. Controlling needs then may make a person mentally sick and disgusted which would have physical impacts. Thus, instead of controlling our needs, we must find ways to satisfy them and march towards a happy and fulfilled life.

Thank you!

4. Migration from villages to cities has led to the spread of urban slums. People living in these slums lead a miserable life. Economic disparity leads to the problems of law and order. Write a debate on 'Solution to the problem of misery in the urban slums lies in creating jobs in the villages'. You are Navtej/Navita.

Ans. For The Motion

Honourable Judges, my worthy opponents and dear students. Today I, Navita of Class XI, will speak in favour of the motion 'Solution to the problem of misery in the urban slums lies in creating jobs in the villages'.

People living in cities are aware that every city has slum areas in which the poor, mostly migrated from nearby rural areas, are leading a miserable existence, doing odd jobs to earn a living. Due to their condition, they sometimes create problems of law and order. We should understand why people migrate to cities, even though they are forced to lead a life of misery there. The reason is that in the rural areas there are no adequate avenues for employment or alternate sources of livelihood. The rural people feel that they can earn better in cities, leading to their migration. Thus, if jobs are created in the villages by setting up more agro-based industries or some other self-employment opportunities people can lead a reasonable livelihood there and will have no reason to migrate to cities.

Consequently, slums will not expand and more people will not lead miserable lives in urban slums. This will also lead to prosperity in the villages and may ultimately give rise to reverse migration, i.e. slum dwellers going back to their villages to lead a more satisfactory life! I'm sure this is possible with adequate planning by our state and central governments.

Thank you!

Against the Motion

Respected Principal, members of the Jury, teachers and my dear opponents. Good morning to you all. Today I, Navtej, take the opportunity to express my disagreement with this view. While creating job is an essential for the growth and development of the country, it is not the primary step that would ensure that the problem at hand will be solved.

The slums and villages of the country have a lot of people who are jobless and aimless because they are unskilled. Hence, the first priority should be providing them with the basic necessities of life as well as making them skilled to get a job. Once they are mentally and physically healthy as well as skilled, they can easily find jobs and end the miseries of their life. Focusing directly on jobs can easily take away the financial stress but the other miseries faced by them are left unresolved. Hence, other problems must be given first priority and then proper jobs as well as good salary will make them come out of their problems forever.

Thank you!

5. A number of your classmates (especially those from science and commerce streams) bunk their classes in order to attend coaching centres. Write a debate on 'Tuition at coaching centres is not essential'.

Ans. **For the Motion**

Honourable Judges, my worthy opponents and dear students, Today I, Saurabh of Class XI, will speak in favour of the motion 'Tuition at coaching centres is not essential'.

We are all aware that coaching centres, particularly for the science and commerce streams, are very popular with students because the parents feel that their children will perform better in their exams by attending coaching. However, this is a misconception, as most coaching centres are literally money making machines for their owners. They have no infrastructure and very high fees. Thus, most coaching centres are not really useful.

In contrast, schools have a better infrastructure with proper classrooms, multimedia facilities and all other requirements for a proper education. The teachers in schools are well-qualified, many of them having adequate teaching experience. Many schools run by registered trusts also have very low fees, because running a school is considered a philanthropic activity by people. However, the schools should reorient their teaching process to make their education competition oriented. This will ensure that schools will be considered essential, while coaching centres will not be at all necessary.

Thank you!

Against the Motion

In this competitive world, students join coaching institutes to score well in exams and be ahead of others.

Good morning honourable judges, my worthy opponents and my dear friends. Today, I will speak against the motion 'Tuition at coaching centres is not essential' While what my worthy opponent has just said is true, the present reality points that students do not get proper guidance in school.

In this cut-throat competitive world, all of us want to score better and thus have no option but to resort to coaching. Coaching centres provide right guidance not only in student's area of study but also in their careers ahead. These institutes can guide students as per their interest and their academic records.

Students gets individual attention at coaching centres, which is not the case in schools where each class has 30-40 students and teachers have limited time in class. This makes it difficult for teachers to guide students as they concentrate on completing the syllabus in time.

Coaching centres develop innovation learning techniques for different types of students, whereas in school, students of the same class get to learn concepts in the same patterns.

When a student misses a day in school, due to any reason, they move out of track in studies. They will not be able to concentrate on the on-going topics. Coaching centres come handy in these cases, where they can cover the missed out classes without losing the on-going classes. Thus, coaching centres cover up all those things missed out by the schools. Hence, they are a necessity.

Thank you!

6. 'Brain drain is not a bane for a developing country like India.' Write a debate either for or against the motion.

Ans. **For the Motion**

Worthy Chairperson, Secretary and Dear Students. Today I, Sameer, stand before you to speak for the motion 'Brain drain is not a bane for a developing country like India'.

What is 'brain drain'? It is defined as the migration of competent people, meaning intellectuals and skilled workers, in search of a better standard of living and quality of life, higher salaries, access to advanced technology and more stable political conditions, to different places worldwide.

Today, from India many people migrate abroad for better prospects and as a result this so called 'brain drain' improves the chances of competent people finding employment. Not only does this brings prestige as the work force gets recognised but this also brings opportunity for talented individual. The 'brain drain' that is considered as a bane actually promotes globalisation and competition. The forex remitted back helps family and also promotes tourism in the country.

Brain drain, thus, enhances socio-cultural and economic relationship. Thus, we can definitely say that brain drain is not a bane for a developing country like India.

Thank you!

Against the Motion

Worthy Chairperson, Secretary and Dear Students. Today I, Kaveri, stand before you to speak against the motion, 'Brain drain is not a bane for a developing country like India'.

Usually, it is the intellectuals and skilled workers of a country who migrate, being dissatisfied the most. This translates into a loss of considerable resources when these people migrate, with the direct benefit going to the recipient countries who have not spent any money on educating them. These migrants are some of the most expensive resources of a developing country like India because of their training in terms of material cost and time, and most importantly, because of lost opportunity. Thus, India's development is severely hampered by these people leaving the country, particularly because it results in many gaps in vital industries and key positions. This significantly hampers the development of the nation.

Thus, we can definitely say that brain drain is a bane for a developing country like India.

Thank you!

7. 'The Internet cannot replace a classroom teacher'. Write a debate either for or against the motion.

Ans. **For The Motion**

Respected Principal, Teachers, honourable members of the Jury and my worthy opponents. Good morning to you all.

Classrooms are the most influential spaces that exist in the world today. These leave a long-lasting impact on the minds of the individuals. As we move in a more globalised and technologically oriented world, the dilemmas of morality, ethics and life are fast increasing and no Internet can ever answer these questions. Thus, the topic that 'Internet can't replace a classroom teacher' has come at the highest time and I stand in favour of it.

Classroom includes teachers who touch the students' lives in innumerable ways. The bond between a teacher and a student is a human bond. It is a human connect which a computer can't replace. A teacher is a person who is able to have a lifelong impact on the students. The teacher can scold, guide and understand a child's emotions as he/she is growing up. They have a positive impact on a student, which builds his/her character from an early stage. These days, we are quite familiar with online classes and online teaching. There is even a designed curriculum, but unlike teachers, the internet cannot provide encouragement and support to the students. Teaching is not just about making sure that the students are learning, it is about creating an interactive environment wherein the student can grow mentally as well as socially.

The Internet can never answer the vastness and depth of questions that exist in the minds of the students. The Internet may give them information which may not even be authentic and it also can't teach them morality or clear their dilemmas of life. The essence of learning is to make individuals capable enough to be able to cope with anger, anxiety, failure and success. The aim of education is to create responsible citizens which the Internet cannot do. It is only a teacher who takes full responsibility for nurturing the child.

Thank you !

Against The Motion

Good morning honourable judges, worthy opponents and my dear friends.

In today's fast moving world, where technology has taken over our lives in all ways possible, the modern-day teacher is the Internet. The view that 'Internet can't replace a classroom teacher' is a thing of the past and has no scope today. Thus, I speak against the motion.

In today's classroom, the students are much more aware of the world. They have answers to all the questions even before a teacher can answer them because the questions can be easily answered by the Internet. The Internet serves not just as a teacher but as an entire library in itself. The internet not only provides different viewpoints but also enhances discussions.

The decline in the number of teachers has paved the way for the Internet to become the new teacher. The quality of teachers today and their consistency is the main cause for the suffering of the education system but with the Internet as the new teacher, there is no problem of quality and consistency. With internet, evaluation becomes faster and unbiased and learning becomes free from time constraints.

On the one hand, where students had to wait for the teachers to solve their doubts, now they can get their questions answered just by the click of the mouse. Their teacher is in their hands and always ready to solve their problems. The Internet is not just limited to the classroom like a teacher but it opens the world to students and allows them to learn.

Thank you!

8. 'The policy of reservation of seats for admission to the professional courses is good for the deprived sections of society.' Write a debate either for or against the motion.

Ans. **For the Motion**

Worthy Chairperson, Secretary and Dear Students. Today I, Sameer, stand before you to speak for the motion 'The policy of reservation of seats for admission to the professional courses is good for the deprived sections of society'.

We all are aware that Indian society still remains a caste based hierarchical system. The lower caste people have remained exploited by the high caste ones and have suffered through the demerits of socio-economic underdevelopment. The aim of reservations in admission is to bring them at par with other sections of society. Though it appears as a violation of the principle of equality, yet its justification is sustained by the obligation of a social welfare state.

Article 46 of the Indian Constitution provides that the state shall promote with special care the educational and economic interests of the weaker sections of the people. Further, the first Constitutional Amendment Act of 1951 provides that nothing shall prevent the state from making any special provision for the advancement of any socially and educationally backward class of citizens. We must remember that a country cannot progress until all the sections constribute together. Thus, the weaker and marginalised must raise themselves from the pits of inequality.

The Constitution was designed to help the deprived sections of society and thus the policy of reservation is justified.

Thank you !

Against the Motion

Worthy Chairperson, Secretary and Dear Students. Today I, Kaveri, stand before you to speak against the motion 'The policy of reservation of seats for admission to the professional courses is good for the deprived sections of society'.

The policy of reservation stated in the Indian Constitution was designed as an ad-hoc policy for ten years. But it is continuing to get extensions after the end of every ten years. These extensions are creating frustrations among other people, as they are deprived of opportunities to take admission in professional courses even after scoring a good and deserving percentage.

In addition, the policy of reservation is contrary to the principle of equality. Equality pre supposes equal treatment to all and equal protection of all people. But special privileges and extra protection to certain classes of people violates it. It violates the very spirit of democracy and does great injustice to the deserving.

Further, the reservation policy has become the main reason for brain drain and the communal disturbance taking place in the society. Due to brain drain, people are fostering resentment as the inequality increases. As a result, the need of the hour is that focus should be on merit.

Today, very high respected positions are occupied by undeserving people due to reservations while the truly deserving is left to struggle. Thus, not only is this policy pushing the morale of the youth downwards but also hindering the efficient growth and development of the nation.

Thank you !

9. 'The policy of no detention till Class VIII is not in the interest of students.' Write a debate either in favour of or against the motion.

Ans. **For The Motion**

Respected Chairperson, honourable members of the Jury and my worthy opponents. Good morning to you all.

Today I, Karuna, stand before you to speak for the motion 'The policy of no detention till Class VIII is not in the interest of students'. It has had a severe impact on the learning outcome in schools and has become a hindrance in the academic growth of a student. Every student knows that with or without studying one will be promoted to the next class till Class VIII. No one checks on the fact that whether or not a student has acquired the bare minimum knowledge before he or she is promoted to the next class.

Cut-throat competition is faced by each and every child. Thus, to become successful students must have a proper base, so that they can excel in every aspects of life. But students do not put 100% efforts in their education. They lack the motivation to excel, first in their academics and later in their life. They become used to not working hard and start expecting to receive benefits without doing anything. Though this policy was implemented with the objective of reducing stress on children, one cannot ignore the fact that the quality of education has to be maintained and the aim of education has to be achieved. Children with weak foundation are unable to perform as their basics are not

clear. It is thus a serious concern that all attempts of educating children is proving to be a waste.

Life, in general, is extremely competitive, so let us not forget that a little bit of pressure is always beneficial in the long run so there is certainly an urgent need to rethink about continuing this policy.

Thank You!

Against The Motion

Respected Chairperson, honourable members of the Jury and my worthy opponents. Good morning to you all.

Today I, Paramjeet, stand before you to speak against the motion 'The policy of no detention till Class VIII is not in the interest of students'. It is universally accepted that each and every child is unique and different. Consequently, each one of us has different learning capacities as well as talents.

While one may be good in studies, other will be good in sports or any other field for that matter. This coupled with the fact that the age group we are talking about generally comprises young children who have very tender hearts, points that every child must be molded and guided in specific ways so that they learn and grow in a positive way.

At such a tender age, a child can get easily affected by any kind of fear and pressures. And the fear of failure in exams is one of the scariest aspects of this. A child from a very young age is forced by parents to excel in studies. He/she is put through endless tuitions so that they top in examinations. As a result, the precious childhood is lost. Further, children do not get time to pursue their hobbies or talents.

In such a situation, the no detention policy till VIII standard is a good initiative by the government which takes away much of the pressure from the child. Children then can not only enjoy their childhood but also work on their talents.

Thank you!

10. 'A career counsellor (not you yourself) is the best person to guide you in the choice of a career.' Write a debate either for or against the motion.

Ans. **For The Motion**

Choosing a definite career and deciding a career goal is very important especially once you have completed your Sr. Sec. Schooling. Unfortunately, not many students are able to discover their potential and interests and that is when the pressure starts building up.

Honourable Chairperson, members of Jury and my dear friends, I am Pulkit and I am here to speak for the motion 'A career counsellor (not you yourself) is the best person to guide you in the choice of a career.' There is no denying the truth that once we finish our school, we are faced with–"what next"? A student at the threshold of a new start has parents, teachers and friends as guides and each person speaks from their own perspective.

It is at this juncture that a career counsellor can help students. They are the best person to guide you and help you decide your career based on your aptitude, skills, performance and personality. Human talent and potential is tremendous and can't be measured as such. Each individual has their strengths and weaknesses. It is here that the career counsellor comes into the picture. They identify that unique quality and provide not just a career mapping but also support and motivation. They boost our morale and give us an analytical vision so that we can make an informed choice.

Thus, I would say that with the help of career counsellors, students end up choosing the best profession well suited to their needs. They perform well and ultimately succeed in life. So, let us make an intelligent and professional move and step ahead in the right direction with the help of those who are more aware and informed.

Thank you!

Against the Motion

Respected Judges, honourable opponents and friends, I will speak against the motion 'A career counsellor (not you yourself) is the best person to guide you in the choice of a career.' I do not agree with the statement that career counsellors are the best persons to help students in the choice of a career. More than career counsellors, the opinion of parents, who are already experienced in career choice making, as well as ourselves, should influence the choice of a career.

All parents wants their children to find happiness and success in life. The right choice of a career will certainly provide happiness. Research in this field has indicated that when children feel supported and loved by their parents, they have more confidence in their own ability to find a career that suits them, and therefore, choose one which will be interesting to them as well as provide them a livelihood. An individual should be the best judge to choose a career of their choice but they can seek guidance from parents and elders. Career counsellors do not know anything about a child before they suggest a career for him, which may ultimately result in failure.

They may fail in identifying interest of the children and even confuse them with multiple career options. Today, this field has become so commercialised that in the desire to earn more and more money, counselors may misinterpret a student's psychology and individual capacities. Therefore, I reiterate, career counsellors are not the best people to guide you in the choice of a career.

Thank you!

11. 'Private cars should be banned in the congested commercial areas of the cities.' Write a debate either for or against the motion.

***Ans.* For The Motion**

Respected jury members, dear teachers, friends and worthy opponents. I stand here to speak for the motion 'Private cars should be banned in the congested commercial areas of the cities' as I believe that it's time we did something about it. Numerous studies have shown that vehicular pollution is on the rise and so is the traffic. Today, every individual owns a car and uses it to travel everywhere without any thought of how it can be detrimental to everyone. More and more cars means less parking space, more accidents, more congestion, etc. While the use of cars cannot be stopped or reduced drastically as it is a transport of convenience, it can be banned in the congested commercial areas of cities.

The advantages of implementing the ban is that it will lead to less congestion, less problem for pedestrians and no road rage incidents. Secondly, less vehicles would mean less exhaust emission and less time wasted on roads which in

turn will increase the efficiency of people. Let my opponents not forget that banning cars in the congested areas will also reduce the noise pollution which has reached alarming levels, the space for movement will be more and the vehicles carrying goods in the commercial hubs and emergency services will ply with more ease thereby saving time too. To conclude, this step should be taken at the earliest as it will immensely benefit the people of the commercial areas and become a path–breaking example for others to follow suit.

Thank you!

Against the Motion

Respected Judges, honourable opponents and friends, I will speak against the motion 'Private cars should be banned in the congested commercial areas of the cities.' I am not in favour of banning private cars from entering congested commercial areas because our public transport system in cities is not efficient enough to satisfy the needs of travel for the people in the cities.

Freedom of travelling is inhibited when one is at the mercy of public vehicles. It has its scheduled places and time of departures and stops. Moreover, it is not a long-term solution. Moreover, if traders and their customers use taxis or autos, it will become a very costly affair. Therefore, trade and business will suffer. Retail prices will increase, causing difficulties for the common man. Thus, both business and the economy will be adversely affected due to such a measure, which we cannot afford. So government should think some other strategy to overcome the problem of pollution like odd-even rule, which was tried earlier with limited success.

Further, the solution must be looked in the real cause of congestion which is to majority commercial vehicles. Roads must be maintained, movement of commercial vehicles must be restricted and traffic signals must be maintained as well as properly managed. One can also not forget that public transport can be made more efficient for the same.

Thus, pollution can be contained without putting a ban on cars being banned in congested commercial areas.

Thank you!

12. Write a debate either for or against the motion : 'Participation in sports is a mere wastage of time'.

***Ans.* For The Motion**

Respected Judges, honourable opponents and friends, I, Rajani, will speak for the motion 'Participation in sports is a mere wastage of time'.

First, I will raise the point regarding the length of the career of a sportsperson. Most sportspersons retire by the age of 35 to 40 years, whereas other persons can have a career normally stretching to the age of 60 or 65. After retirement, a normal sportsperson finds it difficult to get a suitable job to make ends meet. The majority of sportspersons in India are neglected after they retire. There are many examples of sportspersons living in poverty in their old age.

Second, particularly in physical sports, there are chances of injuries, which may cause permanent bodily harm or reduce their efficiency. This may shorten the career of many sportspersons too.

My third point is regarding the time consumed in practising, participating in competitions, maintaining physical fitness, etc. All these consume a large amount of time, thus reducing a sportsperson's social life significantly. What it amounts to is that many sacrifices have to be made for a sportsperson to be successful even if the person is talented.

Summing up, we can understand that participation in sports is really a wastage of time, which cannot lead to a productive career.

Thank you!

Against The Motion

Respected Judges, honourable opponents and friends, I, Ram, will speak against the motion 'Participation in sports is a mere wastage of time'.

Sports has become a viable career option today. With the government launching schemes like 'Khelo India' and others to identify sports talent at the primary school level, any child who is talented will be trained effectively using government funds to develop their talent. Talent for a particular sport can be recognised at this age and developed accordingly. Then it is the duty of the child's parents to allow the child adequate time for practising and participating in competitions.

There are many cases of sportspersons being successful and gaining recognition at a local, national or international platforms. Even if a child is not found talented in a particular sport, participation in sports is definitely not a mere wastage of time because it keeps one mentally and physically fit. Regular participation in sports develops the body and keeps the child physically fit. It also develops a competitive attitude, besides developing other qualities like leadership, cooperation and a sportsman's spirit. Thus, sports develops a person in every sense.

In addition, even a moderately successful sportsperson gets to travel abroad for training or competition and meet sportspersons of other countries, thus developing their personality in an all-round manner. Thus, we can conclude that participation in sports is not a mere wastage of time.

Thank you!

13. You are Ram/Rajani, Participating in a debate. Write a debate either for or against the motion : 'Hard work, and not good luck helps us achieve success in life.'

Ans. **For The Motion**

Hard work means putting a lot of effort into our projects. Luck means things happening by chance rather than through our own efforts.

Respected Judges, honourable opponents and friends, I, Rajani, will speak for the motion 'Hard work and not good luck helps us achieve success in life.'

Luck is some invisible force connected with your life which may turn your life anywhere it may find worthy. It doesn't care about the hard work you have put into something or how useless you were before luck struck you. This goes beyond the fundamental principles of life. It's very complicated and highly illogical I would say. By saying its illogical I do not mean that luck has no role to play. It is just that important hard work is a pre-requisite for success.

Every passionate person could relate to it easily because every passionate person who has some goals to achieve, has worked very hard. It defines goals. Hard work defines life and as result they get the success they always desired. Those opportunities become reality with hard work only.

Not just that, hard work can give us more of a sense of personal satisfaction. Hard work not only improves discipline but also teaches time management. Remember slow and steady wins the race. Here, slow means hard work and we know hard work always pays. Further, it brings its own 'luck' in the form of unexpected benefits. Remember, a hard-working man can make his luck on his own. See the example of Ratan Tata.

It is said that 'luck favours those who work hard'. We should never think that we don't need to work hard. A successful man is successful because he failed before. And he worked hard and achieved success.

Thank you!

Against The Motion

Respected Chairperson, honourable member of the Jury, my worthy opponents and dear audience, I, Ram, would like to speak against the motion 'Hard work and not good luck helps us achieve success in life'. My worthy opponent has just mentioned that luck is an invisible force connected to our lives with the power to turn our life anywhere it may find us worthy and I believe in it without questioning the importance of hard work. Yes, I agree hard work is essential to success but it is not the only aspect that leads to success.

Without luck, even hard-working individuals falter. We will come across many people who had worked hard but circumstances had prevented them from success. These circumstances are driven by luck. Take an example of students who are preparing for competitive exams. They all work hard, but do they always succeed?

Thus, luck is required for success in all aspects. Hard work alone cannot always pay-off.

Thank you!

14. 'Academic excellence is the only requirement for a successful career.' Write a debate either for or against the motion.

Ans. **For The Motion**

Good morning Respected Chairperson, honourable members of the Jury and my dear friends.

Today I, ABC, stand before you to speak in favour of the topic 'Academic excellence is the only requirement for a successful career'. Success in life is a dream of every person in this world. Every person has their own vision of success in life. The basic of all requirements is knowledge. People get knowledge via education received at schools, colleges, universities and other institutions.

A good education strengthens competencies and developing skills required in the practical world. It helps in clearer understanding of the subject and gives an in-depth knowledge. It helps in developing resource fulness and improves the decision making ability of a person. Academic excellence also ensures admission to higher institutes of learning, which in turn ensures better job opportunities.

This excellence results in better salaries and perks at big and reputed organisations. Academics prepares one for competitions and helps one learn from them.

Although we need other attributes like social, language and communication skills to get success in life, still academic excellence is the pre-requisite.

Thank you!

Against the Motion

Good morning Respected Chairperson, Honourable members of the Jury. Today I, ABC, stand before you to speak against the motion 'Academic excellence is the only requirement for a successful career'. I strongly believe that success has little connection with one's academic excellence.

We all know many highly successful personalities such as Steve Jobs, Bill Gates, Henry Ford, etc., who have achieved great success in spite of not being academically brilliant. However, parents and teachers seem to mainly focus the student's attention on scoring good marks instead of focusing on developing skills. They strongly opine that the student's caliber and future career depends solely on their academic scores. But, academic excellence may not be sufficient to ensure success. There are other life skills such as communication skills, social skills, language skills, etc., that are more important than academics. Life skills along with various talents can give more options to the students. They ensure an all-round personality development, multitasking abilities and leadership qualities, and help to develop confidence in the student. New age careers don't necessarily need academic excellence. In fact, non-formal learning helps to broaden spectrum of careers.

So, it is time for all of us to change our mindsets and encourage talent. Every student should be made to realise that they are is a unique individual and have the right to follow their dreams without being in competition with nobody.

Thank you!

15. 'Everyone should become vegetarian.' Write adebate either for or against the motion.

Ans. **For the Motion**

Respected Chairperson, honourable judges, members of the Jury and friends. People should consume more vegetables and fruits and as little meat as possible because intake of high amount of meat can cause serious health issues. In my opinion, the consumption of a vegetarian diet is a better way to live a healthy life and thus, I agree with the motion.

Life is very precious, and everyone has the right to live, even the animals. Just because animals can't speak that doesn't mean they don't feel pain. Just think about their pain and their suffering when you kill them just for your taste. When it is perfectly possible to lead a healthy life by eating

plant-based food, I see no justification for killing birds or animals for our food. Not to mention, producing vegetarian food is more ecologically sustainable, and it reduces damage to the environment.

One should be vegetarian because it is very cheaper, healthier and better for us and also for our environment. By becoming vegetarian, you live longer, stronger and stay fit. There is strong medical evidence which proves that the consumption of meat is very unhealthy. It also causes heart problems and diabetes.

A vegetarian diet reduces the risk of chronic degenerative diseases such as obesity, coronary artery disease, high blood pressure and diabetes. We should consume fruits and vegetables because they are very rich in proteins and vitamins. To conclude, vegetarian diets are healthy and do not contribute to animal cruelty.

Therefore, I believe that everyone should adopt vegetarianism.

Thank you!

Against the Motion

Good morning Respected Principal, teachers and my dear friends. Today, I have the opportunity to speak against the motion 'Everyone should become Vegetarian'.

Vegetarian diets are devoid of the proteins and fats that animal meat contains. I believe that people should have meat in every their meals in order to have a good health. On one hand, there are several reasons why vegetarianism benefits the human body. On the other hand, people are likely to face some difficulties if they do not eat meat like, lack of energy.

Vegetarians believe that meat is unhealthy because of the diseases it has been connected with. However, there are strong arguments for eating meat. Firstly, as humans we are designed to eat meat, which suggests it is not unhealthy, and we have been eating meat for thousands of years. For example, cave men made hunting implements so that they could kill animals and eat their meat. Secondly, meat is a rich source of protein which helps to build muscles and bones. Vegetarians often have to take supplements to get all the essential vitamins and minerals. According to medical science, a diet constituting sea food like fish, and eggs sharpens our intellect and promotes the smooth functioning of our brain. This ultimately accelerates our wisdom.

Also, vegetarians have a limited choice of food compared to meat eaters. They also face difficulties while travelling abroad as vegetarian food is not available at all places.

To sum up, I do not agree that everyone should turn to a vegetarian diet. Although, the over consumption of meat could possibly be unhealthy, a balanced diet of meat and vegetables should result in a healthy body.

Thank you!

Chapter Test (Writing Skills)

Posters

1 Repeated floods in various flood-prone areas in India have resulted in unprecedented damage and destruction to both life and property. Educating people on the precautions to be taken is the need of the hour. Prepare a poster for creating this awareness.

2 Design a poster to highlight the evils of the dowry system.

3 Design an attractive poster for a 'Dog Show' that your Kennel Club is going to organise.

4 The police of your city needs a poster to raise public awareness on the increase in the number of cases of violence against women. Draft the poster for them.

5 You are Gaurav, the Secretary of the Science Club of Avinash Public School, Rewari. Your school is organising an Exhibition on the cultural variety of India. Draft a poster to bring awareness among the school students about the importance of culture.

6 You are the Mayor of your town. The Municipal Corporation of your town has decided to conduct a 'Tree Plantation Programme' to make your city, a 'Green City'. Design a poster to invite participation from the public for this noble cause.

Letter Writing

1 You are Roshni/ Rahul of Delhi Public School, RK Puram, New Delhi. You cannot take your pre-board exams due to illness. Write an application to the Principal of your school requesting him to grant you leave for four days and to allow you to take your exams at a later date.

2 You are Priya/ Prateek of St Francis School, Delhi. Write a letter to the Principal of your school asking him to make arrangements for conducting more tests before the exams to better equip the students for the board exams and to help them assess the level of their preparation.

3 You are Krishna Kant, Administrative Officer of ET&T Computer Education, Mansarovar Garden, New Delhi. Ms. Aparna Ghose of Lajpat Nagar has made certain enquiries about the Computer Programming Course. Write a letter to her supplying information regarding the course. Give specific reply to the points raised and supply other details as well.

4 You are K. Srinivas of C-7, North Avenue, Rajaji Square, Chennai. You have passed the All India Senior Secondary School Certificate Examination securing 85 per cent marks in PCB. Write a letter to the Registrar of some Medical College of Tamil Nadu asking for the terms and conditions for admission in MBBS against a paid seat.

5 There is a lack of clean toilets in your brother's school. Write a letter to the Principal, Evergreen Senior Secondary School, Daryaganj, New Delhi, complaining about this most essential problem. You are Karan/Divya living at F-311, Ekta Colony Delhi.

Debate

1 You are Ram/ Rajani. Write a debate either for or against the motion: 'Hard work, and not only good luck helps us to achieve success in life.

2 You are Ram/ Rajani. Write a debate either for or against the motion "It is cruel to put stray dogs to sleep."

3 'Our large population is not a cause of poverty but an asset, a resource.' Write a debate either for or against the motion. Write a debate either for or against the motion.

4 'Brain drain is not a bane for a developing country like India'. Write a debate either for or against the motion.

5 'The Internet cannot replace a classroom teacher.' Write a debate either for or against the motion.

6 'Rising prices can be controlled only by the government.' Write a debate either for or against the motion.

CHAPTER 01

Determiners

In this Chapter...

- Classification of Determiners
- Chapter Practice

Determiners are the words that modify nouns. In other words, they are words that are to be used with nouns to determine or to modify or add extra information about a noun. Determiners function like adjectives. They are also called 'fixing words'.

Determiners can tell us about or clarify

- the amount or number of people and other noun
- the state of possession
- specificity of noun
- distribution of nouns
- definition of nouns

Classification of Determiners

Determiners can be classified into

1. **Articles** Article show the position, importance and number of nouns. They are

   A, an, the.

2. **Demonstrative Adjectives** Demonstratives show or point out particular nouns out of a group. They are

   This, that, these, those.

3. **Quantifiers** A quantifier is a word or phrase which is used before a noun to indicate the amount or quantity. Types of quantifiers are as follows

   (i) **Definite** One, two, hundred, ..., first, second, both, etc.
   (ii) **Indefinite** Some, many, much, enough, few, a few, all, little, a little, several, most, etc.
   (iii) **Distributive** Each, every, all, either, neither.
   (iv) **Difference** Another, other.
   (v) **Comparative** More, less, fewer.

4. **Possessives** They show possession or ownership of a noun. My, your, his, her, its, our, their, mine, hers, yours, ours, theirs, etc.

1. Articles— A, An, The

Use of Indefinite Articles : A/An

'A' is used before singular nouns beginning with a consonant sound.

e.g.   **a** woman, **a** horse, **a** university

(*Here* woman, horse *and* university *are words beginning with a consonant sound.*)

'An' is used before singular nouns beginning with a vowel sound.

e.g. **an** orange, **an** egg, **an** elephant, **an** hour

(*Here* orange, egg, elephant *and* hour *are words beginning with a vowel sound.*)

Use 'A' and 'An'

- The use of 'a' and 'an' is determined by sound. The following words begin with a vowel, but not with a vowel sound. A 'unique' thing, a 'one' rupee coin, a 'European', a 'unicorn', a 'university', a 'useful' thing, a 'union'. So here 'a' is used.

  On the other hand, with the following words, 'an' is used. An 'hour', an 'honest man', an 'heir' to the throne, an 'MCA'. These words begin with a vowel sound, so 'an' is used.

Use of Definite Article : The

'The' is used before singular countable nouns, plural countable nouns and uncountable nouns.

'The' is used

I. While talking about a particular person or thing or one already referred to

   e.g. **The** book you want is not available.

II. When a singular noun represents the whole group.

   e.g. **The** dog is a faithful animal.

III. With some proper names that denote physical features.

   (i) Oceans and seas e.g. **the** Pacific ocean, **the** Arabian Sea

   (ii) Rivers e.g. **the** Yamuna, **the** Thames

   (iii) Canals e.g. **the** Suez Canal

   (iv) Deserts e.g. **the** Thar Desert, **the** Sahara Desert.

   (v) Group of islands e.g. **the** West Indies, **the** Netherlands

   (vi) Mountain ranges e.g. **the** Himalayas, **the** Satpura Ranges

   (vii) A few names of countries, which include words like States, Republic or Kingdom e.g. **the** People's Republic of China, **the** United Kingdom, **the** USA, etc.

IV. With the names of religious or mythological books.

   e.g **the** Vedas, **the** Puranas, **the** Mahabharata

V. With the names of things which are unique

   e.g. **the** Sun, **the** Moon, **the** Pacific Ocean

VI. With a proper noun, when it is qualified by an adjective or a defining adjectival clause.

   e.g. **the** Great Caesar, **the** King of Rome

   The Mr Verma whom you met last night is my boss.

VII. With superlative degrees.

   e.g. This is **the** worst performance I have ever seen.

VIII. With ordinals.

   e.g. He was **the** first man to walk on the Moon.

IX. With musical instruments.

   e.g. He can play **the** tabla very well.

X. With an adjective when the noun is understood.

   e.g. **The** rich always exploit **the** poor.
      (*Here the word 'people' is understood.*)

XI. As an adverb with comparatives.

   e.g. **The** more money we have, **the** more we want.

Omission of Article 'The'

- With material, abstract and proper nouns used in a general sense.

   e.g. Honesty is the best policy.

- With plural countable nouns used in a general sense.

   e.g. Children like toys.

- With names of people.

   e.g. Rohit.

- With names of continents, countries, cities, etc., e.g. Europe, Pakistan, Nagpur.

- With names of individual mountains

   e.g. Mount Everest.

- With names of meals used in a general sense.

   e.g. Dinner is ready.

- With languages and words like school, college, university, church, hospital.

   e.g. I learn English at school.

2. Demonstrative Adjectives
(This, That, These, Those)

This, that, these, those are used with uncountable nouns.

I. **That** (in case of plural, **those**)

   (a) It refers to person(s) or thing(s) far from the speaker.

      e.g. • Get **that** dog out of here.
         • **Those** houses are for sale.

   (b) It is used to avoid the repetition of the preceding noun(s).

      e.g. • My bat is better than **that** of my friend.
         • Our soldiers are better equipped than **those** of Pakistan.

II. **This** (in case of plural, **these**)

   (a) It refers to person(s) or thing(s) near the speaker.

      e.g. • **This** book is very interesting.
         • **These** flowers are very beautiful.

3. Quantifiers

Quantifiers can be used in affirmative sentences, questions, requests or commands with both countable and uncountable nouns.

e.g. • There are **some** books on the desk.
   • How **much** money have you got?

Some quantifiers can go only with countable nouns and some with uncountable nouns while some are used with both countable and uncountable nouns.

Only with Uncountable Nouns	With both Countable and Uncountable Nouns	Only with Countable Nouns
a little	no, none, not any	a few
a bit of	some, all	a number of
—	any	several
a great deal of	a lot of, lots of	a great number of
a large amount of much	plenty of	a large number of

Usage of quantifiers are as follows

I. Use of few/a few and little/a little

(a) **Few, a few** and **the few**.

Few emphasises the lack of something.

e.g. There are **few** sweets left in the jar.

A few emphasises that something still remains.

e.g. We still have **a few** minutes left before the class gets over.

The few means not many, but all of those left.

e.g. I ran back **the few** yards to where the figure had disappeared.

(b) **Little, a little** and **the little**

Little emphasises the lack of something.

e.g. We have **little** money right now; we should go out for dinner another day.

A little emphasises that something still remains.

e.g. There's **a little** ice-cream left; who will eat it?

The little means not much but all that is.

e.g. The cat has knocked over **the little** milk in the jug.

II. Use of much and many

We use **much** with singular uncountable nouns and **many** with plural nouns.

e.g. • I haven't got **much** change.
• Are there **many** campsites near your place?

III. Use of more, less and fewer

(a) We use **more** or **less** before singular uncountable nouns for comparison. It can also be used to refer to an additional or lesser quantity of something.

e.g. • I do **more** work than Suresh.
• Please give me some **more** salad.

(b) We use **fewer** before plural countable nouns to refer to a group of things smaller than another.

e.g. • **Fewer** students succeeded in passing than last year.

IV. Use of each and every

(a) We use **each** for two or more than two items and **every** is always used for more than two items. Both of these are followed by singular verbs.

e.g. • **Each** of the two boys has won a prize.
• **Every** student in the school is present today.

(b) We use **each** when the number in the group is limited or definite, but **every** is used when the number is indefinite or unknown.

e.g. • **Each** student in my class was promoted.
• **Every** person in the world has a parent.

V. Use of most, several and all

(a) We usually use **most** with plural uncountable nouns.

e.g. • **Most** of the time I am not at home.

(b) We usually use **several** with plural nouns, but it refers to a number which is not very large.

e.g. • **Several** people were crushed in the stampede.

(c) **All** requires a plural verb when used with a countable noun, but requires a singular verb with an uncountable noun.

e.g. • **All** are going to Delhi.
• **All** that glitters is not gold.

VI. Use of another and other

We use **another** only with singular countable nouns, whereas **other** can be used with singular countable, plural countable or uncountable nouns.

e.g. • Bring me **another** knife, as this one is blunt.
• I would prefer the **other** house.
• The **other** students went back home.
• He is a better human being than **others**.

VII. Use of either and neither

(a) We use **either** to refer to two things, people, situations etc. It means one of the two.

e.g. I don't agree with **either** Ram or Shyam.

(b) We use **neither** with only singular countable nouns and a singular verb.

It allows us to make a negative statement about two people or things at the same time.
e.g. Neither France nor Belgium won the 2021 Euro Cup.

4. Possessives
(My, Your, His, Her, Its, Our, Their, etc)

We use a possessive determiner before a noun to show who owns the noun we are talking about.

e.g. • This is **your** book.

The possessive determiners **my, her, his** and **its** are used with singular nouns, while **our** and **their** are used with plural nouns. **Your** can be used with either singular or plural nouns, depending on the sense.

e.g. • This is **my** book.
• The dog licked **its** paw.
• Which is **their** car?

Chapter Practice

Objective Questions

• Multiple Choice Questions

Directions (Q. Nos. 1-15) Choose the correct determiners to fill in the blanks in the given sentences.

1. The train doesn't stop at .... station along the way, but it stops at .... of the main ones.
(a) all , either
(b) every , most
(c) each , much
(d) both , some

Ans. (*b*) every , most

2. Unfortunately, our local library had .... books on the subject, so I'm going to the city library tomorrow hoping to find .... more.
(a) much , a little
(b) a little , a lot
(c) a few , much
(d) few , some

Ans. (*d*) few , some

3. If there is .... food in the world for everyone, why do so .... people die of starvation?
(a) little , much
(b) enough , many
(c) much , few
(d) any , a lot of

Ans. (*b*) enough , many

4. There is ....information available on recycling, but unfortunately, ... of it is known by ordinary people.
(a) a lot of , little
(b) plenty of , much
(c) several , less
(d) much , little

Ans. (*a*) a lot of , little

5. If I had .... fabric left, I could make a dress, but I think I've only got .... to make a skirt.
(a) plenty , a few
(b) a few more , much
(c) a number of , some
(d) a little more , enough

Ans. (*d*) a little more , enough

6. Cyanide leaked into .... Mersey Canal, and .... nine mile stretch of .... canal was affected.
(a) the , the , a
(b) —- , —- , a
(c) the , a , the
(d) a , a , —-

Ans. (*c*) the , a , the

7. The word deafness is used to describe .... degree of hearing loss, though it is most commonly used where there is .... total inability to hear.
(a) some , much
(b) the , some
(c) a , many
(d) any , a

Ans. (*d*) any , a

8. A: Which of these wallpaper designs would you like in the living room?

B: ...... · ...... look horrible. Why can't we just paint the walls?
(a) All , None
(b) Neither , Both
(c) None , Some
(d) Every , Each

Ans. (*b*) Neither , Both

9. Diamonds have .... uses. In addition to the obvious use in jewellery, they have .... number of industrial applications.
(a) much , any
(b) many , a
(c) plenty of , the
(d) some , each

Ans. (*b*) many , a

10. .... albatross, ...largest and most majestic skybird, has .... wing span of over nine feet.
(a) —- , the , —-
(b) The , a , the
(c) The , the , a
(d) An , a , a

Ans. (*c*) The , the , a

11. The teacher said that we could write on ....sides of the paper, but to start a new page for ....question.
(a) either , every
(b) both , each
(c) some , all
(d) all , some

Ans. (*a*) either , every

12. The wildlife of............region is under threat and .... rare animal species may become extinct.
(a) each , others
(b) another , both
(c) every , either
(d) the whole , some

Ans. (*d*) the whole , some

13. After .... years passed, I decided to have an operation to have .... wrinkles taken away from around my eyes.

  (a) several , all   (b) many , a good many

  (c) the whole , both   (d) some , many

Ans. (*b*) many , a good many

14. Although .... in the group knew that .... had ever tried to climb the mountain by this path before, they all seemed very confident.

  (a) someone , nowhere   (b) no one , anywhere

  (c) everyone , no one   (d) anyone , somebody

Ans. (*c*) everyone , no one

15. .... of the soldiers was given two complete uniforms, ... of which they were expected to keep spotlessly clean.

  (a) Every , either   (b) Each , both

  (c) Some , all   (d) The whole , many

Ans. (*b*) Each , both

• Gap filling

Directions (Q. Nos. 16-20) Choose the correct option to fill in the blanks in the given passage.

Once, there was a very rich man. He was neither handsome nor clever but he worked hard and saved ......(16)...... money. There was a beautiful lady who lived just two doors away from his house. She was a widow with ....(17)...... children. Every morning, the rich man would steal a few glances at the widow when she came out to do her chores in the garden. One evening, the man decided to pay her a visit. He brought with him ......(18)...... presents, one for each child. ......(19)...... the children liked him and so every time he visited her, he brought presents for the children. This went on for ......(20)...... months.

16. (a) more   (b) a lot of

    (c) much   (d) a whole lot

Ans. (*b*) a lot of

17. (a) little   (b) a few

    (c) small   (d) few

Ans. (*d*) few

18. (a) much   (b) many

    (c) lots of   (d) whole

Ans. (*b*) many

19. (a) All   (b) Every

    (c) Each   (d) Either

Ans. (*a*) All

20. (a) quite   (b) many

    (c) several   (d) few

Ans. (*c*) several

Directions (Q. Nos. 21-25) Choose the correct option to fill in the blanks in the given passage.

Pampore, a small town on the banks of the river Jhelum, near Srinagar, is the main centre of ......(21)...... saffron cultivation in India. The best saffron comes from Spain, which is the world's largest producer. Saffron, the ......(22)...... expensive spice in the world, is known as 'kesar' in ......(23)...... parts of India. It adds a golden colour to food and gives it ......(24)...... unique flavour. Moreover, ...(25)...... saffron goes a long way – for example, half a teaspoon is sufficient to flavour a litre of kheer.

21. (a) most   (b) much

    (c) lot of   (d) whole

Ans. (*a*) most

22. (a) very   (b) too

    (c) most   (d) lot

Ans. (*c*) most

23. (a) many   (b) several

    (c) every   (d) each

Ans. (*b*) several

24. (a) a   (b) an

    (c) the   (d) No article

Ans. (*a*) a

25. (a) few   (b) a little

    (c) small   (d) quite

Ans. (*b*) a little

• Transformation of Sentences

Directions (Q. Nos. 26-40) Transform the given sentences without changing their meaning.

26. How gorgeous is the sunset!

  (a) The sunset is gorgeous.

  (b) The sunset is not just gorgeous.

  (c) The sunset is very gorgeous.

  (d) The sunset is most gorgeous.

Ans. (*c*) The sunset is very gorgeous.

27. No other metal is as expensive as gold.

  (a) No other metal except gold is expensive.

  (b) Gold is expensive of all the metals.

  (c) Isn't gold the most expensive of all metals.

  (d) Gold is the most expensive of all metals.

Ans. (*d*) Gold is the most expensive of all metals.

28. That chocolate is not as sweet as this one.

  (a) The chocolates vary in their sweetness.

  (b) This chocolate is sweeter than that chocolate.

  (c) This chocolate is not sweeter than that chocolate.

  (d) This chocolate is sweeter than that one.

Ans. (*d*) This chocolate is sweeter than that one.

29. This tea is too hot for me.
   (a) This tea is so hot that I cannot take it.
   (b) This tea is very hot for me.
   (c) This tea is hot for me.
   (d) This tea is hot that I cannot take it.
Ans. (*a*) This tea is so hot that I cannot take it.

30. The oranges are too cheap to be good.
   (a) The oranges are cheap and good.
   (b) The oranges are cheap as well as good.
   (c) The oranges are very cheap good.
   (d) The oranges are so cheap that they cannot be good.
Ans. (*d*) The oranges are so cheap that they cannot be good.

31. Mary had hardly said a word since the party began.
   (a) Mary had not spoken much after the party began.
   (b) In the beginning, Mary did not speak much.
   (c) Mary did not speak anything in the party.
   (d) The party started and Mary did not speak much.
Ans. (*a*) Mary had not spoken much after the party began.

32. Rajdhani Express is the fastest train.
(Positive Sentence)
   (a) There is no other train as fast as Rajdhani Express.
   (b) No other train is as fast as Rajdhani Express.
   (c) Both (a) and (b)
   (d) None of the above
Ans. (*c*) Both (a) and (b)

33. Buy one shirt and get one free.
   (a) If you buy one shirt, you get another shirt free.
   (b) If you buy one shirt, you get one free.
   (c) A shirt free on purchase of a shirt.
   (d) Buy one shirt to get one free.
Ans. (*b*) If you buy one shirt, you get one free.

34. Samay writes more neatly than any other boy in the class.
   (a) No other boy of Samay's class writes as neatly as he does.
   (b) Samay writes neatly than all his classmates.
   (c) Samay's writing is very neat.
   (d) Samay's writing is neater than all the boys in his class.
Ans. (*a*) No other boy of Samay's class writes as neatly as he does.

35. The students were not able to solve the problem. It was too difficult for them.
   (a) It was too difficult to solve the problem.
   (b) To the students it was too difficult to solve the problem.
   (c) The problem for the student was too difficult to solve.
   (d) The problem was too difficult for the students to solve.
Ans. (*d*) The problem was too difficult for the students to solve.

36. He must work hard to make up for the lost time.
   (a) He should make up the lost of time working hard.
   (b) He worked hard and up for the lost time.
   (c) Working hard he can make up the lost time.
   (d) He has to make up the lost time working hard.
Ans. (*b*) He worked hard and made up for the lost time.

37. How childish are your talks!
   (a) Your talks are childish.
   (b) You should not talk childish.
   (c) Your talks are most childish.
   (d) Your talks are very childish.
Ans. (*d*) Your talks are very childish.

38. She is as happy as her sister.
   (a) She is not happier than her sister.
   (b) She is happier than her sister.
   (c) Her sister and she are not happy.
   (d) Her sister is as happy as she.
Ans. (*a*) She is not happier than her sister.

39. She stayed at her aunt's everyday during the holidays.
   (a) She stayed at her aunt's few times during the holidays.
   (b) She stayed at her aunt's plenty of times during the holidays.
   (c) During the holidays, she stayed at her aunt's most of the time.
   (d) During the holidays, she stayed at her aunt's all the time.
Ans. (*d*) During the holidays, she stayed at her aunt's all of the time.

40. Most of the Bottle is filled with gel.
   (a) There is enough gel in the Bottle.
   (b) There is little gel in the Bottle
   (c) There is much gel in the Bottle.
   (d) There is some gel in the Bottle.
Ans. (*a*) There is enough gel in the Bottle.

CHAPTER 02

Tenses

In this Chapter...

- Classification of Tenses
- Chapter Practice

Tense is defined as the form of verb that gives the relation between **Time** and **Action**. In other words the time when the action is done.

There are three phases of time and as a result there are three tenses.

(i) **present** (time that is now)
(ii) **past** (time that has passed)
(iii) **future** (time that is yet to come)

Classification of Tenses

The three kinds of tenses are further divided into four forms each as given in the chart:

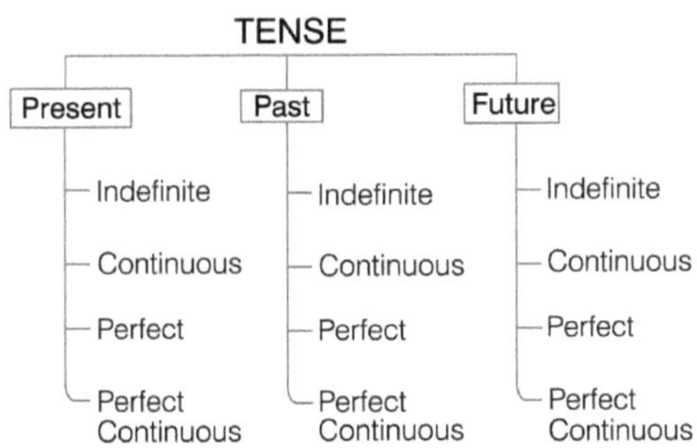

Present Tense (Present Indefinite Tense)

This tense is also called simple present tense.
It is used in the following ways

(i) To express a habit or custom.
e.g. She gets up every morning at 6 o'clock.

(ii) To talk about a general or universal truth.
e.g. The Earth revolves around the Sun.

(iii) To indicate a definite future event.
e.g. The school reopens next week.

(iv) To introduce quotes with the verb 'says'.
e.g. Newton says, "Every action has an equal and an opposite reaction."

Rules for Affirmative Sentences

- Singular subject + first form of verb + s/es + ...
- Plural subject + first form of verb + ...
e.g. (a) They play cricket in the ground.
(b) Water boils at 100°C.
(c) She advises me not to smoke.

Rules for Negative Sentences

- Singular subject + does not + first form of verb + ...
- Plural subject + do not + first form of verb + ...
e.g. (a) Reena does not watch television.
(b) We do not smoke.

Rules for Interrogative Sentences

- Do/does + subject + first form of verb + ...?
- Question word + do/does + subject + first form of verb + ...?

  e.g. (a) Do you play cricket?

  (b) Does she wash clothes?

  (c) Why do you weep now?

  (d) Whose book do you read?

Present Continuous Tense

This tense is used in the following ways

(i) To describe an action in progress and the continuity of the action.

e.g. The passengers are wandering to and for.

(ii) An action that has been pre-arranged to take place in the near future.

e.g. The wedding is going to take place on Sunday.

(iii) Persistent and undesirable habit, especially with adverbs like *always, continually, constantly etc.*

e.g. (a) You are always running me down.

(b) He is constantly gazing at me.

Rules for Affirmative Sentences

- Singular subject + is/am + first form of verb+ ing +.......
- Plural subject + are + first form of verb + ing +.......

  e.g. (a) I am playing a game.

  (b) She is reading a book.

  (c) We are going to Shimla.

Rules for Negative Sentences

- Singular subject + is/am + not + first form of verb + ing +.......
- Plural subject + are + not + first form of verb + ing +.......

  e.g. (a) Ram is not surfing the internet.

  (b) They are not watching a movie.

  (c) I am not swimming in the water.

Rules for Interrogative Sentences

- Is/are/am + subject + first form of verb + ing + ...?
- Question word + is/are/am + subject + first form of verb + ing + ... ?

  e.g. (a) Is Reena cooking the food?

  (b) Are you not writing a letter?

  (c) What is Raveena doing here?

  (d) Why was the camel not drinking water?

Present Perfect Tense

This tense is used in the following ways

(i) To express an action that has recently been completed.

e.g. She has just taken tea.

(ii) To describe an action whose time is not given.

e.g. Have you done M. Sc in Maths?

(iii) To describe past events whose effect still exists.

e.g.   I have finished my work and now I am free.

(iv) To show how a past situation relates to the present.

e.g. I've done my homework, so I can help you with yours now.

Rules for Affirmative Sentences

- Singular subject + has + third form of verb + ...
- Plural subject + have + third form of verb + ...

  e.g. (a) She has gone to the market.

  (b) They have bathed.

Rules for Negative Sentences

- Singular subject + has + not + third form of verb + ...
- Plural subject + have + not + third form of verb + ...

  e.g. (a) I have not called him.

  (b) The train has not gone.

Rules for Interrogative Sentences

- Has/have + subject + third form of verb +.....?
- Question word + has/have + subject + third form of verb + ... ?

  e.g. (a) Has she gone to Delhi?

  (b) Have they not seen the Taj Mahal yet?

  (c) What have they eaten today?

  (d) Why has the peon not come yet?

Present Perfect Continuous Tense

This tense is also called present perfect progressive tense.

This tense is used in the following ways

(i) To describe an action that began in the past and is still continuing.

e.g. They have been staying in the village for a long time.

(ii) To express an action already completed, but whose effect is still continuing.

e.g. I have been running around for the job all day and am now tired.

Rules for Affirmative Sentences

- Singular subject + has + been + first form of verb + ing + ... + for/since +......
- Plural subject + have + been + first form of verb + ing + ... + for/since +......

  e.g. (a) Arpit has been sleeping since 6 o'clock.

  (b) They have been running for three hours.

Rules for Negative Sentences

- Singular subject + has + not + been + first form of verb + ing + ... + for/since +......

- Plural subject + have + not + been + first form of verb + ing + ... + for/since +......

  e.g. (a) You have not been suffering from fever for one week.

     (b) Reena has not been going to music class for 2 months.

Rules for Interrogative Sentences

- Has/Have + subject + been + first form of verb + ing + ... + since/for +.....?
- Question word + has/have + subject + been + first form of verb + ing + ...+ since/for + ...?

  e.g. (a) Have you been sleeping since 8 o'clock?

     (b) Has he not been living in this house for a long time?

     (c) Why have they been playing football since morning?

Past Tense (Past Indefinite Tense)

This tense is also called simple past tense.

It is used in the following ways

  (i) To indicate an action that happened in the past. It is used often in recounts and narratives.

    e.g. I visited the Taj Mahal three months ago.

 (ii) To indicate past habits or repeated events that are now over.

    e.g. In those days, my mother gave me some pocket money every day.

Rule for Affirmative Sentences

- Subject + second form of verb +......

  e.g. (a) I played football in the ground.

     (b) She sang a song in the party.

Rule for Negative Sentences

- Subject + did not + first form of verb +......

  e.g. (a) I did not attend the function.

     (b) They did not watch television.

Rules for Interrogative Sentences

- Did + subject + first form of verb + ... ?
- Question word + did + subject + first form of verb +........?

  e.g. (a) Did you play a game?

     (b) Why did she abuse her friends?

Past Continuous Tense

This tense is used in the following ways

  (i) To indicate an action that was happening at some time in the past.

    e.g. We were watching TV the whole evening.

 (ii) The past continuous is also used for an action that was going on during a given period or at a period of time in the past.

    e.g. While Rohan was filling in the hole, his dog was digging another.

Rules for Affirmative Sentences

- Singular subject + was + first form of verb + ing +.....
- Plural subject + were + first form of verb + ing + ...

  e.g. (a) She was driving her car.

     (b) They were making a noise.

Rules for Negative Sentences

- Singular subject + was + not + first form of verb + ing +.....
- Plural subject + were + not + first form of verb + ing +.....

  e.g. (a) She was not singing a song.

     (b) They were not eating mangoes.

Rules for Interrogative Sentences

- Was/were + subject + first form of verb + ing +......?
- Question word + was/were + subject + first form of verb + ing +.....?

  e.g. (a) Were you eating a mango?

     (b) When was the milkman milking the cow?

     (c) Why was the blind boy crying?

Past Perfect Tense

This tense is used in the following ways

  (i) To indicate an action that was completed before a definite time or before another action that took place in the past.

    e.g. The patient had died before the doctor reached the hospital.

 (ii) It indicates desires in the past that have not been fulfilled.

    e.g. I wish I had not wasted my time.

Rule for Affirmative Sentences

Subject + had + third form of verb + ...

  e.g. She had cooked the food.

Rule for Negative Sentences

Subject + had + not + third form of verb + ...

  e.g. They had not attended the function.

Rule for Interrogative Sentences

Had + subject + third form of verb + ... ?

Question word + had + subject + third form of verb +.........?

e.g. (a) Had she watched a movie?

   (b) Why had you not gone to Delhi?

Past Perfect Continuous Tense

This tense is also called past perfect progressive tense.

This tense indicates an action which began in the past and continued up to a certain point of time in the past.

e.g. When we met in Lucknow, she had been studying in city college for 3 years.

Rule for Affirmative Sentences

- Subject + had been + first form of verb +ing + ... + since/for +.....

  e.g. (a) You had been suffering from fever since Tuesday.

    (b) I had been studying for three hours.

Rule for Negative Sentences

- Subject + had + not + been + first form of verb + ing + ... + since/for +......

  e.g. They had not been going to office since the 5th of July.

Rules for Interrogative Sentences

- Had + subject + been + first form of verb + ing + ... + since/for + ...?
- Question word + had + subject + been + first form of verb + ing + ...since/for+..... ?

  e.g. (a) Had you not been reading the book since morning?

    (b) Where had he been playing since morning?

Future Tense (Future Indefinite Tense)

This tense is also called simple future tense.

It is used to say what we believe or think will happen in future.

e.g. I believe she will join the office tomorrow.

Rules for Affirmative Sentences

- You/He/She/It/They (Second and Third Person Pronouns) + will + first form of verb + ...
- I/We (First Person Pronouns) + shall + first form of verb + ...

  e.g. (a) He will sell his house.

    (b) I shall purchase a new car.

Rules for Negative Sentences

- You/He/She/It/They (Second and Third Person Pronouns) + will + not + first form of verb + ...
- I/We (First Person Pronouns) + shall + not + first form of verb + ...

  e.g. (a) My friend will not host dinner this evening.

    (b) We shall not skip the exams.

Rules for Interrogative Sentences

- Will/Shall+ subject + first form of verb +......?
- Question word + will/shall + subject + first form of verb + ...?

e.g. (a) Will she not come in the party?

  (b) Who will help him?

  (c) Why will your friend not come here?

Future Continuous Tense

This tense is used in the following ways

 (i) To indicate an action that will occur in the normal course.
    e.g. She will be cooking the food tomorrow.

 (ii) To indicate an action that will be in progress at a given point of time in the future.
    e.g. At this time tomorrow, we shall be attending the party.

Rules for Affirmative Sentences

- You/He/She/It/They (Second and Third Person Pronouns) + will + be + first form of verb + ing + ...
- I/We (First Person Pronouns) + shall + be + first form of verb + ing + ...

  e.g. (a) Next year my teacher will be going to China.

    (b) I shall be teaching my students.

Rules for Negative Sentences

- You/He/She/It/They (Second and Third Person Pronouns) + will + not + be + first form of verb + ing + ...
- I/We (First Person Pronouns) + shall + not + be + first form of verb + ing + ...

  e.g. (a) They will not be studying in city college.

    (b) I shall not be bathing this evening.

Rules for Interrogative Sentences

- Will/shall + subject + be + first form of verb + ing + ...?
- Question word + will/shall + subject + be + first form of verb + ing +.....?

  e.g. (a) Will this boy be wandering in the forest?

    (b) How long will they be travelling?

Future Perfect Tense

This tense is used to describe an action which will be completed at some point of time in the future.

e.g. I shall have finished this work by tomorrow.

Rules for Affirmative Sentences

- You/He/She/It/They (Second and Third Person Pronouns) + will + have + third form of verb + ...
- I/We (First Person Pronouns) + shall + have + third form of verb + ...

  e.g. (a) Your examination will have been over by Tuesday.

    (b) We shall have cooked the food by the evening.

Rules for Negative Sentences
- You/He/She/It/They (Second and Third Person Pronouns) + will + not + have + third form of verb + ...
- I/We (First Person Pronouns) + shall + not + have + third form of verb + ...

  e.g. (a) The passengers will not have reached the station before the train starts.

  (b) Your brother will not have read this novel before next Saturday.

  (c) I shall not have written the letter by noon.

Rules for Interrogative Sentences
- Will/shall + subject + have + third form of verb +.......?
- Question word + will/shall + subject + have + third form of verb ......?

  e.g. (a) Will he not have gone before I reach?

  (b) What will he have eaten before he sleeps?

Future Perfect Continuous Tense

This tense is also called future perfect progressive tense.

This tense is used in the following ways

It describes an action that will be in progress over a period of time that will end in the future.

e.g. At noon, Anuradha will have been singing songs for an hour.

Rules for Affirmative Sentences
- You/He/She/It/They (Second and Third Person Pronouns) + will + have + been + first form of verb + ing + ... + since/for + ...
- I/We (First Person Pronouns) + shall + have + been + first form of verb + ing + ... + since/for + ...

  e.g. By next April we shall have been leaving for the USA.

Rules for Negative Sentences
- You/He/She/It/They (Second and Third Person Pronouns) + will + not + have + been + first form of verb + ing + ... + since/for + ...
- I/We (First Person Pronouns) + shall + not + have + been + first form of verb + ing + ... + since/for + ...

  e.g. (a) Mahima will not have been going to Kanpur for a long time.

  (b) I shall not have been writing for half an hour.

Rules for Interrogative Sentences
- Will/shall + subject + have + been + first form of verb + ing + ... + since/for + ... ?
- Question word + will/ shall + subject + have + been + first form of verb + ing + ... + since/for + ... ?

  e.g. (a) Will she have been playing for some time?

  (b) Why will you not have been going to school since 8 o'clock?

Chapter Practice

Objective Questions

• Multiple Choice Questions

Directions (Q. Nos. 1-15) Choose the correct option to fill in the blanks in the given sentence.

1. In 1619, the first African slaves .... in Virginia, USA and by 1790, their numbers .... nearly 700,000.
(a) were arriving / have been reaching
(b) arrived / had reached
(c) have arrived / were reaching
(d) were going to arrive / reach

Ans. (*b*) arrived / had reached

2. We .... a lovely view of the Bosphorus and the bridges over it while the plane .... over Istanbul.
(a) are getting / flies   (b) had got / is flying
(c) got / was flying   (d) get / has flown

Ans. (*c*) got / was flying

3. When they .... in Sydney Harbour, they .... nonstop for three months.
(a) anchor / will have been sailing
(b) were anchoring / sailed
(c) have anchored / were sailing
(d) are anchoring / have been sailing

Ans. (*a*) anchor / will have been sailing

4. According to the new schedule the whole team has accepted, we .... every Monday and Wednesday next term, but I'm sure we .... back to our normal routine of once a week before long.
(a) had trained / revert
(b) train / have reverted
(c) are training / reverted
(d) are going to train / will revert

Ans. (*d*) are going to train / will revert

5. The prospector ran into town in excitement because, at last, he .... some gold at the site which he .... for months.
(a) was finding / was panning
(b) will find / is going to pan
(c) will have found / has panned
(d) had found / had been panning

Ans. (*d*) had found / had been panning

6. I expect you .... bored with working at the Post Office by this time next year and .... for a more interesting job.
(a) have become / will have looked
(b) will have become / will be looking
(c) had found / had been panning
(d) found / will have panned

Ans. (*b*) will have become / will be looking

7. Listen! The coach .... the strengths of our opponents because our team .... against them before.
(a) has explained / weren't playing
(b) explains / won't play
(c) is explaining / hasn't played
(d) will explain / hadn't been playing

Ans. (*c*) is explaining / hasn't played

8. When I .... the alterations to the company accounts, I was left in no doubt that the accountant .... money from the firm.
(a) saw / had been stealing
(b) am seeing / has stolen
(c) was seeing / was stealing
(d) have seen / will have stolen

Ans. (*a*) saw / had been stealing

9. According to the doctor, this time next week, I .... around as normal and the cut on my foot .... completely.
(a) am walking / healed
(b) will be walking / will have healed
(c) walked / was healing
(d) have been walking / heals

Ans. (*b*) will be walking / will have healed

10. Shadow puppets .... in China and .... as far as Turkey and Greece today.
(a) will originate / have been spreading
(b) are originating / will be spreading
(c) originate / had spread
(d) originated / have spread
Ans. (*d*) originated / have spread

11. Over recent years, many skilled craftsmen and women .... their jobs in the pottery trade in the UK, but gradually English porcelain .... its reputation.
(a) will have lost / will regain
(b) had been losing / has regained
(c) are losing / regained
(d) have lost / is regaining
Ans. (*d*) have lost / is regaining

12. After she .... to turn up for our appointment for the third time, I .... to meet her again.
(a) is failing / am refusing
(b) has failed / had refused
(c) was failing / will refuse
(d) had failed / refused
Ans. (*d*) had failed / refused

13. Since I took part in my first debating match, I .... a member of the debating club, which I .... most weekends.
(a) will have been / have attended
(b) have been / attend
(c) will be / was attending
(d) am / had been attending
Ans. (*b*) have been / attend

14. By the first half of the 19th century, potato .... the staple food in the Ireland. In 1854, a disease ...., which resulted in widespread starvation.
(a) was becoming / has struck
(b) will become / was going to strike
(c) had become / struck
(d) was going to become / strikes
Ans. (*c*) had become / struck

15. The origins of domestic poultry .... uncertain, but experts believe that some breeds are descended from the Indian jungle-fowl, which still .... in India today.
(a) had been / will have existed
(b) were / had been existing
(c) are / exists
(d) have been / existed
Ans. (*c*) are / exists

• Gap Filling

Directions (Q. Nos. 16-20) Choose the correct option to fill in the blanks in the given passage.

The first half of the 20th century was dominated by the two World Wars. The wars resulted in unprecedented numbers of casualties. Eight and a half million people are believed ....(16)....... fighting in the First World War of 1914-1918. During the Second World War as many as 60 million ....(17)....... in Asia and the Pacific. From all the total number of casualties, half ....(18)......... civilians. The scale of ....(19)........ was largely due to the destructive power of weaponry. With the use of atomic bomb at the end of the Second World War, this reached too terrifying a peak that the major powers ....(20) .... to prevent international wars.

16. (a) that they died   (b) having died
      (c) to have died   (d) died
Ans. (*c*) to have died

17. (a) killed   (b) killing
      (c) having been killed   (d) were killed
Ans. (*d*) were killed

18. (a) were   (b) had been
      (c) are   (d) is believed to be
Ans. (*a*) were

19. (a) kills   (b) killing
      (c) killed   (d) kill
Ans. (*b*) killing

20. (a) have tried   (b) will have been trying
      (c) tried   (d) will try
Ans. (*c*) tried

Directions (Q. Nos. 21-25) Choose the correct option to fill in the blanks in the given passage.

Turkey's annual information technology fair, CEBIT Bilisim Eurasia, this year aims to attract a diverse crowd into a society debate, especially ....(21)....... the use of Internet technologies in government. CEBIT Bilisim Eurasia ....(22)....... to host visitors from over 70 countries as well as members of the press from nearly 20 countries. Under the theme of 'Competitive Edge', Bilisim Summit 2007 and Forum Bilisim ....(23) .... how to improve the competitive power of countries, organisations and individuals by ....(24) .... ICT technologies. CEBIT Bilisim Eurasia ....(25)......... this year at the TUYAP Beylikdüzü Fair.

21. (a) being concerned   (b) concerned
      (c) having concerned   (d) concerning
Ans. (*d*) concerning

22. (a) expects   (b) is expected
    (c) will be expected   (d) had expected
Ans. (*a*) expects

23. (a) discussed   (b) will be discussing
    (c) will discuss   (d) has discussed
Ans. (*c*) will discuss

24. (a) having used   (b) used
    (c) using   (d) use
Ans. (*c*) using

25. (a) has staged   (b) had been staged
    (c) was staged   (d) will be staged
Ans. (*d*) will be staged

● Transformation of Sentences

Directions (Q. Nos. 26-40) Change the tense of the following sentences as directed without changing their meaning.

26. Change into Simple Present Tense.
Anand was breathing oxygen from the cylinder.
(a) Anand breathe oxygen from the cylinder.
(b) Anand breathes oxygen from the cylinder.
(c) Anand is breathing oxygen from the cylinder.
(d) Anand took a breath of oxygen from the cylinder.
Ans. (*b*) Anand breathes oxygen from the cylinder.

27. Change into Simple Past Tense.
But I have taken my revenge at last.
(a) But I had taken my revenge at last.
(b) But I taken my revenge at last.
(c) But I took my revenge at last.
(d) But I have my revenge at last.
Ans. (*c*) But I took my revenge at last.

28. Change into Future Perfect Continuous Tense.
I had been working for Anil.
(a) I will have worked for Anil.
(b) I will work for Anil.
(c) I will be working for Anil.
(d) I will have been working for Anil.
Ans. (*d*) I will have been working for Anil.

29. Change into Past Continuous Tense.
Dingko Singh had inspired many youngsters in Manipur.
(a) Dingko Singh did inspiring many youngsters in Manipur.
(b) Dingko Singh had been inspiring many youngsters in Manipur.
(c) Dingko Singh was being inspired many youngsters in Manipur.
(d) Dingko Singh was inspiring many youngsters in Manipur.
Ans. (*d*) Dingko Singh was inspiring many youngsters in Manipur.

30. Change into Simple Future Tense.
What are we doing?
(a) What shall we be doing?
(b) What shall we have been doing?
(c) What shall we do?
(d) What shall be done?
Ans. (*c*) What shall we do?

31. Change into Present Perfect Tense.
She had an eager interest in athletics.
(a) She had have an eager interest in athletics.
(b) She had had an eager interest in athletics.
(c) She has an eager interest in athletics.
(d) She has had an eager interest in athletics.
Ans. (*c*) She has an eager interest in athletics.

32. Change into Past Perfect Tense.
The chairs were being arranged.
(a) The chairs had arranged.
(b) The chairs had been arranged.
(c) The chairs were arranged.
(d) The chairs had had arranged.
Ans. (*b*) The chairs had been arranged.

33. Change into Simple Future Tense.
He was kidnapped by an extremist militia.
(a) He will be kidnapped by an extremist militia.
(b) He will have been kidnapped by an extremist militia.
(c) He will be kidnapping by an extremist militia.
(d) He will kidnapped by an extremist militia.
Ans. (*a*) He will be kidnapped by an extremist militia.

34. Change into Present Continuous Tense.
Will you train your child to be a boxer as well?
(a) Are you training your child to be a boxer as well?
(b) Were you training your child to be a boxer as well?
(c) Will you have been training your child to be a boxer as well?
(d) Are you being trained to be a boxer as well?
Ans. (*a*) Are you training your child to be a boxer as well?

35. Change into Future Perfect Tense.
I had a cup of coffee in the morning.
(a) I will have had a cup of coffee in the morning.
(b) I will have a cup of coffee in the morning.
(c) I shall be having a cup of coffee in the morning.
(d) I will had a cup of coffee in the morning.
Ans. (*b*) I will have had a cup of coffee in the morning.

36. Change into Past Perfect Continuous Tense.
I shall be telling you three stories.
(a) I am telling you three stories.
(b) I had been telling you three stories.
(c) I was telling you three stories.
(d) I was being told to tell you three stories.
Ans. (*b*) I had been telling you three stories.

37. Change into Future Perfect Continuous Tense.

I had been working for Anil.
 (a) I will have been worked for Anil.
 (b) I will be working for Anil.
 (c) I shall had been working for Anil.
 (d) I will have been working for Anil.

Ans. (d) I will have been working for Anil.

38. Change into Simple Future Tense.

Every Fortnight a flower blooms on it.
 (a) Every Fortnight a flower will bloom on it.
 (b) Every Fortnight a flower will be blooming on it.
 (c) Every Fortnight a flower will have bloomed on it.
 (d) Every Fortnight a flower will have bloomed on it.

Ans. (a) Every Fortnight a flower will bloom on it.

39. Change into Present Continuous Tense.

Manolin had been forced by his parents.
 (a) Manolin has been forced by his parents.
 (b) Manolin is being forced by his parents.
 (c) Manolin is forced by his parents.
 (d) Manolin was forced by his parents.

Ans. (b) Manolin is being forced by his parents.

40. Change into Past Continuous Tense.

Do you remember your first arithmetic lesson?
 (a) Were you remembering your first arithmetic lesson?
 (b) Did you remember your first arithmetic lesson?
 (c) Had you remembered your first arithmetic lesson?
 (d) Are you remembering your first arithmetic lesson?

Ans. (a) Were you remembering your first arithmetic lesson?

Re-ordering of Sentences

In the re-ordering of sentences, single sentence is divided into parts named with certain alphabets (For example – PQRS) and then jumbled up.

A student is expected to arrange these four parts in a meaningful sequence and mark the correct order from among the alternatives provided. For *example*

1 : It is well-known that
P : youngsters in the cities and the villages
Q : the effect
R : of the cinema
S : on the school and college going
6 : is very bad

(a) Q S P R   (b) Q R S P
(c) R S P Q   (d) R Q P S

The correct sequence is (b) Q R S P.

Chapter Practice

Objective Questions

• Multiple Choice Questions

Directions (Q. Nos. 1-25) The questions given below consists of certain phrases. Rearrange these phrases to form a meaningful sentence.

1. A. I wanted to tell her
   B. not to talk to him
   C. not listen to me
   D. but she would
   (a) ABCD   (b) ABDC   (c) ADBC   (d) BCAD

Ans. (*b*) ABDC

2. A. The managing director
   B. in listening to her
   C. was not interested
   D. explain about why profits were lessening
   (a) ABCD   (b) ABDC   (c) ACBD   (d) BCDA

Ans. (*c*) ACB-D

3. A. for thousands of years
   B. famous symbols of ancient civilisations
   C. Monuments have been created
   D. and they are often the most durable and
   (a) CADB   (b) ABCD   (c) BADC   (d) DCBA

Ans. (*a*) CADB

4. A. is one of the most widely used indicators
   B. of ecosystems and their biodiversity
   C. for assessing the condition
   D. The conservation status of plants and animals
   (a) DACB   (b) DCBA   (c) BCAD   (d) ABCD

Ans. (*a*) DACB

5. A. photos which were submitted
   B. in the fire last night
   C. for the exhibition
   D. have been totally burnt
   (a) ADCB   (b) BACD   (c) ACDB   (d) CADB

Ans. (*c*) ACDB

6. A. supported by soft term loans
   B. to supply the raw material worth ₹ 5 lakh
   C. the dealer has agreed
   D. with a very low rate of interest
   (a) CBAD   (b) DBAC   (c) ADCB   (d) BACD

Ans. (*a*) CBAD

7. Mrs Dalal had a soft spot for Boori Ma,
   A. occasionally she gave the old woman
   B. flavor her stew
   C. some ginger paste
   D. with which to
   (a) ABCD   (b) DCAB   (c) BCAD   (d) ACDB

Ans. (*d*) ACDB

8. You're obviously wrong,
   A. all by yourself-you needn't imagine that
   B. you'll have to walk to the nearest garage
   C. and because of such foresight
   D. I will keep you company
   (a) DCAB   (b) CBAD   (c) ABCD   (d) DCBA

Ans. (*b*) CBAD

9. A. the only creature
   B. laughter
   C. blessed with the power of
   D. man is
   (a) BACD   (b) DACB   (c) ACBD   (d) DCBA

Ans. (*b*) DACB

10. A. by keeping
   B. oblige me
   C. your
   D. to yourself
   E. suspicion
   (a) CBAED   (b) CEDBA   (c) BACED   (d) BACDE

Ans. (*c*) BACED

11. A. do with the
   B. time that is given to us
   C. All we have to
   D. decide is what to
   (a) CABD   (b) BACD
   (c) CDAB   (d) DABC

Ans. (*c*) CDAB

12. We are
   A. rounded with a sleep
   B. are made on, and
   C. such stuff as dreams
   D. our little life is
   (a) CBDA   (b) CADB   (c) ACBD   (d) ADBC
Ans. (*a*) CBDA

13. A. when meat
   B. the food poisoning occurred
   C. added in the food preparations
   D. of low quality was
   (a) CBAD   (b) BCDA   (c) ADBC   (d) BADC
Ans. (*d*) BADC

14. A. She saw her opportunity
   B. to make amends
   C. when he came to her home
   D. to borrow some sugar
   (a) BCDA   (b) BCAD   (c) ADBC   (d) ABCD
Ans. (*d*) ABCD

15. The statement
   P. therefore you must listen carefully
   Q. what the speaker has said
   R. in order to understand
   S. will be made just once
   (a) SRPQ   (b) SPQR   (c) SPRQ   (d) RSPQ
Ans. (*c*) SPRQ

16. Reading books
   P. is a habit
   Q. but also enlarges the mind
   R. because it not only increases knowledge
   S. which must be cultivated by everybody
   (a) PSRQ   (b) PQSR
   (c) SRPQ   (d) PQRS
Ans. (*a*) PSRQ

17. Towards midnight
   P. so that the sky was lighted with
   Q. and the clouds drifted away
   R. the rain ceased
   S. the incredible lamp of stars
   (a) SPQR   (b) SQPR   (c) RPQS   (d) RQPS
Ans. (*d*) RQPS

18. The exhibition committee
   P. attractive and useful
   Q. to make the exhibition
   R. making efforts
   S. has been
   (a) SRQP   (b) QPRS
   (c) SRPQ   (d) QPSR
Ans. (*a*) SRQP

19. They are plant eaters
   P. and various kinds of vegetation
   Q. browsing on grass
   R. and consume
   S. vast quantities of pasture
   (a) RSQP   (b) QSRP   (c) QPRS   (d) RSPQ
Ans. (*c*) QPRS

20. It is a rule
   P. by anyone and admit
   Q. that must not
   R. of no variation
   S. be violated
   (a) QSPR   (b) PSQR   (c) QPRS   (d) RQPS
Ans. (*a*) QSPR

21. I read an advertisement that said
   P. posh, air conditioned
   Q. gentlemen of taste
   R. are available for
   S. fully furnished rooms
   (a) SRPQ   (b) PSQR   (c) PQRS   (d) PSRQ
Ans. (*d*) PSRQ

22. The Indian woman wants
   P. in a male dominated society
   Q. as an equal partner
   R. and it is not too much to demand
   S. her rightful place
   (a) RSQP   (b) QPSR   (c) SQPR   (d) SRPQ
Ans. (*c*) SQPR

23. Little
   P. that he had been let down
   Q. stood by all these years
   R. did he realise
   S. by a colleague whom he had
   (a) QSPR   (b) RPSQ   (c) QSRP   (d) RSQP
Ans. (*b*) RPSQ

24. All religions are
   P. to advance the cause of peace
   Q. in a holy partnership
   R. justice and freedom
   S. bound together
   (a) PQRS   (b) PRQS   (c) SPQR   (d) SQPR
Ans. (*d*) SQPR

25. As lightning accompanies thunder
   P. was mingled with
   Q. so in my character
   R. the mutterings of my wrath
   S. a flash of humour
   (a) QSPR   (b) PRSQ   (c) QPRS   (d) QRPS
Ans. (*d*) QRPS

Integrated Grammar Exercises

Category I : Gap Filling

Directions (Q. Nos. 1-36) Choose the correct option from the given options.

1. Comrades, you all .... about the strange dream that I .... last night.
(a) heard, had
(b) will heard, has
(c) have heard, had
(d) hear, has

Ans. (c)

2. They .... to play cricket every day when they were in the college.
(a) ought
(b) used
(c) may
(d) might

Ans. (b)

3. A stapler is a thing .... you use to attach papers together.
(a) which
(b) where
(c) who
(d) whose

Ans. (a)

4. There are plenty of tomatoes in the fridge. You .... buy any.
(a) mightn't
(b) couldn't
(c) mustn't
(d) needn't

Ans. (d)

5. I always keep .... money in my wallet for emergencies.
(a) any
(b) some
(c) many
(d) much

Ans. (b)

6. When I was living in London, a strange thing .... to me.
(a) has happen
(b) happen
(c) could happen
(d) happened

Ans. (d)

7. Hiroshima is the place .... the first atomic bomb was dropped.
(a) whose
(b) which
(c) where
(d) when

Ans. (c)

8. There must be .... way to knock .... nail in without using .... hammer.
(a) some, the, a
(b) any, the, an
(c) much, a, the
(d) many, a, the

Ans. (a)

9. Tony .... in Manhattan now but he .... home to Brooklyn at least twice a year.
(a) live, go
(b) live, went
(c) had live, went
(d) lives, goes

Ans. (d)

10. You .... leave small objects lying around. Such objects .... be swallowed by children.
(a) needn't, might
(b) shouldn't, may
(c) can't, must
(d) mustn't, may

Ans. (b)

11. The man sitting next to me on the plane was nervous because he .... before.
(a) hasn't flown
(b) didn't fly
(c) hadn't flown
(d) wasn't flying

Ans. (a)

12. This is ....new TV; yet, we have been having .... problems with it over.................. last few weeks.
(a) a, some, the
(b) the, many, a
(c) the, any, a
(d) a, much, the

Ans. (a)

13. The teacher said we .... read this book for our own pleasure as it is optional. But we .... read it if we don't want to.
(a) may, mustn't
(b) might, needn't
(c) can, needn't
(d) can, shouldn't

Ans. (c)

14. John .... tennis once or twice a week.
(a) is playing usually
(b) is usually playing
(c) usually plays
(d) plays usually

Ans. (c)

15. We're good friends. We .... each other for a long time.
   (a) know   (b) have known
   (c) have been knowing   (d) knew
Ans. (b)

16. Yasser Arafat is the person .... is the Palestinian leader.
   (a) which   (b) whose
   (c) who   (d) when
Ans. (c)

17. Napoleon is the man ....wife was called Josephine.
   (a) who   (b) whose
   (c) what   (d) which
Ans. (b)

18. He had been working for .... than 11 hours. He must be tired after such hard work. He .... prefer to get some rest.
   (a) more, may   (b) much, can
   (c) lot, may   (d) many, might
Ans. (a)

19. Shirley .... a book about China last year but I don't know whether she has finished it.
   (a) has written   (b) wrote
   (c) had written   (d) was writing
Ans. (b)

20. Hey, look where you are going! Oh, I'm terribly sorry, ...
   (a) I'm not noticing   (b) I wasn't noticing
   (c) I haven't noticed   (d) I don't notice
Ans. (b)

21. The rain was pouring down in torrents but there wasn't .... wind.
   (a) a few   (b) little
   (c) much   (d) fewer
Ans. (c)

22. .... students succeeded in passing than last year.
   (a) A little   (b) A few   (c) Much   (d) Fewer
Ans. (d)

23. Nancy is not coming tonight. But she ....!
   (a) promises   (b) promised
   (c) will promise   (d) had promised
Ans. (d)

24. I bought .... grapes from a stall. On .... way home, I ate them and had none left when I reached home.
   (a) some, the   (b) much, a   (c) fewer, the   (d) many, the
Ans. (a)

25. It's a secret. You .... tell anybody.
   (a) mightn't   (b) mustn't   (c) needn't   (d) daren't
Ans. (b)

26. You .... study hard to achieve success in your entrance exam.
   (a) used to   (b) ought to
   (c) need to   (d) have to
Ans. (b)

27. My mother doesn't drink .... coffee.
   (a) any   (b) many
   (c) much   (d) some
Ans. (c)

28. When I went back to my hometown three years ago, I found that a lot of changes ....
   (a) are taken place   (b) were taken place
   (c) have taken place   (d) had taken place
Ans. (c)

29. I'm sorry the house is not available any longer. It .... to a timber tycoon.
   (a) is sold   (b) was being sold
   (c) has been sold   (d) will be sold
Ans. (c)

30. Passengers .... to smoke in the train.
   (a) are not allowed   (b) was not allowed
   (c) had not allowed   (d) will not allow
Ans. (a)

31. We invited .... friends over to our house for a barbecue.
   (a) each   (b) much
   (c) a little   (d) a few
Ans. (d)

32. The student's .... to leave the building immediately.
   (a) ordered   (b) will order
   (c) have ordered   (d) have been ordered
Ans. (d)

33. Sunday is the day .... most countries respect a day of rest in the week.
   (a) which   (b) when
   (c) what   (d) whose
Ans. (b)

34. The roof may have been leaking for the past few weeks but you do not have to worry about it any longer. It .... now.
   (a) was repaired
   (b) is repairing
   (c) has been repaired
   (d) is being repaired
Ans. (c)

35. .... short stories that he published were critically acclaimed.
   (a) Few
   (b) Little
   (c) The few
   (d) A little

Ans. (c)

36. The price ...., but I doubt whether it will remain so.
   (a) went down
   (b) will go down
   (c) has gone down
   (d) was going down

Ans. (a)

Directions (1-4) In the given passages there are blanks, each of which has been numbered. These numbers are printed below the passage and against each, four words are suggested, one of which fits the blank appropriately. Find out the appropriate word in each case.

1. Primary school enrolment in India has been a success story, ...(i) ...... due to various programmes and drives to increase enrolment even in remote areas. With enrolment reaching at least 96 percent since 2009, and girls ......(ii)....... up 56 percent of new students between 2007 and 2013, it is clear that many ....(iii)...... of access to schooling have been ....(iv)...... .

Improvement in infrastructure has been the ......(v)....... behind achieving this and now in India 98 percent habitations have a primary school ....(vi)...... one kilometre and 92 percent have an upper primary school within a three kilometre walking distance.

   (i) (a) most
       (b) properly
       (c) totally
       (d) largely

   (ii) (a) coming
        (b) reaching
        (c) counting
        (d) making

   (iii) (a) issue
         (b) opportunities
         (c) problems
         (d) efforts

   (iv) (a) accustomed
        (b) addressed
        (c) met
        (d) forwarded

   (v) (a) main
       (b) forced
       (c) force
       (d) compulsion

   (vi) (a) within
        (b) in
        (c) from
        (d) for

2. Education has been a problem in our country for ....(i) .... The lack of it has been blamed for all ....(ii)....... of evil for hundreds of years. Even scholars have written lengthy articles about how the Indian education system needs to change. The funny thing is that from colonial times, things have ......(iii)....... changed. We have established reputed business schools, law schools and other institutions of excellence. Students, now, so routinely score 90% marks that even with this percentage they find it ......(iv)....... to get into the colleges of their choice. The problem thus lies ......(v)....... us doing more of the same old staff. This needs to change by bringing about ......(vi)....... in education.

   (i) (a) time
       (b) take
       (c) ever
       (d) long

   (ii) (a) possession
        (b) abundance
        (c) typical
        (d) sorts

   (iii) (a) bare
         (b) hardly
         (c) little
         (d) highly

   (iv) (a) simple
        (b) easy
        (c) irregular
        (d) difficult

   (v) (a) with
       (b) in
       (c) for
       (d) from

   (vi) (a) innovation
        (b) dreams
        (c) creating
        (d) foreign

3. Economic development of country is ......(i)....... to their industrial growth. In a developing country like India, Small Scale Industries play a significant role in economic development of the country. They are a ......(ii)....... segment of Indian economy in terms of their contribution towards country's industrial production, exports employment and creation of an entrepreneurial base. These industries by and large represent a stage in economic ......(iii)....... from traditional to modern technology. Small industry plays a very important role in widening the base of entrepreneurship. The development of small industries ......(iv)....... an easy and effective means of achieving broad based ownership of industry, the diffusion of enterprise and initiative in the industrial field. Given their importance, the Government policy framework right from the First plan has ......(v)....... the need for the development of SSI sector keeping in view its ......(vi)....... importance in the overall economic development of India.

   (i) (a) related
       (b) relating
       (c) concentrated
       (d) resembled

(ii) (a) mean   (b) vital
    (c) insignificance   (d) visual

(iii) (a) translation   (b) transferring
    (c) transition   (d) transitional

(iv) (a) offer   (b) offers
    (c) differ   (d) differs

(v) (a) highlighting   (b) highlighted
    (c) heighten   (d) demeaning

(vi) (a) strategy   (b) less
    (c) complex   (d) strategic

4. Agriculture is a ....(i)...... sector of our economy and credit plays an important role in increasing agriculture production. Availability and access to adequate, timely and low cost credit from institutional sources is of great ....(ii)...... especially to small and marginal farmers. Along with other inputs, credit is essential for establishing sustainable and ....(iii)...... farming systems. Most farmers are small producers engaged in agricultural activities in areas of widely ......(iv)....... potential.

Experience has shown that easy access to financial services at affordable cost ....(v)...... affects productivity, asset formation and income and food security of the rural poor. The major concern of the Governmenttherefore ,is to bring all the farmer households within the banking ....(vi)...... and promote complete financial inclusion.

(i) (a) integral   (b) centre
    (c) dominant   (d) proven

(ii) (a) view   (b) importance
    (c) urgency   (d) source

(iii) (a) isolated   (b) apportioned
    (c) abject   (d) profitable

(iv) (a) justified   (b) true
    (c) most   (d) varying

(v) (a) not   (b) seriously
    (c) must   (d) positively

(vi) (a) loans   (b) fold
    (c) premises   (d) area

Category II : Sentence Reordering

Directions (Q. Nos. 1-20) The questions given below consists of certain phrases. Rearrange these phrases to form a meaningful sentence.

1. the only creature (1) / laughter (2)/ blessed with the power of (3)/ man is (4)
  (a) 2134   (b) 4132
  (c) 1324   (d) 4321

Ans. (b)

2. by keeping(1) /oblige me (2) /your (3) / to yourself (4)/ suspicion (5)
  (a) 32154   (b) 35421
  (c) 21354   (d) 21345

Ans. (c)

3. the managing director (1)/ in listening to her (2)/ was not interested (3) /explanation about why profits were lessening (4)
  (a) 1234   (b) 1243
  (c) 1324   (d) 2341

Ans. (c)

4. Supported by soft term loans (1) / to supply the raw material worth ₹ 5 lakh (2) / the dealer has agreed (3) / with a very low rate of interest (4)
  (a) 3214   (b) 4213
  (c) 1432   (d) 2134

Ans. (a)

5. when meat (1) / the food poisoning occurred (2)/ added in the food preparations (3)/ of low quality was (4)
  (a) 3214   (b) 2341
  (c) 1423   (d) 2143

Ans. (d)

6. I wanted to tell her(1)/not to talk to him(2)/not listen to me (3)/but she would(4)
  (a) 1234   (b) 1243
  (c) 1423   (d) 2314

Ans. (b)

7. The managing director(1)/ in listening to her(2)/ was not interested(3)/ explanation about why profits were lessening (4)
  (a) 1234   (b) 1243
  (c) 1324   (d) 2341

Ans. (c)

8. for thousands of years(1)/ famous symbols of ancient civilizations(2)/ Monuments have been created(3)/ and they are often the most durable and(4)
  (a) 3142
  (b) 1234
  (c) 2143
  (d) 4321

Ans. (a)

9. is one of the most widely used indicators(1)/ of ecosystems and their biodiversity(2)/ for assessing the condition(3)/ The conservation status of plants and animals(4)
(a) 4132   (b) 4321
(c) 2314   (d) 1234

Ans. (a)

10. photos which were submitted (1)/ in the fire last night (2)/ for the exhibition (3)/ have been totally burnt(4)
(a) 1432   (b) 2134
(c) 1342   (d) 3142

Ans. (c)

11. supported by soft term loans (1) / to supply the raw material worth ₹ 5 lakh (2) / the dealer has agreed (3) / with a very low rate of interest (4)
(a) 3214   (b) 4213
(c) 1432   (d) 2134

Ans. (a)

12. In the wintertime (1)/ the 2022 World Cup in Qatar (2) / would best be staged (3) / will not be held in June and July but (4)
(a) 2314   (b) 3412
(c) 1432   (d) 2431

Ans. (d)

13. She saw her opportunity (1) / to make amends (2) / when he came to her home (3) / to borrow some sugar (4)
(a) 2341   (b) 1234
(c) 2314   (d) 1423

Ans. (b)

14. the mutterings of (1)/ As lightning accompanies thunder(2)/ so was mingled with in my character(3)/ my wrath a flash of humour (4)
(a) 2314   (b) 2413
(c) 1342   (d) 2134

Ans. (a)

15. coal as a fuel(1)/ in place of wood(2)/ during this period (3)/ people were beginning to use (4)
(a) 2413   (b) 1342
(c) 3412   (d) 4312

Ans. (c)

16. The CEO (1)/ of making the right decision (2)/ was not scared (3) /despite a loss in profits (4)
(a) 1234   (b) 1243
(c) 1324   (d) 2341

Ans. (c)

17. Half its beauty and usefulness (1)/ knowledge would lose (2)/ without hard toil (3)/ if we could acquire it (4)
(a) 3241   (b) 2143
(c) 3421   (d) 4312

Ans. (a)

18. containing memorable letters of Churchill(1)/ Recently a book(2)/ has been published(3)/ by a reputed publisher(4)
(a) 2134   (b) 1234
(c) 2314   (d) 2314

Ans. (a)

19. We can give him (1)/ and let him do nothing (2)/ to lock up a man (3)/ is one ofthe cruelest punishments (4)
(a) 1432   (b) 3241
(c) 2431   (d) 4312

Ans. (b)

20. The managing director(1)/in listening to her (2)/was not interested(3)/ explanation about why profits were lessening(4)
(a) 1234   (b) 1243
(c) 2341   (d) 1324

Ans. (d)

Category III : Transformation of Sentences

Directions (Q.Nos. 1-20) Transform the following sentences without changing their meaning as given in the question.

1. Mumbai is one of the biggest Indian cities.
(a) Mumbai is biggest than most other Indian cities.
(b) Mumbai is bigger than any other Indian cities.
(c) Mumbai is big than any other Indian cities.
(d) Mumbai is bigger than most other Indian cities.

Ans. (a)

2. Bring me aa Axe. This one is blunt.
(a) Bring me another Axe, as this one is blunt.
(b) Bring me a few axes. This one is blunt.
(c) Bring me a little Axe, as this one is blunt.
(d) Bring me many axes, as this one is blunt.

Ans. (a)

3. Villages must be connected by road.
(a) Any of the villages must be connected by road.
(b) Every village must be connected by road.
(c) Much of the villages must be connected by road.
(d) Some of the village must be connected by road.

Ans. (b)

4. There is no flower more beautiful than Daisy in the entire world.
   (a) Daisy is the more beautiful flower in the entire world.
   (b) Most flowers are more beautiful than Daisy in the entire world.
   (c) Daisy is the most beautiful flower in the entire world.
   (d) Some flowers are more beautiful than Daisy in the entire world.

Ans. (c)

5. Many cases of money laundering were pending against him in the court.
   (a) There were several cases of money laundering pending against him in the court.
   (b) There were a few cases of money laundering pending ainst him in the court.
   (c) There were some cases of money laundering pending against him in the court.
   (d) All the cases pending in the court were against him.

Ans. (a)

6. Today a laptop and air conditioner can be seen in each house.
   (a) Today a laptop and air conditioner can be seen in every house.
   (b) Today a laptop and air conditioner can be seen in some houses.
   (c) Today a laptop and air conditioner can be seen in enough houses.
   (d) Today a laptop and air conditioner can be seen in more houses.

Ans. (a)

7. A lot of people went to welcome the President of the USA.
   (a) Some people went to welcome the President of the USA.
   (b) Much people went to welcome the President of the USA.
   (c) Many people went to welcome the President of the USA.
   (c) None people went to welcome the President of the USA.

Ans. (c)

8. His apologies didn't mean anything to me.
   (a) His apologies didn't make no difference to me.
   (b) His apologies made some difference to me.
   (c) His apologies made a little difference to me.
   (d) His apologies didn't make any difference to me.

Ans. (c)

9. Many would like to have your job.q
   (a) Much would like to have your job.
   (b) Plenty of people would like to have your job.
   (c) Your job is liked by some.
   (d) Fewer of people would like to have your job.

Ans. (b)

10. That chocolate is not as sweet as this one
   (a) The chocolates vary in their sweetness.
   (b) This chocolate is sweeter than that chocolate.
   (c) This chocolate is not sweeter than that chocolate.
   (d) This chocolate is sweeter than that one.

Ans. (d)

11. Change into future continuous tense.
She ran as fast as she could.
   (a) She will be running as fast as she could.
   (b) She will have been running as fast as she could.
   (c) She am running as fast as she can.
   (d) She will run as fast as she could.

Ans. (a)

12. Change into past perfect tense.
The visitor is spoiled for choice.
   (a) The visitor had spoiled for choice.
   (b) The visitor had been spoiled for choice.
   (c) The visitor had been spoilt for choice.
   (d) The visitor has spoiled for choice.

Ans. (b)

13. Change into present perfect tense.
A new breed of jellyfish is recently discovered by the biologists.
   (a) A new breed of jellyfish have been recently discovered by the biologists.
   (b) The biologists have recently discovered a new breed of jellyfish.
   (c) The biologists will have recently discovered a new breed of jellyfish.
   (d) The biologists had recently discovered a new breed of jellyfish.

Ans. (b)

14. Change into past perfect continuous tense.
He was bathing in the rain since morning.
   (a) He had being bathed in the rain since morning.
   (b) He had been bathing in the rain since morning.
   (c) He had being bathing in the rain since morning.
   (d) He has been bathing in the rain since morning.

Ans. (b)

15. Change into simple future tense.
How long had you been studying Turkish?
   (a) How long you study Turkish?
   (b) How long will you have studied Turkish?
   (c) How long will you study Turkish?
   (d) How long will you study Turkish?

Ans. (b)

16. Change into future continuous tense.
I am leaving for London tomorrow after my meeting with the traders.
   (a) I would be leaving for London tomorrow after my meeting with the traders.
   (b) I will have been leaving for London tomorrow after my meeting with the traders.
   (c) I will leaving for London tomorrow after my meeting with the traders.
   (d) I will be leaving for London tomorrow after my meeting with the traders.

Ans. (d)

17. Change into present continuous tense.

She will be waiting for us at the Huda City Centre metro station.

(a) She is being waited for us at the Huda City Centre metro station.

(b) She has been waiting for us at the Huda City Centre metro station.

(c) She is waiting for us at the Huda City Centre metro station.

(d) She was waiting for us at the Huda City Centre metro station.

Ans. (c)

18. Change into simple future tense.

Vikram must not be late to avoid punishment.

(a) In the event of being late, Vikram will be punished.

(b) In the event of being late, Vikram is punished.

(c) Vikram should not be late to avoid punishment.

(d) Vikram will be late to avoid punishment.

Ans. (a)

19. Change into present perfect continuous tense.

He earns a five figure salary at Pandora Hotelier Services.

(a) He have been earning a five figure salary at Pandora Hotelier Services.

(b) He has been earning a five figure salary at Pandora Hotelier Services.

(c) He has being earned a five figure salary at Pandora Hotelier Services.

(d) He will have been earning a five figure salary Pandora Hotelier Services.

Ans. (b)

20. Change into present perfect tense.

The South makes an equally strong claim as the North.

(a) The South has make an equally strong claim as the North.

(b) The South has made an equally strong claim as the North.

(c) The South have made an equally strong claim as the North.

(d) The South has been making an equally strong claim as the North.

Ans. (b)

CHAPTER 01

The Ailing Planet
The Green Movement's Role

–by Nani Palkhivala

In this Chapter...
- Chapter Summary
- Word Meaning
- Chapter Practice

Chapter Sketch

This newspaper article is a sad commentary on the gradual deterioration of Earth's environment. Our planet is no longer a pleasant place to live in. Fisheries, forests, grasslands and croplands need to be preserved and protected. The article suggests that we should try to limit the rise in population and stop the perpetuation of poverty. The Green Movement, started in 1972, is the only hope for the survival of this planet as well as that of the human race.

Chapter Summary

The chapter is based on an article written by Nani Palkhivala. The article was published in the Indian Express on 24th Novemer, 1994 and raised the issue of environmental degradation of the planet.

The Green Movement

The Green Movement, which started nearly 25 years earlier than the publication of the article, is one of the most important movements that captivated the entire human race. The movement gained popularity in 1972 after the creation of the world's first nationwide Green party in New Zealand.

Since then a revolutionary change has been seen in the perception of human beings. There has been a shift from the scientific understanding developed by Copernicus to a holistic and ecological view of the world.

For the first time, there is a growing worldwide realisation that the earth itself is a living organism. It has its own metabolic needs and fundamental processes which need to be respected and preserved. With the Earth showing signs of declining health, humans have realised their ethical obligations to protect and preserve the planet for the futher generations.

The Concept of Sustainable Development

The concept of Sustainable Development was popularised in 1987 by the World Commission on Environment and Development. It was defined as the development that meets the needs of the present without compromising the needs of the future generations. In other words, we should pursue development without emptying the resources the future generations will need.

Man and the Other Living Species

A cage in the zoo at Lusaka contains a mirror with the notice that reads 'The world's most dangerous animal'. This along with numerous efforts of many agencies across the world has made human beings come to the realisation that they should live in harmony with other living beings of the planet and not seek to control them anymore.

Scientists till then had listed 1.4 million living species on Earth and believed that about 3 to a 100 million species still remain unknown and endangered.

Earth's Principal Biological Systems

The Brandt Commission was one of the first international commissions which dealt with the question of ecology and environment. It had Mr LK Jha as its member. The First Brandt Report raised a question of how we want to leave our planet for our successors.

Mr Lester R Brown, in his book, 'The Global Economic Prospect', points out that the Earth has four major biological systems. They are fisheries, forests, grasslands and croplands. These four form the foundation of the global economic system. Besides providing us food, they provide nearly all the raw materials for industries except minerals and petroleum derived synthetics. In many parts of the world, humans are over-exploiting these systems due to which their productivity is hampered.

The unsustainable and excessive demand has resulted in deterioration and depletion of resources leading to the breakdown of fisheries, disappearance of forests, deterioration of croplands and turning of grasslands into barren lands. Overfishing for protein and deforestation to obtain fuel for working are some examples of these excessive demands.

A consequence of meeting these excessive demands is the extinction of many species and the increase in the land area covering deserts.

Mankind Destroys Forests

The unsustainable dependence of these systems has a drastic negative impact on the forest area. The ancient inheritance of tropical forests is now eroding at the rate of 40 to 50 million acres per year. In addition, the growing use of dung for combustion deprives the soil of an important natural fertiliser.

The World Bank estimates that a five-fold increase in the rate of forest planting is needed to cope with the expected fuelwood demand in the year 2000.

James Speth, the President of the World Resources Institute, revealed that we are losing the forests at the rate of an acre-and-a-half a second.

Article 48A of the Indian Constitution states that it is the duty of the state to make efforts to "Protect and improve the environment and safeguard the forests and wildlife of the country". Unfortunately, such laws are neither respected nor enforced in India. A report by the Parliament's estimates committee highlights that India is exhausting 3.7 million acres of forest lands every year. The large areas of official forest lands are virtually tree less. The actual loss of forests at present is about eight times the rate presented by the government data.

The Menace of Overpopulation

A three year study by the United Nations found that the environment is in a critical state in many of 88 countries investigated.

One of the most prominent factors for such a condition is the growth of world's population. Mankind took than more a million years to reach the first billion in 1800. Another billion was added in 1900 and 3.7 billion was added in the twentieth century. As of 1994, the world population was at 5.7 billion with one million being added to it every four days.

In 1994, India's population was estimated to be 920 million, pointing to the need of giving population control the top-most priority. Development can be the best contraceptive, as with increased income, education level and health, fertility falls. However, with rising population it is impossible.

The increase in population also increases the economic gap, making the rich richer and the poor poorer. The increase can't be dealt with forceful control of population, hence leaving the only choice to be between control of population and never ending growth in of poverty.

Era of Responsibility

The new holistic view of the world towards the environment has began the era of responsibility. In this view, the concern has shifted to the survival of not only the people but also the planet. In this ecological view, the world is seen as an integrated whole and not a collection of parts.

Industries play a central role in this new era with business's excelling in environmental performance.

The chapter (article) ends with the words of Margert Thatcher and Mr. Lester Brown stating that no one has a freehold on earth and that it is not our property. We need to keep the resources and the environment intact for the future generations.

Word Meanings

The given page numbers correspond to the pages in the prescribed NCERT textbook.

Word	Meaning
Page 43	
irrevocably	permanently
holistic	complete and comprehensive
ecological	concerned with the relation of living creatures to the environment of a place

Word	Meaning
Page 44	
metabolic	related to a chemical process in living things that changes food into energy and materials for growth
ethical	connected with beliefs and principles about what is right and wrong
stewards	caretakers
trustees	trusted people
legacy	inheritance
languish	deteriorate
in ignominious darkness	unknown
scorched	burnt
impoverished	deprived
Page 45	
synthetics	chemical compounds
unsustainable	not possible to replace

Word	Meaning
decimated	largely reduced
procure	obtain
evolution	development
patrimony	inheritance
eroding	gradually disappearing
depletion	reduction
designated	named
Page 46	
contraceptive	way to control population
beget	give birth to
coercion	use of force
transcending concern	major anxiety
Page 47	
felicitous	appropriate
tenancy	temporary

Chapter Practice

Objective Questions

• Multiple Choice Questions

1. The movement has not looked back means that
(a) it is still evident
(b) it has become popular
(c) it is still continuing as a success
(d) it has resulted in positive and long-term changes

Ans. (c) The movement has not looked back means that the movement is still continuing to be a success.

2. What is the meaning of holistic and ecological view?
(a) The preservation of the environment
(b) Saving of the water resources
(c) Savings tees
(d) Rainwater harvest

Ans. (a) The phrase 'holistic and ecological view' means a view that focuses on the preservation and the maintenance of the environment.

3. "The Earth's vital signs reveal a patient in declining health".

In the statement above, which literary device is used to signify 'Earth'?
(a) Hyperbole
(b) Metaphor
(c) Imagery
(d) Personification

Ans. (d) Personification means to attribute human characteristics to non-human things.
By comparing Earth to a patient, the author is personifying it.

4. Select the suitable option for the given statements, based on your reading of 'The Ailing Planet'.
(i) The Green Movement became popular amongst common man in 1972.
(ii) The first green party was formed in New Zealand.
(a) (i) is false (ii) is true
(b) Both (i) and (ii) are false
(c) (ii) is a fact but unrelated to (i)
(d) (ii) is the precursor of (i)

Ans. (d) After the first Green party was formed in New Zealand in 1972, the Green movement gained popularity in the world.

5. Select the roles assigned to humans with respect to 'The Ailing Planet'.
(i) Trustee
(ii) Caretaker
(iii) Owner
(iv) Partnership
(v) Borrower
(a) (i), (ii), (iii) and (iv)
(b) (i), (ii), (iv) and (v)
(c) (ii), (iii), (iv) and (v)
(d) (i), (iii), (iv) and (v)

Ans. (b) The chapter refers to humans as the 'stewards' and 'trustees' of the Earth. Later, through Mr. Lester Brown's words, they have been referred to as the 'borrowers'. And, the chapters suggests that in order to protect the environment, it and humans have to live in harmony as 'partners'.
Hence, option (b) is the correct answer.

6. What is the concept of sustainable development?
(a) Development of the future such that the present is not effected
(b) Development for the present with the purpose of comfort for the future
(c) Development that meets the needs of the present, without compromising the ability of future generations
(d) Environmental development

Ans. (c) The concept of sustainable development suggests that natural resources should be used in such a manner that does not compromise the ability of the future generations to use those resources.

7. By calling man "the most dangerous animal in the world", the author is ....man for its activities.
(a) condemning
(b) taunting
(c) labelling
(d) criminalising

Ans. (c)

8. The author states that man is moving to a system based on partnership.

This indicates a system where
(a) resources are used with care
(b) resources are rarely used
(c) alternative resources are used
(d) resources are given rehabilitation time.

Ans. (a) A system based on partnership is a system wherein all the resources are used with care.

9. The first Brandt Report raised the question-"Are we to leave our successors a scorched planet of advancing deserts, impoverished landscapes and ailing environment."

Select the option that explains it.

(a) The report highlights the exponential increase in the negative impact of activities of development
(b) The report points to the need to shift towards the principle of sustainable development
(c) The report reflects that man has to be environmentally conscious
(d) The report takes data from various countries and justifies its stance of sustainability

Ans. (b) The report and the question it asks are significant as they highlight how humankind needs to shift towards the principle of sustainable development.

10. What will the grassland turn into if systems become unsustainable?

(a) Turn into a barren wasteland
(b) Turn into desert
(c) Soil quality will deteriorate
(d) Drought lands

Ans. (b) The grasslands will turn into desert if systems become unsustainable.

11. At what rate is the world's ancient patrimony of tropical forests eroding?

(a) At the rate of one million per year
(b) At the rate of forty to fifty million acres a year
(c) At the rate of 90 million per year
(d) None of the above

Ans. (b) The world's ancient patrimony of tropical forests is eroding at the rate of forty to fifty million acres a year.

12. Classify (1) to (4) as Fact (I) or Opinion (O), based on your reading of 'The Ailing Planet'.

1. The Indian people do not understand the significance of the green movement.
2. Article 48A puts the responsibility of preservation of environment on the government.
3. The government is to be held responsible for the current state of the environment.
4. Even the government data is based on estimations.

(a) F-1, 2; O-3, 4
(b) F-2, 3, 4 ; O-1
(c) F-1, 4 ; O- 2, 3
(d) F-2, 4 ; O- 1, 3

Ans. (d)

13. Which of the following is TRUE for the study conducted by the United Nations?

(a) Environment is deteriorating critically
(b) Forest land is exponentially reducing
(c) Natural resources are not renewing properly
(d) Fossil Fuels are not sustainable

Ans. (a) The three-year study shows that the environment has deteriorated and that it is critical in eighty-eight countries.

14. Select the correct options with reference to the given statements on the basis of your reading of 'The Ailing Planet'.

(i) Increasing population is one of the major reasons for the exploitation of the environment.
(ii) Education is considered to be the best contraceptive for overpopulation.

(a) Only (i) is correct
(b) Only (ii) is correct
(c) Both (i) and (ii) are correct
(d) Neither is correct

Ans. (a) Only (i) is correct as development is considered to be the best contraceptive for overpopulation.

15. When Margaret Thatcher says, "No generation has a freehold on this earth. All we have is a life tenancy — with a full repairing lease", what does she highlight?

(a) The need to find alternate sources of natural resources
(b) The need to become environment conscious
(c) The need to understand the negative impact of man's actions
(d) The need for the change in the relationship shared with nature

Ans. (b) By making the statement, Margaret Thatcher highlights how the society needs to become environment conscious and make efforts for its benefit.

• Extract Based MCQs

1. Read the extract given below and answer questions that follow.

"We have shifted — one hopes, irrevocably — from the mechanistic view to a holistic and ecological view of the world. It is a shift in human perceptions as revolutionary as that introduced by Copernicus who taught mankind in the sixteenth century that the earth and the other planets revolved round the sun. For the first time in human history, there is a growing worldwide consciousness that the Earth itself is a living organism — an enormous being of which we are parts. It has its own metabolic needs and vital processes which need to be respected and preserved.

The earth's vital signs reveal a patient in declining health. We have begun to realise our ethical obligations to be good stewards of the planet and responsible trustees of the legacy to future generations."

(i) What is meant by the 'mechanistic view' in the extract?

(a) A worldview of machinery
(b) A worldview without human beings in it
(c) Depleting value of mankind
(d) None of the above

Ans. (a) The 'mechanistic view of the world' means looking at the world as if it was a machine that needs to be recklessly used.

(ii) The phrase 'holistic and ecological view' harbors the relationship based on

(a) Subservience   (b) Partnership

(c) Trustee   (d) Owner

Ans. (b) The holistic and ecological view harbors a relation based on partnership wherein both nature and mankind are interdependent on each other.

(iii) The passage mentions that the earth has metabolic needs. It means that

(a) it needs time to heal

(b) it has its own processes and functions

(c) it needs time to renew and maintain balance

(d) it has to make sure that man gets everything

Ans. (c) Saying that the Earth has metabolic needs means that the Earth needs it own time to renew itself so that it can maintain the ecological balance.

(iv) Why does the writer exemplify Copernicus to comment on the issue?

(a) To justify the need to save trees

(b) Because he was a fan of Copernicus

(c) As Copernicus fought for the cause

(d) To contrast the change in human perspective

Ans. (d) The writer uses the impact of Copernicus' research and time to contrast it with the need to bring change in the human perspective.

(v) In what tone does the writer present their concerns?

(a) Preaching   (b) Condescending

(c) Informative   (d) Inspiring

Ans. (d) The tone is inspiring as it tends to inspire people to take action.

2. Read the extract given below to answer the questions that follow.

"In poor countries, local forests are being decimated in order to procure firewood for cooking. In some places, firewood has become so expensive that "what goes under the pot now costs more than what goes inside it". Since the tropical forest is, in the words of Dr Myers, "the powerhouse of evolution", several species of life face extinction as a result of its destruction.

It has been well said that forests precede mankind; deserts follow. The world's ancient patrimony of tropical forests is now eroding at the rate of forty to fifty million acres a year, and the growing use of dung for burning deprives the soil of an important natural fertiliser. The World Bank estimates that a five-fold increase in the rate of forest planting is needed to cope with the expected fuelwood demand in the year 2000."

(i) From the above lines, what relation can be made in the statements below?

  I. The cost of what is being cooked is much lower than what is being used for cooking that.

  II. Firewood is so expensive that one cannot afford it anymore, the resources for cooking have become far more expensive than the ingredients

(a) I is true but II is not

(b) II is the explanation of I

(c) There is no relation between the statements

(d) II is true but I is not

Ans. (b) The connection between the two statements is that while statement I issues the problem, statement II explains and adds more to the given information.

(ii) "What goes under the pot costs more than what goes inside the pot" indicates.

(a) Increasing demand of the fuel

(b) Increase in inflation

(c) Increasing ecological costs

(d) Increasing uses of wood

Ans. (a) The given lines indicates how the natural resource of fuel wood is so in demand that its prices are soaring sky high.

(iii) The reference of the growing use of dung is to highlight the ....

(a) depleting forest land

(b) Conversion of grasslands into wastelands

(c) Over dependence on alternate fuels

(d) All of the above

Ans. (d)

(iv) What has been the result of the tropical forests being "the powerhouse of evolution"?

(a) They promoted technical tools

(b) They caused eradication of livelihoods of species

(c) They improved the search for fodder

(d) All of the above

Ans. (b) The result of tropical forests' exploitation by humans has led to evolution, thus becoming the powerhouse for the same, but it has also led to eradication of livelihoods of many species and their extinction.

(v) Select the correct meaning of 'forests precede mankind'.

(a) Forests provide everything to the mankind

(b) Forests have taught mankind how to grow and build

(c) Forests were in existence on this planet much before the coming of man

(d) None of the above

Ans. (c) The correct meaning of the phrase is that forests were in existence on this planet much before the coming of man.

PART 2
Subjective Questions

• Short Answer Type Questions

1 What is the significance of Green Movement in the modern world?

Ans. The Green Movement has brought a great awareness among people. It has taught us that we are just partners on the earth sharing this planet with other living organisms.

Having learnt this, human beings worldwide have reduced the large amount of destruction being caused on the Earth. People have realised that the earth's existence has been threatened and have begun to do whatever is possible.

2. What shift in human perception has been seen as a result of the Green Movement?

Ans. Human perception has gone through a revolutionary shift as a result of the Green Movement replacing the mechanistic view of the Earth with a more holistic and ecological view of the world.

For the first time in human history, there is a growing worldwide consciousness that Earth itself is a living organism, an enormous being of which we are parts. It has its own metabolic needs and vital processes which need to be respected and preserved.

3. Why is the Earth referred to as 'the ailing planet'?

Ans. Due to the insensitive exploitation of Earth's resources by humans for their survival and development, Earth has lost almost all its vital resources. With drying rivers, depleted and polluted environment and deteriorated forests and greenery, Earth is having a difficult time surviving and thus, it is referred to as 'the ailing planet'.

4. What does the notice 'The world's most dangerous animal' at a cage in the zoo at Lusaka, Zambia, signify?
(**NCERT**)

Ans. The notice signifies that man is responsible for the depletion of resources and deterioration of the environment on Earth. This is so serious that even man's survival is threatened.

5. What question did the First Brandt Report raise?

Ans. One of the early international commissions which dealt with the question of ecology and environment was the Brandt Commission. The First Brandt Report raised the question, "Are we to leave our successors a scorched planet of advancing deserts, impoverished landscapes and ailing environment?"

6. How are Earth's principal biological systems important?

Ans. Mr. Lester R. Brown recognises four principal biological systems of Earth, namely 'fisheries', 'forests', 'grasslands' and 'croplands'.

They form the foundation of the global economic system. They fulfil our entire needs of food, besides providing virtually all the raw materials for industry except minerals and petroleum derived synthetics. Hence, they are extremely important.

7. What is the cause of the collapse of fisheries?

Ans. Fisheries have collapsed due to over-fishing. Fish is an important source of protein which is essential for growth. With the spread of education, people all over the world have become conscious about consuming proteins. This has led to fishermen trying to meet the demand for fish by over-fishing, leading to the collapse of fisheries.

8. Why and how are our grasslands being converted into barren wastelands, and croplands deteriorating?

Ans. One of the greatest reason of the deterioration of these grasslands and croplands is the growth of population. Population has been increasing drastically. As a result, the pressure on land is increasing.

Over-grazing of animals has caused havoc to our grasslands. Due to this, grasslands are becoming barren wastelands. In the same way, the pressure of population on croplands is affecting their productivity. More mouths mean more food and hence, more pressure on croplands.

9. Why are tropical forests called 'the powerhouse of evolution'?

Ans. Tropical forests are called 'the powerhouse of evolution' because it is in the heart of tropical forests where newer plants and animals evolve to more adaptable forms. If they are drastically reduced, as at present, it will affect evolution as a whole and many species of plants and animals will be rendered extinct in this process.

10. What do you understand by the statement, "Forests precede mankind; deserts follow?"

Ans. Forests are one of the principal biological systems of Earth. They form the foundation of the global economic system. It is true that if forests disappear, deserts will replace them.

Forests were in existence much before the coming of man on this planet. Local forests are disappearing to provide firewood and timber. The world is losing 40 to 50 million acres of forests a year. If this continues, nothing will be left except deserts and wastelands.

11. Explain the unusually alarming statistics about the population that the author mentions.

Ans. According to the author, the increase in human population over the years is alarming. The first billionth was reached in a million years, in 1800, followed by the second billionth reached in just a century, in 1900.

It is even more frightening that in just 94 more years, another 3.7 billion was added, making the world population 5.7 billion.

This exponential growth in human population is a threat to the planet.

12. How can the growth of population be checked or controlled?

Ans. The growth of population can be checked by spreading education and awareness among the masses. The people, especially the ones below the poverty line, think that if they have more children they will have more earning members, which is not true. In order to stop the people from thinking in this manner, development by means of education is the only solution. This will lead to a better life among the masses and will indirectly contribute towards curbing the population explosion.

13. What do you understand by this statement of Margaret Thatcher, "No generation has a freehold on this earth. All we have is a life tenancy—with a full repairing lease"?

Ans. We understand from her statement that man has been the victim of many false illusions. In his view, he is the lord of this world. This attitude man has caused untold havoc and destruction. He has always indulged himself in plundering natural resources. However, man should remember that he has to hand over this planet to the coming generations. He should not forget that he is only a trustee and not the master. It is his foremost duty to leave this earth in good health and shape for future generations.

14. What did Mr Lester R Brown mean when he said "We have not inherited this Earth from our forefathers; we have borrowed it from our children"?

Ans. Mr Lester R Brown believes that the present generation of people has no right to think that the Earth is their property. In fact, everyone should believe that they are responsible to leave Earth for future generations in the same condition as they found it. He further says that human beings have no right to misuse Earth because we are accountable to future generations.

15. Justify the title of the article by Nani Palkhivala.

Ans. The title of the article by Nani Palkhivala, 'The Ailing Planet: The Green Movement's Role', is totally justified and appropriate. The Earth's vital signs are that of a patient in declining health. We have overexploited its resources. But the Green Movement has changed our thinking. We have started to understand that earth is also a living organism and we have to respect its needs.

• Long Answer Type Questions

1. In spite of knowing the deplorable condition of the environment, human beings only make a show of doing something about it. Elaborate.

Ans. The issue of indiscriminate exploitation of nature has become an essential feature of human existence. Although sustainable development of resources is a goal for most nations, the reality is hardly so.

This uncaring behaviour is manifested in practices such as deforestation, destruction of wetlands, excessive mining for oil and mineral supplies, over-fishing and so on. The root causes for such practices are overpopulation, inefficiency in resource utilisation, over-consumption, poverty and ineffective structures such as human institutions, regulatory bodies and attitudes.

Moreover, the funds meant to help in conservation of critically endangered species are being siphoned off for other causes and the concerned authorities are not taking this matter seriously.

2. "Laws are never respected nor enforced in India." Explain. **(NCERT)**

Ans. It is a very sad state of affairs that in India laws are neither respected nor enforced. There is a very well written Constitution of India that covers all the aspects of the running of the country. New laws are also made and reforms take place. But generally, Indians can be seen exploiting these laws in order to get benefits from them.

There is a general apathy towards the system of law. There could be a lot of reasons behind this. Corruption is one of them. We, in India, know that everyone and everything can be bought for a price. The second reason could be that, in our country, the course of justice takes a long time.

We believe in the words that, 'Justice delayed is justice denied.' So, there is a possibility that people take law in their own hands and try to meet their demands according to what they want. What needs to be done is to make people more aware about right and wrong.

People should respect laws rather than break them. Corrupt officials should be punished strictly and justice should be delivered quickly. Only after some serious measures have been taken can the situation be improved.

3. "Are we to leave our successors a scorched planet of advancing deserts, impoverished landscapes and an ailing environment?" Explain. **(NCERT)**

Ans. The ever-rising inflation, the high cost of living, paucity of drinking water and frequent power cuts are some of the problems we face every day. We fall sick with all kinds of new ailments. These are the assets we have inherited from our ancestors. But the question is, if we are suffering, should we not think of finding solutions to these problems and give a better world to our successors.

We certainly have to take corrective measures to ensure that we do not leave our successors a planet that has been exhausted of landscapes and has a suffering environment and barren lands. We should not make unreasonable claims on the planet's biological systems.

Over-fishing should be avoided and forests should be preserved. New plants should be planted. We should try to avoid using cow dung for burning, so as not to deprive soil of its natural fertiliser.

If utmost care is not taken now, then the future of all of mankind would become endangered. It is high time that we keep our selfish motives in check and try to build a healthy future.

4. "We have not inherited this Earth from our forefathers; we have borrowed it from our children." Expain. **(NCERT)**

Ans. Man suffers from many misconceptions. He considers himself to be the lord of this world. Perhaps he doesn't know that his actions are leading to the degradation and destruction of this Earth. He thinks that he has a freehold on this Earth.

The hungry world has been ruined by over fishing. Forests are disappearing at the rate of an acre and a half every second. Grasslands and croplands are being converted into wastelands and deserts. Man's greed and claims have made this earth a scorched planet of advancing deserts and an ailing environment.

Man should remember that he has to hand over this planet to the coming generations. He is only the trustee and not the master. It is the duty of every living being to leave this Earth in good health and shape. According to Margaret Thatcher, we have only a life tenancy and not the ownership. At any cost, we have to maintain sustainable development in order to meet our present needs without harming the interests and needs of the future generations.

5. "The problems of overpopulation directly affect our everyday life." Explain. **(NCERT)**

Ans. There is no doubt that the growth of world population is one of the strongest factors distorting the future of human society. World population is increasing at a rapid speed.

This is a very alarming situation. Every day, we face the brunt of this menace. There is not a single utility location where there are not long queues, be it a hospital, ration shops or educational institutes.

Overpopulation makes the poor still poorer. More children only means more people without work and more mouths to feed. There are not enough houses for everyone, so we find slums everywhere.

In government hospitals, where the treatment is available at a reduced cost, there are not enough beds for the patients. Every day, there are new colleges and schools opening, but still the rate of illiteracy is not reducing.

Moreover, high population affects the environment adversely. Trees are cut to make new settlements. As a result, forests recede. More food is needed to support an increasing population. A protein hungry world creates a perpetual pressure on fisheries and croplands. Ultimately, it also adds to impaired productivity.

● Extract Based Questions

1. Read the extract to attempt the questions that follow.

"In the zoo at Lusaka, Zambia, there is a cage where the notice reads, 'The world's most dangerous animal'. Inside the cage there is no animal but a mirror where you see yourself. Thanks to the efforts of a number of agencies in different countries, a new awareness has now dawned upon the most dangerous animal in the world. He has realised the wisdom of shifting from a system based on domination to one based on partnership.

Scientists have catalogued about 1.4 million living species with which mankind shares the earth. Estimates vary widely as regards the still-uncatalogued living species — biologists reckon that about three to a hundred million other living species still languish unnamed in ignominious darkness."

(i) Why is man referred to as 'the most dangerous animal'?

(ii) Do you agree with the author's opinion?

(iii) What is the purpose of placing a mirror inside the cage?

(iv) The author says that man has realised the wisdom of shifting to a new system. What does it mean?

(v) What is the significance of the lines 'biologists reckon that about three to a hundred million other living species still languish unnamed in ignominious darkness.'?

Ans. (i) Man is referred to as 'the most dangerous animal' because he is using up the resources at an exponential rate. He is also killing animals for his own benefit without any consideration of the planet.

(ii) Yes, I agree with the author's opinion that man is the most dangerous animal on earth for using the natural resources recklessly.

(iii) The placing of a mirror inside the cage serves to remind man of his own actions so that he can shift to a more sustainable system.

(iv) The fact that man has realised the wisdom of shifting to a new system means that man has seen the consequence of his actions. The Earth and its resources are depleting which can affect the presence of mankind itself.

(v) The given lines show how some species which are still undiscovered are becoming extinct.

2. Read the extract given below and answer the questions that follow.

"In addition to supplying our food, these four systems provide virtually all the raw materials for industry except minerals and petroleum-derived synthetics. In large areas of the world, human claims on these systems are reaching an unsustainable level, a point where their productivity is being impaired. When this happens, fisheries collapse, forests disappear, grasslands are converted into barren wastelands, and croplands deteriorate. In a protein-conscious and protein hungry world, over-fishing is common every day."

(i) What are 'these four systems'?

(ii) Why are these systems important?

(iii) How is the productivity of these systems impaired?

(iv) What is the impact of mankind of on these systems?

(v) Whom does the author blame for the collapse of fisheries?

Ans. (i) These four systems are — fisheries, forests, grasslands, and croplands.

(ii) These systems are important as they form the foundation of living. They provide us with raw material for food, shelter, etc.

(iii) The productivity of these systems gets impaired when mankind overexploits these systems without giving them a chance to renew properly.

(iv) Because of the overexploitation of these systems by mankind, fisheries are depleting, forests and grasslands are becoming wastelands and croplands are deteriorated.

(v) The author blames the protein hungry or specifically non-vegetarian people for the collapse of fisheries.

3. Read the extract given below and answer questions that follow.

"But what causes endless anguish is the fact that laws are never respected nor enforced in India. (For instance, the Constitution says that casteism, untouchability and bonded labour shall be abolished, but they flourish shamelessly even after forty-four years of the operation of the Constitution.) A recent report of our Parliament's Estimates Committee has highlighted the near catastrophic depletion of India's forests over the last four decades. India, according to reliable data, is losing its forests at the rate of 3.7 million acres a year. Large areas, officially designated as forest land, "are already virtually treeless". The actual loss of forests is estimated to be about eight times the rate indicated by government statistics."

(i) Which law does the author mention in the given extract?

(ii) What is the cause of anguish for the author?

(iii) Why has the author used the example of caste based laws?

(iv) Explain 'virtually treeless'.

(v) "The actual loss of forests is estimated to be about eight times the rate indicated by government statistics." Comment.

Ans. (i) The author mentions Article 48A in the given extract. This law states that the State is responsible for the protection and the improvement of the environment and for safeguarding the forests and wildlife of the country.

(ii) The author feels anguished because he knows that no matter how many laws are enacted by the Government for environment, these laws will never be efficiently enacted and enforced.

(iii) The author has deliberately used the example of caste-based laws to make man realise that their actions are shameful and worthy of punishment. At the same time, the author also feels that because of lack of action on the part of the government, man will go unpunished.

(iv) The phrase 'virtually tree less' has been used to refer to the area which has been officially designated as forest area. However, contrary to its categorisation, it does not have any trees at all.

(v) The given line highlights that all the statistical data regarding the loss of forest land is just an estimation. The real loss is much greater then we could imagine.

CHAPTER 02

The Browning Version

—by Terence Rattigan

In this Chapter...

- Chapter Summary
- Word Meaning
- Chapter Practice

Chapter Sketch

This extract, from the play 'The Browning Version', highlights the attitude of a teenaged student towards his teacher. His comments are shocking because they are very close to the truth. He calls the teacher almost inhuman, though not a sadist. He is mortally afraid of his teacher because his promotion depends on his teacher's goodwill. When another teacher encourages him, the student becomes more frank. It appears that the teacher was strict and seemed to hate people who like him. This reflects on the teacher's quality.

Chapter Summary

Mr Frank Converses with Taplow

The scene of the play is set in a school. The play opens with a sixteen year old boy, Taplow, who has been detained by his teacher to compensate for one day's absence. He is waiting for his teacher, Mr Crocker-Harris, who has not yet arrived. Another teacher, Frank, finds Taplow waiting in the room and starts talking to him.

Taplow introduces himself and informs him that he is a student in the lower fifth grade. He adds that he would specialise next term if he got promoted. He also tells Frank that Mr Crocker-Harris does not tell the students their results beforehand like the other teachers. Frank is surprised.

Frank admits that there is a rule that results should be announced on the last day only by the principal but no one follows it. Taplow remarks that only Crocker-Harris follows the rule.

Then Frank asks Taplow which specialisation would he take. Taplow readily tells him that he will take science as he is extremely interested in science. Frank tells Taplow that he is not interested in the science he teaches. But Taplow retorts that it must be better than the 'Agememnon' written by Aeschylus. Seeing Frank's reaction, Taplow clarifies that he likes the plot of the book but not the way it is taught.

Taplow's Extra Work

Frank thinks that Taplow sounds a little bitter as he has not been promoted. Taplow informs him that he is there for extra work. Frank is more than surprised to hear that Taplow is doing extra work on the last day of the term.

Taplow informs him that he had missed a day of school the previous week due to illness and so Mr Crocker-Harris had asked him to do extra work to make up for that. Mr Frank tries to calm him by telling him that he would certainly get his result the next day for taking extra work. But Taplow feels that such things do not work with Mr Crocker-Harris, as he is not like other teachers who appreciate students who do extra work.

Taplow's Criticism of Mr Crocker-Harris

Taplow adds that when he had asked Mr Crocker-Harris about his result, he had told him that he had given him what he deserved, no less and no more. Taplow feels that Mr Crocker-Harris would have rather marked him down for doing extra work.

He believes that Mr Crocker-Harris is hardly human. When he realises that he had gone too far, he apologises to Frank. Frank had been listening to Taplow in seriousness and asks Taplow to repeat it. He then gets more serious and asks Taplow to read Aeschylus. When Taplow expresses his dislike, Franks asks Taplow to leave for Crocker-Harris is 10 minute late.

Frank's suggestion shocks Taplow. He tells Frank that he wouldn't do it for the fear of Crocker Harris's reaction. Frank admits that he envies how students are scared of him. Taplow informs him that Crocker-Harris is not a sadist as he does not beat anyone.

Mr Crocker-Harris's Personality

However, Taplow believes that it would have been better if Crocker-Harris were a sadist, as it would mean he had some feelings. He feels that Crocker-Harris hates that people like him. Taplow finds it funny that in spite of all the crankiness, he likes Mr Crocker-Harris.

He feels that Crocker-Harris knows it but it makes him more hard and strict.

Taplow recalls an incident when Crocker-Harris made a joke. No one laughed at it as no one understood it. Out of sheer courtesy, Taplow laughed. Instead of understanding his intention, Crocker-Harris asked Taplow to explain the joke to the class for only he could understand the advanced Latin.

As this conversation was going one, Millie Crocker-Harris entered the scene unnoticed.

Millie Crocker-Harris Brings Relief to Taplow

Millie Crocker-Harris, Crocker-Harris' wife, is a thin woman in her late thirties. She is smartly dressed, unlike other schoolmasters' wives. Taplow was still imitating Crocker-Harris when Frank noticed her and suddenly broke off. Taplow gets scared and asks Mr Frank if Millie Crocker-Harris could have heard their conversation.

Mr Frank thinks that she did. Taplow fears that if she tells anything to Mr Crocker-Harris, then he will surely not get promoted.

Millie Crocker-Harris asks Taplow if he was waiting for her husband. She further informs him that her husband is busy at the Bursar's and might get late. She asks him to leave. Taplow is doubtful and says Mr Crocker-Harris had particularly asked him to come.

She tells him that she will take the blame and advises him to go away for a quarter of an hour. Taplow is scared if so, she gives him a prescription and sends him to the chemist to get it filled. Convinced, Taplow accepts the proposal and leaves.

Word Meanings

The given page numbers correspond to the pages in the prescribed NCERT textbook.

Word	Meaning
Page 50	
excerpt	a short extract from a piece of writing
remove	promotion
Page 51	
form	class
muck	rubbish
kept in	detained
Page 52	
got carried away	got excited and lost control
Page 53	
cut	go away without permission
sadist	person who gets pleasure from inflicting pain or suffering on others
all shrivelled up	having no feelings
Page 54	
shrivel him up	reduce his feelings
general run	normal group
cape	a shawl or stole
Page 55	
frantically	in a hurried way
It made up	prepare or put together

Chapter Practice

Objective Questions

• Multiple Choice Questions

1. What is Taplow doing on the last day of school?
   (a) Extra work   (b) Can't say
   (c) Passing time   (d) Doing his homework
Ans. (a) On the last day of school, Taplow is doing his extra work as he waits for Mr Crocker-Harris.

2. Why is Taplow waiting for his teacher, Mr. Crocker-Harris?
   (a) To apologise to him   (b) To talk about Frank
   (c) To receive his result (d) To give him a present
Ans. (c) Taplow was waiting for Mr. Crocker-Harris to receive his remove, i.e. his result.

3. How is Mr. Crocker-Harris different from other teachers?
   (a) As he is not biased   (b) As he is strict
   (c) As he is old   (d) As he is rude
Ans. (a) Mr Crocker-Harris is an unbiased teacher who does not favour any child. He gave results according to the academic performance of his students.

4. Select the suitable option for the given statements, based on your reading of 'The Browning Version'.
   (i) Taplow did not really hate the play 'Agamemnon' by Aeschylus.
   (ii) Taplow disliked the way Crocker Harris taught the play.
   (a) (i) is false but (ii) is true.
   (b) Both (i) and (ii) are true.
   (c) (ii) is a fact but unrelated to (i).
   (d) (i) is the cause for (ii).
Ans. (b) Taplow states that he liked the story of Agamemnon but he disliked the way it was taught to him by his teacher Mr. Crocker-Harris.

5. Why does Taplow have to do extra work?
   (a) Because he missed a day previous week as he was sick
   (b) Because he didn't performed well in his studies
   (c) Because he was there to help his teacher
   (d) Because he was called by his teacher

Ans. (a) Taplow had to do extra work because he missed a day previous week as he was sick.

6. "Yes, sir, and I might be playing golf. You'd think he'd have enough to do anyway himself, considering he's leaving tomorrow for good — but oh no, I missed a day last week when I was ill — so here I am — and look at the weather, sir."

   In the given lines, Taplow sounds ....
   (a) Despairing   (b) Disdainful
   (c) Bitter   (d) Regretful
Ans. (c) In the given lines, Taplow sounds bitter because instead of enjoying the weather and playing golf, he had to stay back in the school and study.

7. Frank asks Taplow to imitate Crocker-Harris again. Select the option that explains it.
   (a) Frank is envious of Crocker-Harris.
   (b) Frank doesn't think Taplow sounds anything like Mr. Crocker Harris while imitating him.
   (c) Frank is stupefied by the student's opinion for Crocker Harris.
   (d) Frank dislikes Crocker-Harris.
Ans. (b) Franks asks Taplow to repeat his imitation because he doesn't think that Taplow sounds anything like Mr. Crocker-Harris.

8. Classify (1) to (4) as Fact (F) or Opinion (O), based on your reading of 'The Browning Version'.
   1. Frank cannot understand why students are afraid of Crocker Harris.
   2. Taplow knows that if he leaves without meeting Crocker Harris he wouldn't get his remove.
   3. Frank does not believe in the school system.
   4. Taplow is a very rational child.
   (a) F-1, 2, 4; O-3   (b) F-2, 3; O-1, 4
   (c) F-2; O-1, 3, 4   (d) F-3, 4; O-1, 2
Ans. (a)

9. Why did Taplow call Mr. Crocker – Harris 'hardly human'?
   (a) Because he is a sadist
   (b) He does not show any emotions
   (c) He is very rude to everyone
   (d) He finds peace in failing students
Ans. (b) He calls his professor 'hardly human' as he is all shriveled up and does not show any emotions.

10. What was Frank's reaction when Mrs Crocker-Harris entered the classroom?
(a) He was happy
(b) He was nervous
(c) He was relieved
(d) Nothing unusual

Ans. (c) Frank seemed relieved to see Mrs. Crocker-Harris as she entered the classroom.

11. Why was Taplow worried that Mrs. Crocker-Harris might have heard what they were saying?
(a) As she had been standing for a few minutes when they were busy talking
(b) As she interrupted them talking about her husband
(c) As she heard them talking about the Principal
(d) It is unclear why he was worried

Ans. (a) Taplow was worried that Mrs Crocker-Harris might have heard what they were saying about her husband as she had been standing there for a few minutes while they imitated Mr. Crocker-Harris.

12. Select the option that correctly describes Frank.
I. Friendly
II. Lenient
III. Humourous
IV. Disrespectful
V. Uninterested
(a) All but IV
(b) I, II and III
(c) III and V
(d) All but II

Ans. (b) Frank seems to be friendly and his approach towards education is lenient. He is also humorous and entertains Taplow with a conversation.

13. Which of the following statements is TRUE about the play?
I. Frank is curious about Taplow's opinion of Mr. Crocker-Harris.
II. Taplow is confused about choosing a subject to study.
III. Taplow is waiting for Mr. Crocker-Harris.
IV. Mrs. Crocker-Harris asks Frank about Taplow's education.
(a) I and III are true
(b) I and IV are true
(c) II and III are true
(d) None of these

Ans. (a) Frank is curious to know about Mr Crocker-Harris and what Taplow thinks about him, which is why he strikes up a conversation with Taplow. It is while Frank arrives that Taplow is waiting for Mr Crocker-Harris to arrive.

14. Select the central thematic concern of the play, from the given options.
I. The uniqueness of Mr. Crocker-Harris
II. The bad behaviour of Taplow
III. Mrs. Crocker Harris's shopping list
IV. The play 'Agamemnon'
(a) II and III
(b) II and I
(c) Only I
(d) III and IV

Ans. (c) The central thematic concern of the play is the uniqueness of Mr. Crocker-Harris.

15. Select the option that lists the characteristics displayed by Taplow.
I. Obedient
II. Strange
III. Unempathetic
IV. Straight Forward
V. Respectful
(a) All but V
(b) I, IV and V
(c) II and III
(d) All but II

Ans. (b) Taplow is obedient, straightforward and respectful as he is dedicated to his professor, expresses himself well and respects his teacher's orders.

• Extract Based Questions

1. Read the extract given below and answer the questions that follow.

"**Frank** What's your name?

Taplow Taplow.

Frank Taplow! No, I don't. You're not a scientist I gather?

Taplow No, sir, I'm still in the lower fifth. I can't specialise until next term — that's to say, if I've got my remove all right.

Frank Don't you know if you've got your remove?

Taplow No sir, Mr Crocker-Harris doesn't tell us the results like the other masters.

Frank Why not?

Taplow Well, you know what he's like, sir.

Frank I believe there is a rule that form results should only be announced by the headmaster on the last day of term."

(i) What does 'remove' mean in this context?
(a) A division in British schools
(b) Take away something
(c) Unfasten
(d) Get rid of

Ans. (a) 'Remove', in this context, means a division in British schools.

(ii) Select the statement(s) that can be inferred from the above extract:
I. Frank is meeting Taplow for the first time.
II. Taplow is a new student of Frank.
III. Mr. Crocker-Harris is a rather unique teacher.
(a) I and II are true
(b) Only II is true
(c) I and III are true
(d) I, II and III are true

Ans. (c) The extract does not inform the reader whether Taplow is a new student of Frank or not.

(iii) What is Frank's reaction when he asks Taplow as to why he does not know about his remove yet?
(a) Sad
(b) Surprising
(c) Angry
(d) Happy

Ans. (b) It is surprising to Frank that Taplow has not received his remove yet.

(iv) What does Frank mean to say when he states that Crocker-Harris is unlike other teachers?

(a) He follows rules

(b) He does not favour any child

(c) He is not flexible

(d) He is strict

Ans. (c) When Frank says that Crocker-Harris is unlike other teachers, he wishes to highlight that Crocker-Harris follows rules. He waits for the headmaster to tell the results as per the rule which other teachers do not follow.

(v) By stating the rule, Frank is .... Mr. Crocker-Harris.

(a) trying to understand   (b) defending

(c) negating   (d) clarifying

Ans. (b)

2. Read the extract given below and answer the questions that follow.

"**Frank** Well, he's ten minutes late. Why don't you cut? You could still play golf before lock-up.

Taplow (really shocked) Oh, no, I couldn't cut. Cut the Crock — Mr Crocker-Harris? I shouldn't think it's ever been done in the whole time he's been here. God knows what would happen if I did. He'd probably follow me home, or something ...

Frank I must admit I envy him the effect he seems to have on you boys in the form. You all seem scared to death of him. What does he do — beat you all, or something?

Taplow Good Lord, no. He's not a sadist, like one or two of the others."

(i) What makes Mr. Crocker-Harris different from other teachers?

(a) He might be a sadist

(b) He treasures his students

(c) He values other teachers

(d) He has a special influence on students

Ans. (d) Mr. Crocker-Harris is different from other teachers as he has a special effect on his students.

(ii) Frank asks Taplow to cut. He means that Taplow should ....

(a) leave   (b) wait

(c) contact   (d) forget

Ans. (a) Frank suggests that Taplow 'cut' i.e. leave, as Mr. Crocker is ten minutes late.

(iii) Why does Taplow correct himself immediately after calling his professor Crock?

(a) Because Mr. Crocker-Harris arrived

(b) Because he is with another teacher

(c) Because he forgot his teacher's actual name

(d) Because he is sad

Ans. (b) As Frank is another teacher, it is important for Taplow to show his respect towards Mr. Crocker-Harris. Thus, he immediately corrects himself after calling his professor Crock.

(iv) Taplow says that Crocker-Harris is not a sadist. Select the option that explains this.

(a) To negate Frank's belief that Crocker-Harris beats them.

(b) To state why they are afraid of Crocker-Harris.

(c) To justify why students are afraid of Crocker Harris.

(d) To claim that Crocker-Harris was not strict.

Ans. (a) Taplow says that Crocker-Harris is not a sadist to clarify that Crocker-Harris does not beat them as Frank misunderstands.

(v) How does Taplow come out in the given extract?

(a) Rational

(b) Matter of fact

(c) Frank

(d) All of the above

Ans. (d)

PART 2
Subjective Questions

● Short Answer Type Questions

1. "We get all the slackers!" What did Mr Frank mean?

Ans. Mr. Frank means that he thinks that most studies who opt for science are poor in studies and the subject frequently attracts 'slackers'.

He further goes on to admit that he himself doesn't like the science he teaches.

2. What did Taplow consider 'muck'? Why?

Ans. Taplow considered the Greek tragedy 'Agamemnon' as 'muck'. Even though he liked the plot of the play, Taplow disliked the way it was taught by Mr Crocker-Harris. Besides, a number of Greek words were to be learnt and if a student went wrong, he had to write each word fifty times as punishment.

3. Why was Taplow bitter?

Ans. Mr Frank found Taplow waiting for Mr Crocker- Harris and they got into a conversation. While talking, Taplow called the 'Agamemnon' rubbish. Mr Frank detected some bitterness in Taplow's voice. Taplow said that he was certainly bitter. The weather was good and he could have been out playing golf but here he was, in the school, doing extra work on the last day of the term.

4. Why would Taplow not get any 'comfort' as mentioned by Mr Frank?

Ans. Mr Crocker-Harris gave no benefit to his students for being good boys in taking up extra work. He gave marks as per the performance and not for doing any extra work. In fact,

Taplow was afraid that his teacher would have rather marked him down for doing extra work.

Hence, he doesn't think he would get any 'comfort'.

5. What did Mr Frank call 'bad luck'?

Ans. The weather was fine and Taplow wanted to go and play golf. But Taplow had been given extra work to do by Mr. Crocker-Harris. He was waiting for his teacher and couldn't dare to defy him. Mr Frank considered Taplow's situation 'bad luck' as he could not go out to play on such a wonderful day.

6. Why did Taplow say that Mr Crocker-Harris was hardly human?

Ans. Taplow could not believe that Mr Crocker-Harris was a normal human being for a number of reasons. Mr Crocker-Harris was extremely strict while teaching. He followed the headmaster's rules of announcing results on the last day of term. He never told the students their results beforehand. He frightened the students in every possible way. He was a man who hated even those who liked him.

7. Did Taplow come to the school only because Mr Crocker-Harris had asked him to?

Ans. Taplow was present at the school on the last day of the term as he had missed a class of Mr Crocker-Harris the previous week and Mr Crocker-Harris had asked him to make amends for it. It is true that Taplow was there because he was scared to death of Mr Crocker-Harris, but he also had another motive. He was waiting for his result and feared that if he did not obey Mr Crocker-Harris then his result would suffer.

8. Why is Taplow worried about his 'remove'? What did Mr Crocker-Harris reply to him?

Ans. Taplow is in the lower fifth class. He can't specialise until he goes into the next class. He is worried about the 'remove' i.e. his result, because much depends on how he performed in the examination.

At the same time, he is very anxious to know his result. So, he had gone to Mr Crocker-Harris and asked him if he had passed him. However, the teacher gave a very mysterious answer and told him that he had given him exactly what he deserved, not less and certainly not more.

9. Why does Mr Frank ask Taplow to 'cut'? How does Taplow react?

Ans. When Mr Frank finds Taplow waiting, he asks him to 'cut' as Mr Crocker-Harris had not arrived even after ten minutes. However, Taplow cannot even imagine doing such a thing. According to him, there is probably not a single student who has insulted Mr Crocker-Harris in his career.

10. Mr Crocker-Harris is not a sadist. Still his students are scared of him. Comment.

Ans. Taplow says that Mr Crocker-Harris is not a sadist. If he had been a sadist then he wouldn't have been so frightening. It would mean that he had some feelings. But Mr Crocker-Harris was devoid of any feelings. He seemed to hate that people liked him and Taplow couldn't think of any teacher who didn't like being liked by his students.

11. What kind of a teacher and a human being is Mr Crocker-Harris, according to Taplow?

Ans. Mr Crocker-Harris appears to be a disciplinarian. Students are scared to death of him. He follows rules and believes in them. He tells Taplow that he will mark him according to what he deserves, neither less, nor more. Taplow thinks that Mr Crocker-Harris is not a sadist, but hates being liked. He is all shrivelled up and without any feelings.

He has a wonderful hold over his students. No student has ever refused any punishment given by Mr Crocker-Harris in his entire career. He appears frightening to his students.

12 What happened when Mr Crocker-Harris made one of his classical jokes?

Ans. One day, Mr Crocker-Harris made one of his classical jokes in class. Nobody understood it and hence nobody laughed. However, Taplow knew that Mr Crocker-Harris meant something funny and he laughed out of sheer courtesy. Mr Crocker-Harris said that he was impressed by the progress made by Taplow as he understood what others in his class couldn't and then asked Taplow to explain to the whole class what he had understood.

13. How does Taplow react to Millie Crocker-Harris' arrival?

Ans. Taplow is nervous on seeing Millie Crocker-Harris. He is unable to control his emotions and whispers to Mr Frank whether he thinks she has heard their conversation. Taplow feels that if she tells Mr Crocker-Harris about what they were talking about, he would surely be failed.

14. How does Millie Crocker-Harris send Taplow away?

Ans. On seeing Taplow, Millie Crocker-Harris points out that her husband was at the Bursar's and would take some time to get back. She suggests him to go away for a quarter of an hour. However, Taplow does not do so due to fear of the teacher. Millie Crocker-Harris assures him that she would take the blame. She given him prescription and requests him to bring some medicines from the chemist. Taplow accepts the proposal and leaves.

15. What do you gather about Mr Frank from the play?

Ans. Mr Frank is a young science teacher. He does not like the subject he teaches. He also admits that he tells results to the students before they are officially announced. He envies Mr Crocker-Harris for the effect he has on the students.

● Long Answer Type Questions

1. Taplow does an imitation of Mr Crocker-Harris. Do you think respect for one's teacher is fast disappearing in the modern world? Give reasons in support of your answer.

Ans. It is true that respect for one's teacher is fast disappearing in the modern world. Improper parenting, lack of restriction in schools and no fear of teachers are some of the reasons why teachers are not being adequately respected.

Too often parents these days blame the teachers for the slightest bit of strictness in schools. No wonder the children have no respect for the teacher when they know they can get away with indiscipline.

Moreover, these days teachers seem to lack the passion to teach. As a result, teachers do not have good knowledge of their subject and are thus not respected by their students.

Moreover, there are teachers who are biased and prejudiced in their approach. Students do not appreciate such teachers and thus lose respect for them. Further, it is rightly said that respect is never demanded but earned. It is the responsibility of the teacher to earn the students' respect. If a teacher comes across students who are disrespectful, he/she should think over it and try to understand where he/she has gone wrong and lost the respect.

2. Do you feel it is proper for students to present their teacher the way Taplow does? What in your opinion should the relation between teacher and student be like?

Ans. It is improper for students to present their teacher the way Taplow does. He should not have criticised his teacher and his ways in front of another teacher. Moreover, Taplow's bitterness arises out of the fact that he is detained by his teacher for extra work when he wanted to play golf. Further, Mr Crocker-Harris is the only one who follows the rules strictly. Had other teachers been like him, Taplow might not have been so critical of his teacher.

The relation between a teacher and his students should be of mutual understanding, respect and cooperation. They should work as a team, as neither is complete without the other. Both should try and create an interactive space where problems can be talked about and brought to a conclusion.

Moreover, it is the duty of the teacher to gain the trust of the students and create a friendly atmosphere where students are not scared of sharing their problems.

3. Comment on the attitude shown by Taplow towards Mr Crocker-Harris.   **(NCERT)**

Ans. Mr Crocker-Harris is a middle-aged schoolmaster. He is a teacher in the traditional mould. He is a strict man who is more feared than respected. He follows rules and regulations with all sincerity.

Taplow is in the lower fifth standard. His attitude towards Mr Crocker-Harris is mixed. He recognises his sense of discipline, sense of devotion and stoic nature. But he has a personal feeling of ill-will against Mr Crocker-Harris. He is given extra work on the last day of the term as punishment because he missed a day the previous week when he was ill. Mr Crocker-Harris is a hard taskmaster. That's why he gave extra work to Taplow. He doesn't bother that it is the last day of the term.

Taplow feels that Mr Crocker-Harris is devoid of feelings, is strict and can never be flattered. In spite of everything, Taplow rather likes him. Mr Crocker–Harris doesn't tell the results like the other masters before they are formally announced. Hence, Mr Crocker-Harris is different from other teachers.

Taplow doesn't consider Mr Crocker-Harris a sadist. He doesn't get pleasure out of giving pain to others. In his view, a sadist shows some feelings but Mr Crocker-Harris has none.

4. Does Mr Frank seem to encourage Taplow's comments on Mr Crocker-Harris?   **(NCERT)**

Ans. Yes, Mr Frank seems to encourage Taplow's comments on Mr Crocker-Harris. Mr Frank is a young school teacher. He teaches in the same school in which Mr Crocker-Harris, his senior colleague, teaches. Actually, he is jealous of Mr Crocker-Harris. He frankly admits that Mr Crocker-Harris enjoys a wonderful hold over his students. They all seem scared to death of him. He is jealous of Mr Crocker-Harris's authority and 'effect' on his students.

He relishes all adverse comments against Mr Crocker-Harris. Not only that, he even encourages Taplow to criticise him. But he doesn't do it openly. He pretends not to like any adverse comments against Mr. Crocker-Harris like when Taplow calls him 'Crock'. However, when Taplow imitates Mr. Crocker-Harris in his throaty voice, Mr Frank relishes it. He even asks Taplow to repeat it. He enjoys Mr Crocker-Harris being ridiculed by his own student.

Mr. Frank also asks Taplow to go away without meeting his teacher. But Taplow can't even imagine doing such a thing. He also encourages Taplow to share Mr. Crocker-Harris's jokes with him. Mr. Frank pretends to have no jealousy against Mr. Crocker-Harris and warns Taplow that he has gone much too far in his criticism of Mr. Crocker-Harris.

5. What do you gather about Mr Crocker-Harris from the play?   **(NCERT)**

Ans. Mr Crocker-Harris is a middle-aged schoolmaster. He is quite reserved and a disciplinarian. He follows rules very strictly. He is a devoted teacher who can't tolerate any relaxation among his students. He is a hard taskmaster. He doesn't leak the results like other masters before they are formally announced. He is very conscious of his duty and he never spares a child who absents himself. He can give extra work to a student even on the last day of the term.

He is quite unpredictable. It is very difficult to read his mind. For instance, when Taplow asked him if he had given him a promotion, Mr Crocker-Harris replied mysteriously that he has given him exactly what he deserves, no less and certainly no more. His junior colleague feels jealous of the effect Mr Crocker-Harris has on the students.

Students seem to be scared to death of him. Taplow says that Mr Crocker-Harris has no feelings. It is quite correct, as he doesn't like flattery, nor does he like anyone who likes him. Sometimes he also cracks jokes but his classical jokes lack humour. In spite of everything, Taplow likes him.

• Extract Based Questions

1. Read the extract given below and answer the questions that follow.

"**Taplow** Well, I'm not so sure, sir. That would be true of the ordinary masters, all right. They just wouldn't dare not to give a chap a remove after his taking extra work. But those sort of rules don't apply to the Crock — Mr Crocker-Harris. I asked him yesterday outright if he'd given me a remove and do you know what he said, sir?

Frank No. What?

Taplow (imitating a very gentle, rather throaty voice) "My dear Taplow, I have given you exactly what you deserve. No less; and certainly no more." Do you know sir, I think he may have marked me down, rather than up, for taking extra work. I mean, the man's hardly human. (He breaks off quickly.) Sorry, sir. Have I gone too far?

Frank Yes. Much too far.

Taplow Sorry, sir. I got carried away."

(i) What is Taplow not sure of ?

(ii) Why does Taplow say that 'those kind of rule don't apply to the Crock'?

(iii) Do you think Taplow is bitter about not knowing whether he got his remove?

(iv) Why does Taplow call Crocker-Harris 'Hardly Human'?

(v) Why does Taplow feel that he got carried away?

Ans. (i) Taplow is not sure of whether he would get his remove from Crocker Harris.

(ii) Taplow says that those kind of rules does not apply to the Crock because if it would have been some other teacher he would have gotten his remove but Mr. Crocker-Harris would not do so.

(ii) No, Taplow is not bitter about not knowing whether he got his remove because this was expected of Crocker-Harris.

(iv) Taplow calls Crocker-Harris hardly human because he felt that Crocker-Harris did not have any emotions.

(v) Taplow feels that he got carried away because he was talking about another teacher disrespectfully in front of Frank who was a teacher himself.

2. Read the extract given below and answer the questions that follow.

"Anyway, the Crock isn't a sadist. That's what I'm saying. He wouldn't be so frightening if he were — because at least it would show he had some feelings. But he hasn't. He's all shrivelled up inside like a nut and he seems to hate people to like him. It's funny, that. I don't know any other master who doesn't like being liked —"

(i) Who is the speaker of the given lines?

(ii) Why does he say that Crock isn't a sadist?

(iii) Do you think Taplow dislikes Crocker-Harris?

(iv) Taplow states that Crocker Harris is shriveled up like a nut. Explain.

(v) Why does the extract end with '-----' ?

Ans. (i) Taplow, a 16 year old boy, is the speaker of the given lines.

(ii) Taplow says that Crock isn't a sadist to clarify to Frank that he does not beat children and boys are afraid of him for some other reason.

(iii) No, I don't think that Taplow dislikes Crocker-Harris because he, in his description of the teacher, does nowhere state so or show any resentment towards him.

(iv) Taplow says that Crocker-Harris is all shriveled up like a nut to highlight that Crocker-Harris does not seem to have any emotions and even if he has any he hides it.

(v) The extract ends with '----' to show that the speaker of the given lines was interrupted in between.

3. Read the extract given below and answer the questions that follow.

"**Millie** He's at the Bursar's and might be there quite a time. If I were you I'd go.

Taplow (doubtfully) He said most particularly I was to come.

Millie Well, why don't you run away for a quarter of an hour and come back? (She unpacks some things from the basket.)

Taplow Supposing he gets here before me?

Millie (smiling) I'll take the blame. (She takes a prescription out of the basket.) I tell you what — you can do a job for him. Take this prescription to the chemist and get it made up.

Taplow All right, Mrs Crocker-Harris. (He crosses towards the door up right.)"

(i) Why does Millie tell Taplow that if she were him she would leave?

(ii) Why is Taplow hesitant to leave without seeing Crocker-Harris?

(iii) Do you think Millie Crocker-Harris wanted Taplow to leave her and Frank alone?

(iv) How do you think is Mrs. Millie Crocker-Harris different from what Taplow thought about her?

(v) What can you say about Taplow's feeling's for Crocker-Harris?

Ans. (i) Millie tells Taplow to leave because she knows that Crocker-Harris would take his time to reach school.

(ii) Taplow is hesitant to leave without seeing Crocker-Harris as he feels that if he does so, he would not get his remove.

(iii) Yes, I think that Millie Crocker-Harris wanted Taplow to leave her and Frank alone for some time.

(iv) When Taplow sees Mrs. Millie Crocker Harris he thinks that she would tell everything to Crocker Harris and then he would not get his remove. However, contrary to his opinion, Millie tells Taplow to leave and that she would take the blame on herself.

(v) From the given extract, we can gather that Taplow is respectful towards Mr Crocker-Harris and is afraid of him and dare not cut the extra work even on the last day of the term.

CHAPTER 03

Silk Road

—by Nick Middleton

In this Chapter...

- Chapter Summary
- Word Meaning
- Chapter Practice

Chapter Sketch

This chapter is part of a travelogue about the author's journey along the ancient trade route called 'Silk Road' regions as they are now. This account of the Silk Road, with its contrasts and exotic detail, describes the challenges and hardships the author faced while journeying to Mount Kailash on a pilgrimage.

Chapter Summary

Departure from Ravu

The author left Ravu along with Daniel, an interpreter, and Tsetan, a tourist guide. Before leaving, Lhamo, the lady who had provided them accommodation at Ravu, gave the author a gift of a long-sleeved sheepskin coat, as they were going to Mount Kailash where it would be very cold. Tsetan knew a short cut to reach the mountain. He added that the journey would be smooth if there was no snow.

Drokbas and Encounter with Tibetan Mastiffs

As they crossed the hills of Ravu, they saw open plains, and arid pastures. As they started climbing the hills again, they saw individual *drokbas* (nomad shepherds) looking after their flocks. Both men and women were seen wearing thick woollen clothes. They would stop and stare at their car, sometimes waving to them as they passed.

On their journey, they also passed isolated nomad tents. These tents were guarded by black dogs called Tibetan Mastiff. These dogs wore red collars and barked furiously with their big jaws. Whenever their car passed through, they would chase the car for some distance while barking furiously. Because of their nature, these dogs were popular in China as hunting dogs and they were brought along from Tibet on the Silk Road as a tribute.

Ice Blocks the Road

By now, the author could see the snow capped mountains. Their car entered a valley wherein the river was wide and clogged with ice. The turns were now more sharper and the ride became bumpier.

As they were climbing up, the author started feeling pressure in his ears. Suddenly, Tsetan stopped the car and got out of it. Snow was covering the area around them. They now could not move around the snow patch or could climb the steep mountain. So, they threw some dirt on the path. To avoid any mishap, the author and Daniel stayed out of the car while Tsetan slowly drove over the ice patch.

They came across a similar blockage in a short while. But this time Tsetan drove around the snow. Rapid ascent had caused a headache to the author who checked his watch to find that they were at the height of 5400 metres. When they reached the top of the pass at 5515 metres, Tsetan unscrewed the top of the car. He was glad that there was no smoking.

Back on the Highway

After making sure that their car was fine, they went down the other side of the pass. At 2'oclock, they had lunch at a place which unlike other places was full of activity. Salt collectors were coming from the plateau that was full of salt flats.

By late afternoon, the author reached Hor, a place that falls on the old trade route from Lhasa to Kashmir. Daniel had to go to Lhasa so he left. Tsetan and the author got the punctured tyres repaired and moved forward on their journey.

Hor-a Miserable Town

The author finds Hor, a town that was located on the shore of holy lake Mansarovar, to be grim and miserable. It had no vegetation and was covered in just dust and rocks. The author now could see Mount Kailash and was eager to move ahead.

However, Tsetan left the author to drink tea for some time. For this solitary time, the author felt his experience at Hor to be in contrast with the emotional outburst of other people.

The Author's Mysterious Experience

It was 10:30 pm when the author reached Darchen. At night, they stayed in a guest house. As the author went down to sleep, his nostrils got clogged. His cold had reappeared and he had trouble breathing. So, the author started breathing from his mouth. When the author felt comfortable and was drifting off to sleep, he woke up. Mysteriously, whenever he laid down to sleep, he could not breathe. He felt that he was not allowed to go to sleep and that if he did, he would die.

The next day Tsetan took the author to the Darchen Medical College. The doctor told him it was just the cold and the altitude which were giving him trouble. He gave him some medicine and that night, after taking one full day course of medicine, the author was able to sleep well.

Tsetan left the author in Darchen and returned to Lhasa. When the author informed him of his experience, Tsetan told him that it didn't really matter if the author died but it would be bad for his business.

Darchen

Darchen, although dusty, was surrounded by a picturesque scene of the Himalayas. It also had some general stores and cafes and was full of people. For the author, it was a relaxed place but there were no pilgrims there.

The author was told that during pilgrimage season, the town was full of tourists. The author had felt that he would reach at the beginning of the season but was infact early.

One day while drinking tea, the author thought about his pilgrimage. He did not want to do the Kora alone for the fear of ice even though, he could see the pilgrimage alone. He also did not find anyone to clear his doubts.

Meeting Norbu

The author finally found someone to accompany him on his Kora. The author was reading a book in a cafe when Norbu sat with him. Norbu spoke English and so they started a conversation.

Norbu was a Tibetan who worked in Beijing at the Chinese Academy of Social Science in the Institute of Ethnic Literature. He was writing academic papers on Kora and had come to do it himself for the first time. It was he who gave the idea of them being a team. He suggested that they could hire Yaks to carry their luggage while they did their Kora.

Word Meanings

The given page numbers correspond to the pages in the prescribed NCERT textbook.

Word	Meaning
Page 74	
French loaves	thin loaf of French bread commonly made from basic lean dough
ducking back	quickly going inside
kora	pilgrimage (in Tibetan language)
drokba	nomad shepherd (here it means, "You look like a nomad shepherd.")
Changtang	plateau in Western Tibet
gazelles	small antelopes
Page 75	
kyang	wild asses
pall	cloud
en masse	together
manoeuvres	exercises involving a large number of animals
billowed	swelled out and went
mastiff	large and strong breed of dog
Page 76	
tribute	payment for tax
clogged	jammed
meanders	winding curves or bends of the river
daubed	spread on the surface
snorted	made a loud sound by forcing breath through a nostril
swathe	long strip
petered out	gradually came to an end
wristwatch	a watch having an altimeter eworn on the wrist

Word	Meaning
Page 77	
four wheel drive	having a transmission system to provide power directly to all four wheels
lurching	moving unsteadily
cairn of rocks	pile of stones marking a special place
festooned	ornamentally decorated
careered down	descended
salt flats	areas of flat land covered with a layer of salt
brackish	slightly salty
vestiges	remains
a hive of activity	full of people working hard
as smooth as my bald head	totally worn out
Page 78	
venerated	respected
cosmology	ancient history
headwaters	streams forming the source
striking distance	a distance from which it can be easily reached
draught	current of air
spread the grease around on	cleaned
solitary confinement	loneliness
prone	inclined

Word	Meaning
kicking around	passing time aimlessly
drifting off	going to sleep
Page 79	
disappearing into the land of nod	going to fall asleep
put my finger on	pinpoint
paraphernalia	dress identifying his profession
screws of paper	small paper packets
Page 80	
derelict	run down
pool	a game similar to billiards
supremely incongruous	totally out of place
babbled	flowed with a babbling sound
cavernous	like a cave
Page 81	
struck up	started
escaped from the library	removed themselves from academic work
tempered	weakened
envisaged	thought of
yaks	Tibetan ox
prostrating	stretching and lying down with face down

Chapter Practice

Objective Questions

• Multiple Choice Questions

1. What is the chapter 'Silk Road' about?
(a) About the author's journey to complete the kora
(b) About the author's journey to Ravu
(c) About the author's journey to Kashmir
(d) None of the above

Ans. (a) 'Silk Road' is about the author's journey to complete the kora, which starts from slopes of Ravu and ends on Mount Kailash.

2. What is meant by 'kora'?
(a) Yoga Aasana
(b) Medication
(c) Name of a small town
(d) Meditation performed by Buddhist believers

Ans. (d) Kora is a meditation that is performed by the Buddhist believers and is a core religious activity that they complete.

3. Why is Mount Kailash important for the author's long journey in the mountains?
(a) To show his essential display in Buddhist beliefs
(b) To show his friends that he is adventurous
(c) To meet a friend that lived in the mountains
(d) None of the above

Ans. (a) Mount Kailash is important for the author's long journey in the mountains as it completes the kora, which is an essential display in Buddhist beliefs. Buddhists believers are to perform meditation in this process as it is important for their religious identity.

4. What does Lhamo's act of giving the coat made of sheepskin reflect on her?
(a) She was charitable
(b) She was native
(c) She was wasteful
(d) She cared for the author

Ans. (d) Lhamo's act of giving the author a long sleeve sheepskin coat as a farewell gift shows that she is a compassionate woman who knew that the author wasn't prepared for the cold of the mountains.

5. Selects the statement(s) that justify(s) the title of the chapter 'Silk Road'.
I. Silk is the lake's name that the author crosses.
II. The author explored the old silk route which was one of the historical routes for trade.
III. The author enjoyed buying silk for his wife.
IV. The author sees the creation of the silk cloth on his entire journey.
(a) II and IV   (b) Only II   (c) I and III   (d) Only IV

Ans. (b) The chapter has been titled 'Silk Road' because the author explored the region of the old silk route which was one of the historical routes for trade.

6. Select the suitable option for the given statements, based on your reading of 'Silk Road'.
(i) The author looks at the passing landscape with childlike curiosity and excitement.
(ii) The author has not expected the landscape to be so beautiful yet grim.
(a) Both (i) and (ii) can be inferred
(b) Both (i) and (ii) cannot be inferred
(c) (i) can be inferred but (ii) cannot be inferred
(d) (i) cannot be inferred but (ii) can be inferred

Ans. (b)

7. Select the option that can be used to describe a Tibetan Mastiff.
(i) Ferocious   (ii) Alert
(iii) Friendly   (iv) Goofy
(v) Loyal
(a) (i) and (ii)   (b) (iii) and (iv)
(c) (iv) and (v)   (d) (i) and (v)

Ans. (a) The description of the Tibetan Mastiff by the author places them as 'ferocious' and 'alert' dogs who are wary of strange people and cars.

8. Why did the driver stop the car at a sharp turn?
(a) He was tired and wanted to rest
(b) Because the author was feeling sick
(c) As the car's tyre got punctured
(d) As a long track of snow was in front of them

Ans. (d) The driver stopped the car at a sharp turn as a long track of snow was in front of them and it would be difficult for them to cross it.

9. 'The slope was steep and studded with major rocks, but somehow Tsetan negotiated them, his four-wheel drive vehicle lurching from one obstacle to the next.

The given line shows that ....

(a) the journey to do the Kora was not easy
(b) the time chosen by the author to do the Kora was not correct
(c) Tsetan was an expert driver who knew how to journey through the roads
(d) Tsetan was bound to damage his vehicle in driving his car in such rough patches.

Ans. (c) The given lines show that Tsetan was an expert in tackling the icy roads that one can encounter on the journey to do the Kora.

10. Why was Hor an ugly and miserable place?

(a) It had no modern markets
(b) It had no vegetation or people
(c) It didn't had any proper medical facilities
(d) It had no place to live

Ans. (b) Hor was an ugly and miserable place as it was devoid of vegetation. It only had dust and rocks, along with garbage.

11. Classify (1) to (4) as Fact (F) or Opinion (O), based on your reading of Silk Road.

1. The author had expected Hor to be a beautiful and spiritual place.
2. The lack of pilgrims made the place look so lonely and miserable.
3. The description he had read about the place also led to his dissatisfaction.
4. Hor was located on a draughted land where the only respite was the lake.

(a) F-1,4; O-2, 3   (b) F-2, 3; O-1, 4
(c) F-2; O-1, 3, 4   (d) F-3, 4; O-1, 2

Ans. (a)

12. What happened when they reached Darchen at night to stay in the Guest House?

(a) The author slept well
(b) Tsetan went missing
(c) The author was sad
(d) The author wasn't able to breathe properly

Ans. (d) When they reached Darchen at night to stay in the guest house, the author wasn't able to breathe properly and demanded urgent medical assistance.

13. "As a Buddhist, he told me, he knew that it didn't really matter if I passed away, but he thought it would be bad for business." Select the option that explains it.

(a) Tsetan's beliefs and business are in contradiction to each other.
(b) Tsetan had become deeply attached to the author.
(c) Tsetan did not believe that it was wrong to die in pilgrimage.
(d) Tsetan as a hospitable man cannot let a guest die under his supervision.

Ans. (a) Tsetan was a Buddhist who believed that death is not the end. He might have gone directly to heaven as Kailash is a holy place. But at the same time he thought it would be bad if the author died because it might affect his business and he could have lost his credibility.

14. Why was meeting Norbu a relief for the author?

(a) Because he finally found some company
(b) Because Norbu could play with him
(c) Because Norbu was a lost friend of his
(d) The author was not relieved to meet Norbu

Ans. (a) The author felt relieved at meeting Norbu because he finally found some company and wouldn't be left alone. He also suggests hiring yaks to carry their luggages, which the author saw as a good sign.

15. What is the tone employed by the author in the chapter?

(a) Informative
(b) Formal
(c) Informal
(d) Serious

Ans. (c) The author employs an informal tone to convey his adventures and a compelling story of himself on the silk route.

• Extract Based MCQs

1. Read the extract given below and answer the questions that follow.

"Now that we were leaving Ravu, Lhamo said she wanted to give me a farewell present. One evening I'd told her through Daniel that I was heading towards Mount Kailash to complete the kora and she'd said that I ought to get some warmer clothes. After ducking back into her tent, she emerged carrying one of the long-sleeved sheepskin coats that all the men wore. Tsetan sized me up as we clambered into his car. "Ah, yes," he declared, "drokba, sir." We took a short cut to get off the Changtang. Tsetan knew a route that would take us South-West, almost directly towards Mount Kailash. It involved crossing several fairly high mountain passes, he said. "But no problem, sir", he assured us, "if there is no snow." What was the likelihood of that I asked. "Not knowing, sir, until we get there."

(i) Why does the author communicate via Daniel as can be understood by when he says "I'd told her through Daniel"?

(a) They did not speak the same language
(b) They were not on speaking terms
(c) They were afraid to see each other
(d) None of the above

Ans. (a) As Lhamo and the author did not speak the same language, Daniel assisted the conversation between them.

(ii) Tsetan says that there will be no problem in their journey if there is no snow.

He means that snow ....
(a) can hasten their movement
(b) determines the smoothness of their journey
(c) can tell if they can reach Mount Kailash
(d) will increase their difficulties in the journey

Ans. (b) Snow determines whether their journey through the short cut would be easy or difficult as it has the power to hamper their travel.

(iii) Choose the correct statement(s) that can be inferred from the passage.
  I. Lhamo was kind and generous to travellers.
  II. Tsetan knew the roads quite well.
  III. Daniel does not know any other language than the author's.
  (a) Only III   (b) Only II
  (c) I and II   (d) All of these

Ans. (c) Lhamo was kind and generous to the travellers. Tsetan knew the roads well as he suggested a short cut to travel through to reach quicker. However, Daniel knows more languages than the author's as he is able to communicate in Tibetan with Lhamo, a language unknown to the author.

(iv) "Ah, yes," he declared, "drokba, sir." Select the option that explains it.
(a) Tsetan says this as the author is looking like a drokba
(b) Tsetan had complimented the author
(c) Tsetan wants to point what the author was going to see
(d) Tsetan wants to thank Lhamo for the coat

Ans. (a) The given line is said by Tsetan who states that the author is looking like a drokba.

(v) Which of the following can be said about Tsetan?
(a) He was an amiable man.
(b) He was expert at his job.
(c) He was going on the first journey of the season.
(d) All of the above.

Ans. (d)

2. Read the extract given below and answer the questions that follow.

"It's a cold," he said finally through Tsetan. "A cold and the effects of altitude. I'll give you something for it." I asked him if he thought I'd recover enough to be able to do the kora. "Oh yes," he said, "you'll be fine."

I walked out of the medical college clutching a brown envelope stuffed with fifteen screws of paper. I had a five-day course of Tibetan medicine which I started right away. I opened an after-breakfast package and found it contained a brown powder that I had to take with hot water. It tasted just like cinnamon. The contents of the lunchtime and bedtime packages were less

obviously identifiable. Both contained small, spherical brown pellets. They looked suspiciously like sheep dung, but of course I took them. That night, after my first full day's course, I slept very soundly. Like a log, not a dead man.

(i) What is the author's reaction to the medicine he is offered?
(a) He is happy to get the treatment
(b) He is doubtful about the treatment but succumbs to it
(c) He is strongly against the medication
(d) He did not believe that it was real medication

Ans. (b) The author is doubtful about the treatment as the pellets looked like sheep dung but he, despite the suspicion, takes the medication to heal himself.

(ii) What is meant by the utterance: 'It's a cold,' in the begining of the extract?
(a) Tsetan knew English but chose not to talk to the author
(b) The doctor was unhelpful and selfish towards the author, so he talked through Tsetan
(c) Tsetan translated the conversation between the doctor and the author
(d) None of the above

Ans. (c) As the author only knew English and the doctor only knew Tibetan, Tsetan translated the conversation between the doctor and the author.

(iii) The author was suspicious about the medicine yet he took it. Why?

This was so because ....
(a) he would not have been able to survive another sleepless night.
(b) he was desperate to complete his kora.
(c) he wanted relief from the cold.
(d) he did not want Tsetan to worry about him and wanted him to continue his journey.

Ans. (b) The author was suspicious but he still took the medicine because he wanted to compete his kora for which he had come there.

(iv) Which of the following describes the author's view about the Medical College?
(a) Scantily maintained
(b) Monastery like
(c) Spiritual
(d) Eye pleasing

Ans. (b) The author finds the Medical College at Darchen to be like a monastery.

(v) Explain the phrase: 'Like a log, not a dead man'.
(a) He slept peacefully
(b) He felt lifeless
(c) He dreamt about dying
(d) He felt disturbed in his sleep

Ans. (a) The phrase meant that he slept peacefully. After going to the Tibetan doctor the author soon recovered. Unpalatable as it seemed, the medicine led him to a quick recovery. Hence, the author had a healthy and sound sleep unlike when he was ailing and restless.

PART 2
Subjective Questions

• Short Answer Type Questions

1. What was the farewell present given by Lhamo to the author when he told her that he was going to Mount Kailash?

Ans. The farewell present given by Lhamo to the author when he told her that he was going to Mount Kailash was a long-sleeved sheepskin coat that normally shepherds wore. She felt that the coat would protect him from the cold weather on the mountain.

2. What did Tsetan say would be the only hurdle while they were on their way to Mount Kailash?

Ans. Tsetan said that their journey to Mount Kailash would involve crossing several high mountain passes. He knew the way very well, but the only hurdle would be snow on the way. He could not say anything for sure until they reached there.

3. Tibetan mastiffs were popular in China's imperial courts. Explain   **[NCERT]**

Ans. Tibetan mastiffs were popular in China's imperial courts as hunting dogs. They were brought along the Silk Road in ancient times as payment of tax from Tibet. They were huge black dogs also used as watchdogs. They exploded into action like bullets when roused. They were furious and fearless.

4. Describe the appearance of Hor.

Ans. Hor, although a town at the shore of the holy lake Mansarovar, was a grim and miserable place. There was no vegetation whatsoever; only dust and rocks, liberally scattered with years of accumulated rubbish left by tourists. There was only one cafe in Hor which also was poorly maintained. The author found no population there except for one youth of chinese military.

5. The author's experience at Hor was in stark contrast to earlier accounts of the place.   **[NCERT]**

Ans. According to the earlier accounts, the town, on the shore of Lake Manasarovar, was abundant in natural beauty. A Japanese monk who had arrived there in 1900 was so moved by the sanctity of the lake that he burst into tears. A couple of years later, the hallowed waters had a similar effect on another traveller. However, now it was a grim and miserable place. There was no vegetation whatsoever, but only dust and rocks liberally scattered with years of accumulated rubbish left by tourists.

6. What troubled the author at Darchen?

Ans. A bad cold troubled the author at Darchen. He was unable to go to sleep at night as his nostrils were blocked. When he was just dozing off, he woke up suddenly. He felt his chest becoming very heavy, as he was not able to breathe-in enough oxygen.

7. How did the author find relief from his breathing troubles?

Ans. The author found relief from his breathing troubles after taking a full day's course prescribed by the doctor at Darchen medical college. The author was diagnosed with cold and the effects of altitude.

8. "As a Buddhist, he told me, he knew that it didn't really matter if I passed away, but he thought it would be bad for business." Comment.   **[NCERT]**

Ans. These were Tsetan's words spoken to the author. After the author's sickness was cured, Tsetan wanted to go back to Lhasa. By saying these words, Tsetan firmly stated that he was a Buddhist, who believed that physical death was not death in the real sense. However, he thought that the death of a tourist could affect his business as his credibility will be at stake in looking after the tourists, due to which he may not get customers anymore.

9. The author was disappointed with Darchen. Explain.

Ans. The author was indeed disappointed in Darchen as the place was dusty, partially derelict and punctuated by heaps of rubble and rubbish left behind by tourists. Further, even though the place was full of people, there were no tourists or pilgrims in whose company he could complete his kora.

10. Briefly comment on the author's meeting with Norbu.

Ans. The author was feeling rather lonely without Tsetan, who had gone back with the car to Lhasa. There weren't any pilgrims at Darchen as he had reached the place too early in the pilgrimage season. The author was sitting in the only cafe in Darchen when he met Norbu. The author was delighted to meet Norbu since he was also planning to do the *kora*. Now, he had a companion with whom he could also complete his pilgrimage.

11. Why had Norbu come to Kailash?

Ans. Norbu had been writing academic papers about the Kailash *kora* and its importance in various works of Buddhist literature for many years, but he had actually never done it himself. Hence, he also was there to do *kora*.

12. The author thought that his positive thinking strategy worked well after all. Justify   **[NCERT]**

Ans. The author felt that his positive strategy was working because, all the while he was in Darchen, he had been worried about completing his kora. He had no companion and no person to clear his doubts. So, he had being trying to convince himself that he would be successful in his endeavour. His positive thinking worked as soon he met Norbu who would be his companion while doing kora.

13. How did Norbu become an ideal companion for the author?

Ans. Norbu was an ideal companion for the author as both were academicians who had come away from their academic work. Both were not devout believers and they did not intend to prostrate themselves all round the mountain like other pilgrims.

14. Explain the purpose of the author's journey to Mount Kailash. **(NCERT)**

Ans. Nick Middleton is an Oxford Professor as well as an adventurer. He follows the most difficult terrain through the Silk Road and reaches the foot of Mount Kailash. The purpose of the author's journey to Mount Kailash was to complete the *kora*, which was a sacred religious ritual according to Hindu and Buddhist tradition.

15. Tsetan's support to the author during the journey. Elaborate. **(NCERT)**

Ans. Tsetan was a good and efficient driver. He drove the car very carefully. During the journey, he spoke to the author giving information about the places they were visiting. He was very caring. At Darchen when he found that the author was not well, Tsetan took him to the medical college and got medicine for him. He was also a good Buddhist.

• Long Answer Type Questions

1. Describe the author's experiences at Darchen.

Ans. Both the author and Tsetan reached Darchen during the late night. They found a guesthouse to stay in. However, the author had serious sleep problems at night as he was suffering from the effects of the high altitude as well as a blocked nose. The next day, Tsetan took him to the Darchen Medical College for getting him treated. The doctor there told them that it was a common problem in this area and gave some medicine for him.

Then Tsetan left him to return to Lhasa as, from here onwards, the author would have to go on foot. At Darchen, he found people very relaxed and unhurried, but he could not find pilgrimage there as he had reached there very early in the pilgrimage season. Then he met Norbu, who was a Tibetan working in Beijing. He also had come for kora. They decided to climb Kailash together, as both were not devout pilgrims and had no desire to prostrate themselves all round the mountain.

2. How was his experience of Hor a stark contrast to the accounts he had read of the earlier travellers?

Ans. Hor was a small town placed in the back on the main East-West highway that followed the old trade route from Lhasa to Kashmir. The author found the place very grim and miserable. There was no vegetation whatsoever, just dust and rocks, scattered all around along with heaps of garbage left behind by people. The town sat on the shore of lake Manasarovar, Tibet's holiest stretch of water. Ancient Hindu and Buddhist scriptures tell that Lake Manasarovar was the source of four great Indian rivers: Indus, Ganges, Sutlej and Brahmaputra. Actually only the Sutlej flows from the lake, the headwaters of the others rise nearby on the slopes of Mount Kailash.

His experience in Hor came as a stark contrast to accounts he had read of earlier travellers' first encounters with Lake Manasarovar. Ekai Kawaguchi, a Japanese monk who had arrived there in 1900, was so moved by the sanctity of the lake that he burst into tears. Similarly, in 1902, Sven Hedin from Sweden was also moved by the vision of the lake. However, now you could only find open-air dumps of rubbish in the town.

3. Justify the title 'Silk Road'.

Ans. The 'Silk Road' is not single highway, but a network of overland routes linking Europe with Asia, making trade possible between those with a passion for silk, horses and exotic fauna and flora. Just about every transaction imaginable has occurred along its many trails over the centuries. It's a thread that links East and West, a network of veins that pumped new lifeblood into mighty empires, a fabled route trodden by innumerable adventurers through the ages.

Yet, underlying this romantic trail is one of the most extraordinary tracts of land on this planet, a vast region separating China from the Mediterranean world that rates as one of the least hospitable areas on Earth. It was the difficulty of crossing such unforgiving territory that kept East and West apart for so long, allowing them to develop in their own distinct ways.

The author records the challenges and hardships he faced in the Silk Road regions as they are now. The reader finds it refreshing to traverse such vast tracts of the natural world that remain largely unchanged from earlier days.

4. "He's an adventurer, but at heart more a meticulous academic than a daredevil". Explain the truth of the statement about the author based on your reading of the travelogue 'Silk Road' by Nick Middleton.

Ans. Oxford professor and travel writer, Nick Middleton is truly an adventurer, but at heart more a meticulous academic than a daredevil adventurer. He is an environmental consultant who has written many articles in journals, magazines and newspapers as well as 16 books. Nick Middleton teaches geography at Oxford University. His main research interest is in the nature and human use of deserts and their margins.

After reaching Hor, what he was struck by was not the natural beauty of the place but the litter all around the area left by tourists. He was disappointed to see how man was ruining the environment. Being an environmental consultant, he was much disturbed at how the environment is slowly deteriorating due to human activity.

He gives a graphic detail of the mountain terrain, the snow covered mountains and the calm and relaxed people he met there. He strongly believes that travelling broadens our mind.

• Extract Based Questions

1. Read the extracts given below and answer the questions that follow.

"He had opened his door and jumped out of his seat before I realised what was going on. 'Snow,' said Daniel as he too exited the vehicle, letting in a breath of cold air as he did so. A swathe of the white stuff lay across the track in front of us, stretching for maybe fifteen metres before it petered out and the dirt trail reappeared. The snow continued on either side of us, smoothing the abrupt bank on the upslope side. The bank was too steep for our vehicle to scale, so there was no way round the snow patch. I joined Daniel as Tsetan stepped on to the encrusted snow and began to slither and slide forward, stamping his foot from time to time to ascertain how sturdy it was. I looked at my wristwatch. We were at 5,210 metres above sea level."

(i) What is going on in the given lines?

(ii) How will the snow impact the journey?

(iii) Do you think that the presence of snow hampered the author's mood?

(iv) Did the problem faced by the author in the given extract repeat itself?

(v) How did Tsetan solve the problem?

Ans. (i) In the given lines, Tsetan has stopped the car because the path in front is covered in snow.

(ii) The snow would impact the journey undertaken by the author because it would be difficult for them to cross the snow easily. The presence of the snow thus would make the journey difficult.

(iii) I don't think that the presence of snow hampered the author's mood. In fact, he remains neutral following Tsetan to reach his destination.

(iv) Yes, the problem of snow repeated itself just after 10 minute of throwing dirt on the snow and driving away described in the given extract.

(iv) To solve the problem, Tsetan threw a handful of dirt on the snow and drove along the path while the author and Daniel walked.

2. Read the extract given below and answer the questions that follow.

"My experience in Hor came as a stark contrast to accounts I'd read of earlier travellers' first encounters with Lake Mansarovar. Ekai Kawaguchi, a Japanese monk who had arrived there in 1900, was so moved by the sanctity of the lake that he burst into tears. A couple of years later, the hallowed waters had a similar effect on Sven Hedin, a Swede who wasn't prone to sentimental outbursts.

It was dark by the time we finally left again and after 10.30 p.m. we drew up outside a guest house in Darchen for what turned out to be another troubled night. Kicking around in the open-air rubbish dump that passed for the town of Hor had set off my cold once more, though if truth be told it had never quite disappeared with my herbal tea."

(i) How did the author feel about Hor?

(ii) "My experience in Hor came in contrast to accounts I'd read." Explain.

(iii) Do you think that the author is dissatisfied with Hor?

(iv) Explain the phase 'another troubled night'.

(v) What is to be blamed for the author's deteriorating cold according to him?

Ans. (i) The author felt that Hor was a grim and a miserable place without any vegetation of population.

(ii) The author could not see the spiritual beauty of Hor which had enamored the earlier travelers. He felt that it was dusty and dirty place in contrast to the earlier travelers who had emotional outbursts at seeing the place.

(iii) Yes, the author is dissatisfied with Hor as he had expected it to be full of spirituality and picturesque scenarios but the reality was completely different.

(iv) The phrase 'another troubled night' refers to the health problem suffered by the author due to his cold. The author was unable to sleep due to his cold.

(v) The author blames the dust found in Hor to be the cause of his deteriorating cold.

3. Read the extract given below and answer the questions that follow.

"'You English?' he enquired, after he'd ordered tea. I told him I was, and we struck up a conversation.

I didn't think he was from those parts because he was wearing a windcheater and metal-rimmed spectacles of a Western style. He was Tibetan, he told me, but worked in Beijing at the Chinese Academy of Social Sciences, in the Institute of Ethnic Literature. I assumed he was on some sort of fieldwork.

"Yes and no," he said. "I have come to do the kora." My heart jumped. Norbu had been writing academic papers about the Kailash kora and its importance in various works of Buddhist literature for many years, he told me, but he had never actually done it himself."

(i) Do you think Norbu was also looking for a companion?

(ii) What was Norbu doing in Darchen?

(iii) How do you think that the author and Norbu are similar?

(iv) Was the author correct in saying that Norbu was doing some fieldwork?

(v) How did the author feel about Norbu?

Ans. (i) Yes, I think that Norbu was also looking for a companion as it is he who suggests that they could be a team.

(ii) Norbu had come to Darchen to do the kora for the first time even though he was a Tibetan.

(iii) The author and Norbu are similar in many aspects. Both of them are academicians who are not well-equipped to do the kora by themselves.

(iv) Yes, the author was correct in saying that Norbu was doing some fieldwork as Norbu was not only doing the kora but was also writing academic paper on it.

(v) The author was excited to meet Norbu as he felt that he had a companion to complete his kora.

CHAPTER 01

The Voice of The Rain

—by Walt Whitman

In this Chapter...

- Stanzawise Explanation of the Poem
- Word Meaning
- Chapter Practice

Central Idea of the Poem

The poem 'The Voice of the Rain' by Walt Whitman signifies the eternal role that the rain plays in nurturing, quenching and purifying the various elements of Earth.

The rain returns the favour to its place of origin from where it rises unseen from the depths of the water and from the land. The rain itself is explaining to the reader about its origin, work and its cyclic movement. A comparison has also been drawn between rain and music as both of them make the world more lively and return to their place of origin after fulfilling their purpose.

Stanzawise Explanation of the Poem

Stanza 1

> And who art thou? said I to the soft-falling shower,
> Which, strange to tell, gave me an answer, as here translated:
> I am the Poem of Earth, said the voice of the rain,

Word Meaning

thou - you; **soft-falling** - dropping softly; **shower** - raindrops when they fall continuously on Earth

Explanation The poem begins with the poet asking for the identity of the soft-falling rain. Much to the surprise of the poet, the rain replies to his question which the poet translates for his readers. The rain in its own voice tells the poet that she is the poem of this Earth. The rain is trying to say that, as music or poetry gives pleasure to human beings, the rain gives happiness to mother Earth.

Stanza 2

> Eternal I rise impalpable out of the land and the bottomless sea, Upward, to
> heaven, whence, vaguely form'd, altogether changed, and yet the same,

Word Meaning

eternal - everlasting; **impalpable** - unable to be felt by touching; **whence** - from where; **vaguely** - unclearly; **form'd** - made into a specific shape or form

Explanation The poet says that the falling of the rain is an eternal process, but it takes different forms at different times. It rises from the land and the deep sea in the form of intangible water vapour and goes up to the sky. There it takes an indistinct shape in the form of clouds.

Although it changes in its form or shape, its core matter remains the same. The words 'impalpable' and 'eternal' indicate that nature is not fully understood and some part of it always remains beyond our reach.

Stanza 3

I descend to lave the droughts, atomies,
dust-layers of the globe,
And all that in them without me were seeds
only, latent, unborn;

Word Meaning

descend - move or fall downwards; **lave** - wash; **droughts** - dry spells; **atomies** - very tiny particles; **latent** - dormant, inactive

Explanation The raindrops pour down from above to wash away droughts and dust layers enveloping Earth. It satisfies the thirst of the dry Earth and heals everything that is degrading and is lying lifeless. The rain also helps in the germination of seeds which were lying dormant due to a dry spell. In other words, rain is responsible for making the Earth clean and green.

Stanza 4

"And forever, by day and night, I give back life to my own origin, And make pure and beautify it;
(For song, issuing from its birth-place, after fulfilment, wandering Reck'd or unreck'd, duly with love returns.)

Word Meaning

issuing - originating/starting; **fulfilment** - completing the cycle; **wandering** - moving from one place to another; **reck'd** - cared about; **unreck'd** - uncared for;

Explanation The rain is involved in a continued process of giving life to Earth by providing water to dormant seeds and making the Earth more beautiful and full of greenery. Rain helps in enhancing the beauty of Earth as, in the absence of water, everything turns dull and lifeless.

The last two lines are the poet's own words and his reflections upon the answers given by the rain. The poet observes that the life of rain is similar to that of a song. A song or poem is creativity at its best. It has the power to calm, heal, rejuvenate, transform and thrill. In the same way, when the entire environment gets drenched in the rain, dust particles settle down and there is greenery everywhere which makes the whole Earth beautiful to look at.

Poetic Devices Used in the Poem

- **Personification** The rain has been personified as it has been given a voice in the poem.
- **Metaphor** "I am the Poem of the Earth". The poet uses a metaphor to compare how the rain leaves the ground to come back to the ground, giving back to it much like a person who leaves its home, only to come back after fulfilling its journey.
- **Parallelism/Simile** In the last two lines, the poet has drawn a parallel between the rain and the song of a poet.
- **Hyperbole** 'Bottomless sea' is an example of hyperbole. The poet describes sea as bottomless which is an exaggerated statement to bring out the desired effect.
- **Imagery** In the first line of the poem, 'Soft-falling shower' gives the reader an image of gentle rain or drizzle. During the dialogue between the poet and the rain, it creates an image of showers or drops of water falling down from the heavens to Earth and infusing it with greenery, purity and beauty.

Chapter Practice

Objective Questions

• Multiple Choice Questions

1. Why does the poet get surprised when he gets an answer from the rain?
  (a) Because he expected a reply from earth
  (b) Because he did not expect rain to reply
  (c) Because he wanted to be alone with his thoughts
  (d) Because he was only dreaming

Ans. (b) The poet gets surprised when he gets an answer from the rain, as it is inanimate and cannot speak. In this poem, to the poet's and reader's amazement, the rain gives a reply which has been translated by the poet for the readers.

2. What answer does the rain give back to the poet?
  (a) That he should leave for home
  (b) That he should wake up
  (c) That rain is a continuous process
  (d) That this is not the Poem of Earth

Ans. (c) The rain answers the poet's question by telling him that it is the poem of Earth and is involved in a continuing process of going up and coming down.

3. How does the rain justify its claim 'I am the Poem of Earth'?
  (a) By explaining its relationship with earth
  (b) By talking to the trees
  (c) By staying quiet
  (d) By bringing a storm to the poet

Ans. (a) The rain calls itself the poem of the Earth because the poem rendered by the poet has the task of bringing joy, happiness, life to its readers. Similarly when the rain falls down over Earth, a rhythm or music is created. That's why the rain calls itself 'the Poem of Earth'.

4. Why does the rain call itself 'impalpable'?
  (a) Because it cannot be felt by touching or seeing.
  (b) Because it is afraid of the poet.
  (c) Because it does not want to change its form.
  (d) Because it is unsure of the future.

Ans. (a) Impalpable means something that cannot be felt by touching or seeing. When water takes the form of vapour, it is not visible to the human eye and nor can we feel its touch. Hence, the rain calls itself impalpable.

5. Why does the rain say "without me were seeds only, latent, unborn" ?
  (a) Because rain shelters the seeds.
  (b) Because rain protects the seeds.
  (c) Because rain provides shadow to the seeds.
  (d) Because rain helps the seeds grow.

Ans. (d) The rain helps the seeds grow into plants and without it, the seeds cannot grow into plants and stay hidden.

6. Choose the correct statement(s) for the poem 'The Voice of the Rain'.
  I. The poem is about rain, its eternal process and its benefits.
  II. The rain is speaking through its own language, via the poet.
  III. The poem is a reflection of the poet's dream.
  IV. The poem translates the message of earth through the rain.
  (a) I and II are correct.
  (b) I, II and IV are correct.
  (c) III and IV are correct.
  (d) I and IV are correct.

Ans. (a) The poem is about the eternal process of rain and its benefits. Through the words of the rain, the poet has tried to bring out the importance of rain for Earth, for plants and for people. As the poet is translating what the rain is speaking through its own language (the sounds it makes when it falls), the whole poem is about the rain talking to the poet.

7. Why does the poet contrast music with rain?
  (a) As rain is loved by the poet as much as music
  (b) Because he was told by the trees to do it
  (c) As rain makes rhythm with earth like music
  (d) None of the above

Ans. (c) The poet contrasts music and rain as when rain falls down, it makes a rhythm with earth.

8. What is the similarity between the rain and music?
  (a) Both abandon the poet
  (b) Both come back to their origin
  (c) Both talk with the trees
  (d) Both are interesting to the poet

Ans. (b) The rain and music both come back to their origin afterwards. Thus, they are similar.

9. Identify the tone of the poem 'The Voice of the Rain'.
(a) Chaotic
(b) Conversational
(c) Sympathetic
(d) Idle

Ans. (b) The tone of the poem is conversational in nature. It helps to maintain continuity of thoughts and ideas of the poet and also bring clarity and vividness in expression.

10. Find the figure of speech in the line 'bottomless sea' from the poem, 'The Voice of the Rain'.
(a) Personification   (b) Alliteration
(c) Hyperbole   (d) Metaphor

Ans. (c) 'Bottomless sea' is an example of hyperbole. The poet describes the sea as bottomless which is an exaggerated statement to bring out the desired effect.

11. Which of the following uses the same poetic device as used in the lines 'I am the poem of the Earth'?
(a) Her tears were a river flowing down her cheeks.
(b) He felt like the flowers were waving hello.
(c) They fought like cats and dogs.
(d) The wind howled in the night.

Ans. (d) In the line 'I am the Poem of Earth' the poetic device used in these lines is personification. The rain addresses itself like a human being with the pronoun 'I'.

12. What does 'Reck'd or unreck'd' mean?
(a) enrichment or no enrichment
(b) cared for or not cared for
(c) to purify or not
(d) to wash or not to wash

Ans. (b) The rain states that it does not care for anyone or their opinions. She is only responsible for her work which she does and leaves.

13. Select the suitable option for the given statements, based on your reading of 'The Voice of the Rain'.
(i) The poet finds the music created by the soft-falling shower to be rain's voice.
(ii) In translating the voice of the rain the poet is describing the process and the purpose of rain.
(a) (i) is false but (ii) is true.
(b) Both (i) and (ii) are true.
(c) (ii) is a fact but unrelated to (i).
(d) (i) is the cause for (ii).

Ans. (b) The poet translates the music created by the falling rain to describe the process of formation of the rain and the importance of rain for Earth.

14. The poet draws a parallel between rain and song to
(a) point out the artistic quality of rain
(b) state the creative expressions of man and God
(c) bring out the similarities between pleasures gained from them
(d) state the healing qualities of both rain and song

Ans. (d) The parallel between rain and song presents the healing quality of both rain and song. The rain heals the Earth just like the song heals the hurt hearts and mind of man.

15. Which of the following is TRUE as per the poem?
(a) The process of rain is an everlasting and ever continuous process.
(b) Rain's purpose is to beautify and purify Earth.
(c) Rain replying to the poet adds a sense of mystery to the poem
(d) All of the above

Ans. (d) All the statements are true as per the poem.

• Extract Based MCQs

1. Read the extract to attempt the questions that follow.

"And who art thou? said I to the soft-falling shower,

Which, strange to tell, gave me an answer, as here translated:

I am the Poem of Earth, said the voice of the rain,"

(i) What is the difference between the two 'I' in the given lines?
(a) One is of the poet and the other is of the rain
(b) One is with love and other is with surprise
(c) One asks the question and the other answer
(d) Both (a) and 9c)

Ans. (d) 'I' in the first line is referred to as the poet asking a question. 'I' in the third line is the raindrop which answers the poets question.

(ii) The poet specifically says that the answer was given by 'The Voice of the Rain'. The emphasis on voice of rain adds a hint of .... to the poem.
(a) mystery   (b) thrill
(c) drama   (d) doubt

Ans. (a) The reference to The Voice of Rain as emphasised in the poem adds a sense of mystery to the poem as the reader is left to wonder how can rain answer.

(iii) What do you understand by the phrase 'strange to tell'?
(a) Unusualness of the answer for the poet
(b) Stupidness of the answer for the earth
(c) Ordinariness of the answer for the poet
(d) Commonness of the answer for the raindrops

Ans. (a) 'Strange to tell' means that it is an unusual and extraordinary answer given by the raindrops to the poet who asked who 'it' was.

(iv) What role does the poet play?
(a) To give voice of rain
(b) Translator
(c) Advocate of rain
(d) None of the above

Ans. (a) The poet assumes the role of the translator for the reader as he translates what the rain tells him.

(v) Select the suitable option for the given statements, based on your reading of the extract.
1. The poet is imagining the rain talking.
2. The rain calls itself the poem of the earth as it beautifies the world
(a) (1) is false but (2) is true.
(b) Both (1) and (2) are true.
(c) (2) is a fact but unrelated to (1).
(d) (1) is the cause for (2).

2. Read the extract given below and answer the questions that follow.

"Eternal I rise impalpable out of the land and the bottomless sea,

Upward to heaven, whence, vaguely form'd, altogether changed, and yet the same,

I descend to lave the droughts, atomies, dust-layers of the globe,

And all that in them without me were seeds only, latent, unborn;"

(i) From where does the rain originate?
(a) Clouds and land   (b) Land and sea
(c) Sky and sea   (d) Sky and land
Ans. (b) The rain originates from the land and the bottomless (deep sea) in the form of water vapour.

(ii) What happens to the raindrops in the sky?
(a) They change their form
(b) They evaporate to become air
(c) They disappear from earth
(d) Nothing
Ans. (a) In the sky, the raindrops form the rain. Their form has changed but the essence has remained the same.

(iii) With what purpose does the rain descend from the sky?
(a) To destroy crop   (b) To flatter the poet
(c) To entertain earth   (d) To give life to the planet
Ans. (d) The raindrops fall from the sky in order to give life to the planet by removing the dry areas and washing the famine-stricken lands.

(iv) What is 'latent' and 'unborn'?
(a) Flowers   (b) Plants
(c) Earth   (d) Seeds
Ans. (d) The seeds are dormant and unborn because of lack of water which is needed for them to germinate and form a new plant.

(v) What quality of rain is highlighted in the extract?
(a) Entertainer   (b) Healer
(c) Preserver   (d) Caregiver
Ans. (b) The rain assumes the role of a healer for the Earth. Before rain, the Earth is draughted and covered in dust. As rain falls, the dust and draught goes away and the land is covered with greenery.

Subjective Questions

• Short Answer Type Questions

1. There are two voices in the poem. Who do they belong to? Which lines indicate this?   (NCERT)
Ans. The poem, 'The Voice of the Rain', presents a dialogue between the poet and the rain itself. In this poem, the poet asks rain who it is. The poet gets an answer as the rain itself gives its introduction.
Hence, the two voices in the poem are those of rain and the poet. These are
(i) In the poet's voice and who art thou? said I to the soft-falling shower.
(ii) In the voice of the rain and I am the poem of the Earth, said the voice of the rain.

2. What does the phrase 'strange to tell' mean? (NCERT)
Ans. The phrase expresses the poet's surprise at the rain's ability to reply and use words. The belief is that rain cannot speak like living beings. The poet believes that the readers will also find it surprising and weird that the rain should speak and answer the poet's question.

3. How does the rain justify its claim 'I am the Poem of Earth'?
Ans. The rain calls itself the poem of the Earth because the poem rendered by the poet has the task of bringing joy, happiness, life to its readers.
Similarly when the rain falls down over Earth, a rhythm or music is created . That's why the rain calls itself the 'Poem of Earth'.

4. Describe the never ending cycle of rain.
Ans. Water rises unperceived in the form of vapour from land and water bodies on the Earth. It goes up, takes the form of a cloud, changes its shape and falls down on Earth in the form of water drops to bathe the small dust particles, land and sea. The water returns through rivers to oceans and seas after it rains on Earth.

5. Why does the rain call itself 'impalpable'?
Ans. 'Impalpable' means something that cannot be felt by touching or seeing. When water takes the form of vapour, it is not visible to the human eye and nor can we feel its touch.
The vapour rises to the sky, condenses and forms clouds which cause rain. Though we are aware of its presence, the process remains invisible to us. Hence, the rain has rightly called itself 'impalpable'.

6. What happens when it rains after a long hot spell?
Ans. After a long hot spell, everything is dried up on Earth. When it rains, all the dust that has accumulated on Earth gets washed away, giving a new fresh look to nature.
Moreover the seeds which were lying latent till now, get germinated with the help of rain and new trees and plants start growing.

7. Latent seeds get a life by rain. Explain.

Ans. The seeds lying on Earth require water to germinate and take shape. When it rains, the seeds start germinating and change into the form of saplings. In this way, the seeds which would have dried up or get wasted get a new lease of life by rain.

8. Why is rain essential for Earth?

Ans. If it doesn't rain then Earth will remain parched, droughts will follow and the dust-layers will not be washed away. There will be nothing to quench the thirst of the plants and trees and their seeds will die.

9. How does the rain become the voice of Earth?

Ans. In the poem, 'The Voice of the Rain', the poet describes how the rain falls on Earth. He also asks a question to the rain about it. He calls the showers of the rain as 'Poem of Earth' as the rain gives a new lease of life to the scorched and parched Earth and falls on Earth in a rhythmic manner.

Actually, it is the voice of Earth as the slowly falling showers produce a very soft music and Earth finds its expression only through the showers falling on it.

10. Why do you think the poet says the phrase 'reck'd or unreck'd'?

Ans. The words have been poetically drafted. 'Reck'd and unreck'd' stand for reckoned and unreckoned. The words literally mean cared and uncared for respectively. The poet says these words to emphasise the fact that when it falls on the Earth, we sometimes take notice of it or sometimes completely ignore it. But even if it is left uncared for, it completes its destiny and returns to absorbed where it started from.

11. Why are the last two lines put within brackets? (NCERT)

Ans. The last two lines of the poem have been put within brackets as they do not form a part of the conversation between the poet and the rain. The lines in the brackets indicate the reflections, observations and thoughts of the poet. He makes observations about the life course of a song and draws similarities between the life cycle of a song and the rain.

12. Justify the title 'The Voice of the Rain'.

Ans. The whole poem is about the eternal process of rain and its benefits. Through the words of the rain, the poet has tried to bring out the importance of rain for Earth, for plants and for man. As the poet is translating what the rain is speaking through its own language (the sounds it makes when it falls), the whole poem is about the rain talking to the poet. Thus, the title is justified.

13. Natural elements such as air and rain make no discrimination and bless everyone equally. Comment on class distinction and inequality, which is a totally human creation.

Ans. Man's existence on this Earth is short-lived but even in this short span, he has been responsible for many wrong doings against other human beings. God has created everyone as equal. But it is very unfortunate that man has divided this society on the basis of class, caste and other factors.

Man must learn from elements of nature which provide us fresh air, heat or water, without making any distinction. But in human society class distinctions and caste distinctions both exist and inequalities prevail in large numbers.

It is high time that man must learn lessons from nature and adopt universal brotherhood for the betterment of our society.

● **Long Answer Type Questions**

1. There is a parallel drawn between rain and music. Which words indicate this? Explain the similarity between the two. (NCERT)

Ans. The last two lines of the poem (in brackets) indicate the parallel drawn between rain and music (here it is called 'song', as a song always has music associated with it). In these lines, the poet observes that the life-cycle of rain and a song are alike. The song issues from the singer and travels to reach others. It wanders and, whether heard and enjoyed or not, eventually returns to its creator with all due love. Similarly, rain originates from Earth, and after fulfilling its role of spreading beauty and purity, returns to its origin. Both are perpetual in nature. Moreover, the sound of the soft-falling rain is in itself a kind of music.

2. How is the cyclic movement of rain brought out in the poem? Compare it with what you have learnt in science. (NCERT)

Ans. In the poem, water rises from the 'land and the bottomless sea' to reach the sky. There, it transforms itself into vague formations of clouds, different in their structure than the water from which they originated. After wandering, these clouds descend to Earth in the form of rain to provide relief to the drought-ridden areas and infuse life into unborn and latent seeds. The rain gives Earth beauty and purity.

In science, we learn the cyclical process of rain using terms like evaporation, condensation, precipitation, flowing rivers, ground water, ocean water etc, while in the poem the same process becomes interesting and unusual. The rain speaks itself to describe its course. Thus, both what is given in the poem and what we learn in science are similar.

3. The poem 'The Voice of the Rain' gives a hidden message that rain is essential for this Earth. Write an article describing the importance of rain.

Ans.

Importance of Rain

by Ali Jawed

As we all know, the three essentials for survival are water, food and air. The most important element of weather is water. We get water in different forms of precipitation but rain is the most beneficial of all types of precipitation.

Rain helps in harvesting our crops that give us food to eat. Without rain, no crops would grow and we would perish. Also, falling showers remove the dust in air, making our air clean, because we need clean air to breathe.

Rain water plays a key role in creating the climate of certain areas. Its presence in the atmosphere provides replenishment of the moisture in cloud systems.

The most well-known and most important effect of rain water is to provide us with water to drink. Without rain, there would be no life.

4. Rain is an eternal process benefiting mankind. Contrast it with human life which is short lived on this Earth. Should we disturb these eternal elements of nature?

Ans. The poem 'The Voice of the Rain' beautifully shows the continued process of rain which sounds like music to human ears, as it fulfils our needs.

It is an ever going process which sustains human life and provides us with food, pure air and green cover. On the other hand, human lives are mortal.

We come on this Earth for a short period and then depart without leaving any mark on this planet.

Moreover human beings, for their greed and selfish motives, indulge in destructive activities which may disturb these eternal processes of nature.

We must learn a lesson from nature. If we want peaceful co-existence, we need not disturb the balance of nature, otherwise the whole of humanity will be in danger.

We must learn a lesson from such eternal processes and do something good for humanity at large.

• Extract Based Questions

1. Read the extract given below and answer the questions that follow.

And who art thou? Said I to the soft falling shower,
Which, strange to tell, gave me an answer, as here Translated:
I am the poem of Earth, said the voice of the rain,
Eternal I rise impalpable out of the land and the bottomless sea,
Upwards to heaven, whence, vaguely form'd, altogether Changed, and yet the Same.

(i) What do you understand by the phrase 'Strange to tell'?
(ii) How has the answer been conveyed to us and what is it?
(iii) Why does the rain call itself 'eternal'?
(iv) Explain 'vaguely formed'.
(v) Explain 'altogether Changed, and yet the Same.'

Ans. (i) The phrase 'Strange to tell' means that it is an unusual and extraordinary thing to receive an answer from the inanimate raindrops.

(ii) To convey the answer, the poet has personified the rain drop and it is answering the poet's question by saying that it is the 'Poem of the Earth'.

(iii) The rain calls itself eternal because the process formation of rain goes on forever.

(iv) The phrase 'vaguely formed' refers to the formation of clouds that are full of rain water vapours. These clouds do not have a particular shape and thus the rain assumes a vague shape.

(v) The given phrase means that in the sky, the rain drops form the rain. In doing so, their form has changed but the essence has remained the same.

2. Read the extract given below and answer the questions that follow.

I descend to lave the droughts, Atomies, dust-layers of the globe,
And all that in them without me were seeds only, latent, unborn;
And forever, by day and night, I give back life to my own origin,
And make pure and beautify it.
(For song, issuing from its birth-place, after fulfillment, wandering
Reck'd or unreck'd, duly with love returns.)

(i) With what purpose does the rain descend from the sky?
(ii) How does the rain help the seeds?
(iii) Why has the poet compared the rain to a song?
(iv) Why are the last lines put within brackets?
(v) Where does the song return?

Ans. (i) The rain drops fall from the sky in order to give life to the Earth which is suffering from dryness and draught.

(ii) Before the rain falls, the seeds are dormant and unborn because of lack of water. With rain they get the water which is needed for them to germinate and form a new plant.

(iii) The poet has compared the life cycle of the rain drops to that of the song saying that they both return to their origin after fulfilling their tasks. On their journey they both heal and beautify the Earth and Man's heart respectively.

(iv) The last lines are put in brackets because they do not form the voice of the rain or the poet. They only certain a general observation by the poet about the course of a song.

(v) The song returns to the place of its origin i.e., comes back to the heart of poet.

Childhood

—by Markus Natten

In this Chapter...

- Stanzawise Explanation of the Poem
- Word Meaning
- Chapter Practice

Central Idea of the Poem

In this poem, the poet thinks deeply over the question of his lost childhood. Childhood is a stage of innocence in which the child believes others and loves unconditionally. The poet has tried to identify some stages of his life when his thoughts and perceptions of the world changed. The poem describes the first step to maturity or loss of childhood as when one is able to think logically and rationally. Forming one's own opinion and not getting influenced by others is also a sign of maturity or loss of childhood.

The poem also hints at the hypocrisy prevalent in our society, where people pretend to be nice to each other but in reality they do not like each other.

Stanzawise Explanation of the Poem

Stanza 1

> When did my childhood go?
> Was it the day I ceased to be eleven,
> Was it the time I realised that Hell and Heaven,
> Could not be found in Geography,
> And therefore could not be,
> Was that the day!

Word Meanings

go - end; **ceased to be** - stopped being;

Explanation The poet wonders when he lost his childhood. He reflects that perhaps it was the day when he crossed the age of eleven. Maybe it was the stage when he realised that the concepts of Hell and Heaven, about which he had been taught since his childhood, did not exist in reality. Geography textbooks did not give the location of any such places. The poet realises that he might have lost his childhood when he gained education.

Stanza 2

> When did my childhood go?
> Was it the time I realised that adults were not
> all they seemed to be,
> They talked of love and preached of love,
> But did not act so lovingly,
> Was that the day!

Explanation In this stanza, the poet reflects that maybe the loss of childhood occurred when he was able to see through the hypocrisy of adults. These people followed double standards, actually following and preaching different standards of behaviour.

They told the poet to be loving and caring; however they themselves were argumentative, violent and discourteous. Their behaviour was far from the love they sermonised about and advocated so reverently to the child.

Stanza 3

When did my childhood go?
Was it when I found my mind was really mine,
To use whichever way I choose,
Producing thoughts that were not those of other people, But my own, and mine alone
Was that the day!

Word Meanings

really mine - when not influenced by others' opinions;

Explanation The poet asks the same question again and again. He is trying to guess when he actually lost his childhood. Perhaps, it was the day when he realised that his mind could think independently, form his own opinions and was able to take his own decisions. He gained a sense of individuality, which set him free from the preconceived opinions of others. His own individual opinions and experiences shape his thoughts now and he realised that this might have been the time when he lost his childhood innocence completely.

Stanza 4

Where did my childhood go?
It went to some forgotten place,
That's hidden in an infant's face,
That's all I know.

Word Meanings

forgotten - unremembered;

Explanation In this stanza, instead of wondering about the time, the poet wonders about the location where his childhood has gone. He realises that his childhood has gone been lost forever. He can never relish his childhood now.

The only way in which he can see his childhood is by looking at. The innocent face of a child who does not have any pretensions and rationality and who trusts others unconditionally. In other words, one can find one's own childhood in a small child's innocent face and that is everything that the poet knows.

Poetic Devices Used in the Poem

- **Alliteration** In this figure of speech, a number of words having the same first consonant sound occur close together in a series. For example: 'Hell and Heaven', 'that the day', 'my mind', 'whichever way,' etc.

- **Antithesis** This figure of speech refers to the placement of opposing or contrasting ideas together. It can be seen in the use of words Hell and Heaven.

- **Enjambent** This figure of speech refers to the practice of running lines of poetry from one to the next without using any kind of punctuation to indicate a stop. The example is in the second line of the second stanza.

- **Personification** It is the attribution of human characteristics to non-human things. In the poem, 'childhood' is personified in the line 'It went to some forgotten place'.

- **Repetition** It is the repetition of a word or a phrase to put emphasis or bring poetic effect. In the poem, the phrases, "when did my childhood go? "and" was it that day!" is repeated to emphasise the difference between childhood and adulthood.

Chapter Practice

Objective Questions

• **Multiple Choice Questions**

1. What did the poet believe about Hell and Heaven when he was a child?
(a) That they were actual places
(b) That they were imaginary
(c) That they belong to the Church
(d) That they were in America

Ans. (a) The poet believed that Hell and Heaven were actual places, when he was child.

2. Antithesis is where two opposite words are used together in a sentence in a poem. Where did the poet use it?
(a) Infant's face
(b) Forgotten place
(c) Hell and Heaven
(d) Preached of love

Ans. (c) Hell and Heaven are opposites of each other and thus, is used by the poet to bring out antithetical elements in his poem.

3. When did the poet begin to feel that his childhood was lost?
(a) When he went on a trip
(b) When he saw the reality of life
(c) When he called his parents
(d) When he read more books

Ans. (b) The poet began to feel that his childhood was lost when he found out about the reality of life which shattered his imagination.

4. The repetition of the questions shows that the poet is ....
(a) helpless
(b) excited
(c) stubborn
(d) desperate

Ans. (d) The poet is desperately looking for the childlike innocence and hence, asks a lot of questions in his attempt.

5. The poet's trust on adults breaks because ....
(a) they lie to the poet
(b) they preach love and fail to act on love
(c) they are selfish
(d) they are lazy

Ans. (b) The adults seem who they are not because they are hypocrites who preach love but fail to act on love.

6. Select the word that suits the poet's description of adults.
(a) Cunning
(b) Intelligent
(c) Smart
(d) Pretentious

Ans. (d) The poet seems to describe adults as 'pretentious' as they are double faced about their ideas of love.

7. The literary device 'refrain' is used in the poem 'Childhood' in the line
(a) When did my childhood go?
(b) Hell and Heaven
(c) Could not be found in Geography
(d) That's all I know

Ans. (a) In poetry, a refrain is a word, line or phrase that is repeated within the lines or stanzas of the poem itself. In the poem it has been employed in "When did my childhood go?"

8. What did the poet sense about himself when he realised he could use his own mind the way he wants?
(a) He sensed that he is as intelligent as his friends
(b) He sensed his own individuality and a separate personality
(c) He sensed that he is very smart
(d) He sensed that he could use his mind in creative work

Ans. (b) The poet sensed his own individuality and separate identity as he realised that he could use his own mind the way he wants.

9. Select the option that justifies 'To use whichever way I choose'.
(a) To form perspective
(b) To create newer ideas
(c) To question
(d) All of the above

Ans. (d) All the options given above justifies 'To use whichever way I choose.'

10. Where could he see his childhood now?
(a) In an infant's face
(b) Only in his memories
(c) Nowhere
(d) Only in the poem

Ans. (a) The poet could see his childhood now in an infant's face as it reminded him of purity and innocence.

11. Which of these is NOT one of the options where the poet thinks that his childhood has gone?

(a) The time when he ceased to be twelve

(b) The time when he realised that hell and heaven could not be found in Geography

(c) The time when he realised that adults were hypocrites

(d) None of the above

Ans. (a) The poet has understood the loss of his childhood as he ceased to be eleven. Thus, it is not the time that he had ceased to be twelve.

12. What is the tone of the poem?

(a) Inspiring   (b) Challenging

(c) Hopeful   (d) Nostalgic

Ans. (d) The poet uses a tone that is nostalgically remembering his childhood.

13. What are the aspects of adulthood that are discussed in the poem?

  I. Individuality   II. Bravery

III. Rationality   IV. Hypocrisy

(a) I and II   (b) I, II and IV

(c) III and II   (d) I and III

Ans. (d) The poet points out that adulthood comes with rationality and individuality.

14. Select the suitable option for the given statements, based on your reading of 'Childhood.'

(i) The poet states that the childhood innocence and the happiness is lost as one becomes an adult.

(ii) The poet want the childlike innocence and happiness to remain forever.

(a) (i) is true but (ii) is false

(b) Both (i) and (ii) are true.

(c) (ii) is a fact but unrelated to (i).

(d) (i) is the cause for (ii).

Ans. (a) The poet believes that childhood innocence and happiness is lost with adulthood. As one becomes an adult one becomes a rational individual as well as a hypocrite.

15. Markus Natten says that his childhood has gone to an 'unremembered place'. Which option indicates the significance of 'unremembered place'?

(a) Childhood is not lost to the rational world.

(b) Childhood is nowhere visible in the hypocritical world.

(c) The loss of childhood is permanent.

(d) Both (a) and (c)

Ans. (c) By stating that childhood had gone to an 'unremembered place', the poet indicates that once gone, childhood will never return. The loss of childhood is permanent.

• Extract Based MCQs

1. Read the extract given below and answer the questions that follow.

"When did my childhood go?
Was it the day I ceased to be eleven,

Was it the time I realised that Hell and Heaven,
Could not be found in Geography,
And therefore could not be,
Was that the day!"

(i) Why is the age of eleven so important to the poet?

(a) Because he can now differentiate between fact and fiction

(b) Because he now know about his parents

(c) Because he can now get a new bike

(d) Because he can now get new gifts

Ans. (a) It is because at the age of eleven, he can differentiate between what is fact and what is fiction.

(ii) What quality has the poet acquired as mentioned in the extract?

(a) Individuality   (b) Rationality

(c) Patience   (d) Imagination

Ans. (b) The poet has gained the quality of a rational person at this stage.

(iii) What shatters the poet's illusion about the world?

(a) When he is unable to find hell and heaven in geography book

(b) When his geography book is torn

(c) When he turns twelve

(d) When he talks to his teacher

Ans. (a) The illusion for the poet shatters when he is unable to find hell and heaven in his geography book.

(iv) What is the cause of the poet's worry?

(a) Loss of purity and innocence

(b) Increase in age

(c) Breaking of trust

(d) Loss of fantasy

Ans. (a) The cause of the poet's worry is that he has lost the purity and innocence in his thoughts while gaining rational thinking.

(v) Which literary device has the poet used in the given lines?

(a) Refrain   (b) Alliteration

(c) Anaphora   (d) All of these

Ans. (d) Refrain is a literary device in which a line or phrase is repeated in every stanza. In the stanza 'When did my childhood go?'. Alliteration is a literary device in which a sound at the beginning of a word is repeated in closest placed words. Herein the sound of 'h' is repeated in 'hell and heaven'. Anaphora is the repetition of a phrase at the beginning of consecutive lines. Herein 'was it' is repeated.

2. Read the extract to attempt the questions that follow.

"When did my childhood go?
Was it when I found my mind was really mine,
To use whichever way I choose,
Producing thoughts that were not those of other people
But my own, and mine alone
Was that the day!"

(i) Explain 'my mind was really mine'.
 (a) The poet was afraid of himself
 (b) The poet was completely in control of himself
 (c) The poet felt strong yet indecisive
 (d) The poet felt confused by his environment
Ans. (b) The poet was completely in control of himself and felt that his mind belonged to him completely.

(ii) What is meant by: "producing thoughts that were not those of other people's"?
 (a) The poet gains confidence in individuality
 (b) The poet gains resilience in tough times
 (c) The poet takes on new challenges without a care in the world
 (d) The poet is still learning to express himself
Ans. (a) This line points that the poet has finally gained confidence in individuality and is able to express himself well.

(iii) Select the statements that justify why the poet is eager to know the lost place of his childhood.
 I. The poet cherishes childhood the most.
 II. The poet is eager to find pieces of his childhood again.
 III. The poet wants to tell his friends about his childhood.
 IV. The poet wants to find the innocence he lost.
 (a) All statements are correct
 (b) I and III are correct
 (c) Only II is correct
 (d) I, II and IV are correct.
Ans. (d) All statements justify the poet's eagerness except statement three which is false about the poet's intention.

(iv) Through the given lines, which characteristic of childhood is highlighted?
 (a) Blind belief (b) Innocence
 (c) Lack of rationality (d) All of these
Ans. (a) Through the given lines, the poet states that in childhood one used to believe what parents or elders told them blindly. But as he became an adult this blind belief on elders broke.

(v) What does the poet feel when he utters these lines?
 (a) Anxiety (b) Dejection
 (c) Regret (d) Disdain
Ans. (b) The poet feels dejected at the loss of his childhood.

PART 2
Subjective Questions

• Short Answer Type Questions

1. How did the poet conclude that Hell and Heaven were imaginary places?
Ans. The poet concluded that Hell and Heaven were imaginary places because Geography books contain names of places, but there was no mention of places like Hell or Heaven in these books.

2. Bring out the hypocrisy that the adults exhibit with regard to love.
Ans. As the poet grew up, he could make out the double standards of the adults. He realised that though adults preached of love and talked of love, their behaviour was totally different and full of manipulation. They were all hypocrites who behaved differently from the way they talked.

3. What did the poet notice about independent thinking? How important was this discovery?
Ans. The poet discovered that he was different from others and could think independently. He could have his own opinions without getting influenced by anyone else.
This discovery was very important to him as it revealed to him his abilities for independent thinking and decision taking.

4. What is the poet trying to convey when he says that childhood is hidden in an infant's face?
Ans. The poet says an infant is really innocent as he trusts everyone and does not try to fool others. The poet brings out this fact by contrasting it with the behaviour of adults, who become manipulative and are hypocrites. As a person develops rational thoughts, his childlike innocence fades away.

5. What do you think are the most poetic lines? Why?
Ans. The most poetic lines in the poem are (NCERT)
 "Where did my childhood go?
 It went to some forgotten place,
 That's hidden in an infant's face,"
These poignant lines explain beautifully what most adults feel. These lines take us back to the innocent world of an infant where the poet thinks his childhood seems to be lying hidden. Naturally, the pure and unadulterated childhood will never come back to us, though we can find it in an infant's face.

6. According to Markus Natten, when does the child become an adult?
Ans. Becoming an adult is a complex process which is associated with physical, mental and social development. A child becomes an adult when he is able to live his own life and takes care of his responsibilities individually. He also develops his own thought process, using which he can form his own beliefs and opinions.

7. What is the poet's feeling towards his childhood?
(NCERT)
Ans. The poet regards childhood as a period of innocence. A child sincerely feels that he is free from all evils and that there is really a Hell and a Heaven. A child knows no hypocrisy. There is no difference between his thoughts and actions. In short, childhood is a state of innocence and purity of heart.

8. How does the poem expose man and present him in true colours?
Ans. According to the poet, childhood symbolises innocence, purity, softness and love. As a child grows up, these qualities start receding. Man adheres to lying, shrewdness, cunningness and hypocrisy. Adults preach about truth and honesty but themselves practise hatred and lying. The simplicity and honesty of childhood evaporates the moment man crosses the threshold of innocent childhood.

9. The poet has discussed two stages of life — childhood and adulthood. How do we differentiate one from another?

Ans. Childhood has been considered by the poet as a blissful period in one's life, where a child trusts everyone.

Adulthood is marked by rational and creative thoughts, ability to perceive and differentiate and learn new things. In this stage of life one also learns to be double faced and crafty.

10. What according to the poem is involved in the process of growing up?   **(NCERT)**

Ans. According to this poem, the process of growing up involves many stages. Attainment of mental maturity can be seen as an indication of growing up.

When a person becomes logical, rational and is able to maintain individual thoughts, he is assumed to be grown up. A grown up can discriminate between reality and fantasy and between reality and hypocrisy.

• Long Answer Type Questions

1. Is independent thinking a step towards adulthood? If yes, then how? Explain with reference to the poem 'Childhood'.

Ans. Yes, independent thinking is a step towards adulthood. As a child, one is not able to make one's own decisions and one's thinking is always influenced and directed by adults. A child is so innocent that it is not able to distinguish between truth and imagination.

As a child's thinking is influenced by others, it has no individuality. Moreover, it is prone to manipulations which lead to fickle-mindedness. Independent thinking makes us what we are. It shapes our personality and we are known among people through what our mind thinks and what decisions we take.

If we want to stay away from evil people who try to influence our thoughts for their selfish purposes, then only independent thinking can help us. We cannot claim to be an individual if we cannot take decisions ourselves.

2. Write an article about childhood and the process of growing up in reference to the poem 'Childhood.'

Ans.
Childhood
by Manav Singh

When I was a child, the world seemed to be a place of joy and happiness to me. There was nothing worth worrying about. Whenever I cried, somebody consoled me. When I did not like to sit alone, I was always in somebody's arms. My mother always looked after me. These are my most cherished memories and I believe that looking at a child playing and enjoying childhood makes me somewhat nostalgic.

Childhood is free from all cares. There are no duties or responsibilities on the shoulders of a child. A child only eats, drinks, sleeps and plays. Thus, a child lives in the bliss of ignorance and innocence. As we grow in age, worries about studies, choice of profession, shouldering responsibilities, etc., keep haunting us. Tensions, stress and worries become a part of adult life and the individual forgets to live a carefree life.

• Extract Based Questions

1. Read the extract to attempt the questions that follow.

"When did my childhood go?
Was it the time I realised that adults were not
All they seemed to be,
They talked of love and preached of love,
But did not act so lovingly,
Was that the day!"

(i) Do you think that the poet is appreciative of the adults?

(ii) Explain 'They talked of love and preached of love, but did not act so lovingly'.

(iii) What had happened with the poet in the given lines?

(iv) The poet is continuously asking questions and answering it himself. What does this show?

(v) What can be said about the feelings of the poet as per the extract?

Ans. (i) I do not think that the poet is appreciative of the adults as he finds his trust on them to be breaking.

(ii) The given lines highlight the hypocrisy of adults. They tell us to be loving and caring but were themselves not very loving and caring.

(iii) In the given lines, the poet depicts how he had grown up. One of the stages of growing up for him was to realize that adults were pretentious.

(iv) The poet's act of continuously asking questions and answering it himself shows that the poet feels that the journey from childhood to adulthood is set in stages.

(v) As per the extract, one can ascertain that the poet is nostalgic about his childhood.

2. Read the extract to attempt the questions that follow.
"When did my childhood go?
Was it when I found my mind was really mine,
To use whichever way I choose,
Producing thoughts that were not those of other people
But my own and mine alone
Was that the day!
Where did my childhood go?

It went to some forgotten place,
That is hidden in an infant's face,
That's all I know."

(i) Why is the poet eager to know the lost place of his childhood?

(ii) Which quality is achieved by the poet in the given extract?

(iii) Explain 'Producing thoughts that were not those of other people but my own and mine alone'.

(iv) The poet says that his childhood has gone to a forgotten place. Comment.

(v) Do you think the poet will be able to see his childhood?

Ans. (i) The poet is eager to know about his childhood because he cherishes childhood the most and once again wishes to lead the innocent life of a child.

(ii) In the given extract, the poet has achieved 'individuality.' He now can form his own opinions and ideas.

(iii) The given lines point out that once a child gains individuality, his trust and blind belief on adults break. Now, the child can form his own perspective and ideas that are unique.

(iv) The poet, in saying that his childhood has gone to a forgotten place, points out that once childhood is lost it will never be seen again. The loss of childhood is a permanent loss.

(v) I don't think that the poet will be able to see his childhood as it is lost to him now. However, he can see the childhood innocence in an infant's face.

CHAPTER 01

Albert Einstein At School

—by Patrick Pringle

In this Chapter...

- Chapter Summary
- Word Meaning
- Chapter Practice

Chapter Sketch

This biographical piece discusses the childhood of Albert Einstein, the famous physicist. The chapter starts with Einstein's disagreement on rote learning with his history teacher. Einstein wanted to get away from the system of education followed in Munich. So he decided to get a doctor's certificate declaring that he has had a nervous breakdown and needs rest for six months. Only his maths teacher admired Einstein for his brilliance. But before Einstein could get an appointment with the head teacher to present the certificate, he was asked by the head teacher to leave the school due to poor conduct. So he felt happy on leaving.

Chapter Summary

Einstein in History Class

The narrative begins with Einstein being asked by his history teacher, Mr Braun, about the year in which the Prussians defeated the French at Waterloo. Einstein frankly replied that he did not remember and he didn't see any point in learning dates. Mr Braun was amazed that Einstein didn't believe in learning facts. According to him, learning facts was essential to education. However, Einstein did not believe that learning facts is education. This enraged Mr Braun who asked Einstein to share his theory of education.

Einstein's Theory of Education

Albert, shyly, states that education should be about ideas and not facts. He elaborates that instead of dates of battles or any other fact, he will be interested in learning why the soldiers were trying to kill each other.

Mr Braun was shocked and furious. He did not agree with Einstein's views on education. He punished Einstein by asking him to stay for an extra period in school. He also told Einstein that he was a disgrace to the school and an ungrateful boy who ought to be ashamed of himself. The teacher suggested Einstein to call his father to take him away.

Einstein's Hatred for the School and the Slum

Einstein felt miserable as he knew he had to come to school the next day again. He wanted his father to take him away but knew that his father wouldn't do so until Einstein got his school diploma. In addition to school, the place where he lived also added to his misery. Einstein's father was poor and so, Einstein could only find a room in the poor corner of Munich. Einstein did not care for comfort or dirt around his home but hated the atmosphere of slum violence. His landlady beat her children and every Saturday her husband came home drunk and beat her. His only source of joy was his violin which he played regularly. But the landlady hated it so he had to stop.

Yuri, Einstein's Friend

When Einstein stated all this to his friend Yuri, he comforted him. He told Einstein about how lucky he is to have his own room while he has to share a room with uncivilised people. He further goes on to tell Einstein about how a boy was killed in a fight and how the other boy is proud of his act.

Yuri's statement intensefies Einsteins' misery as he feel that he would never be able to join college. He feels he would never be able to pass the exams for his school diploma.

Einstein Met his Cousin, Elsa

When Einsten's cousin Elsa came to visit him from Berlin, he informed his doubts to her. She tried to counsel him. Elsa told him that she knew a lot of boys who were more stupid than him and they all had passed the exam. She adds that he only needs to learn his school books by heart and repeat it in exams.

Einstein tells Elsa that he cannot learn like a parrot. Elsa tells him that he can if he tries. She adds that Einstein always has a book with him but Einstein tells her that he was reading Geology which was not taught in the school.

Einstein's Plan to Get Away from School

When Einstein met Yuri, he told him that he found it meaningless to stay in Munich. It was no use wasting his father's money and everyone's time. Einstein suddenly got an idea. He asked Yuri if he knew a doctor. Einstein wanted to get a medical certificate to show that he had a nervous breakdown and he should stop going to school. Yuri doubted that the doctor will believe Einstein. Einstein commented that he would have a real nervous breakdown to make matters easier for the doctor. He believed that a day or two in school will make him reach the state of nervous breakdown.

The next time Einstein met Yuri, he was miserable. Yuri informed him that he had found a doctor and that Einstein has to visit him the next day in the evening. Yuri adds that the doctor's name is Ernst Weil and Einstein may be his first patient. He also warns Einstein to not lie to Ernst.

When Einstein met Dr Ernst the next day, he was nervous. Dr Ernst told him that Yuri had informed him about Einstein's case. He also tells Einstein that he believes that he was infact on the verge of a nervous breakdown and writes a prescription for six months stating that Einstein needed to stay away from school. As a payment, he asks Einstein to take Yuri for a meal which he does.

Einstein gets the Reference

The next day, Einstein reached his mathematics teacher for a reference. Mr. Koch willingly gave it as he found that Einstein had learned all the maths that he could learn at school and even more than that. Mr Koch expresses his

dejection at Einstein leaving the school which shocks him. It puzzled Einstein that his teacher knew he was leaving even before Einstein knew about it himself.

Einstein is asked to Leave

Einstein was summoned to the head teacher's room where he was told to leave the school by his own self. The head teacher clarifies that Einstein's presence disturbs the class. The teachers as well as the pupils can't study when he continuously rebels against the system.

When Einstein heard this, he felt sad that he had unnecessarily wasted time and effort in procuring a medical certificate. Einstein was tempted to tell the head teacher what he thought about the school or about the teachers but somehow stopped himself. When he left the school, he did not look back to see the school for the last time.

The only person he wanted to meet before leaving was Yuri, who wished him good luck and said that he would be happier in Milan.

Word Meanings

The given page numbers correspond to the pages in the prescribed NCERT textbook.

Word	Meaning
Page 25	
physicist	scientist who studies physics
unthinking	spontaneous
Page 26	
heavy sarcasm	mockery
flushed	became red in confusion
stay in	remain
lodgings	place of residence
squalor	filth
slum violence	fights in the poorest areas of the town
duel	fight between two people
badge of honour	mark of pride
Page 27	
glumly	sadly
learning things by heart	remembering things perfectly
wailing	long and loud sound made by the violin
gets on one's nerves	annoys
howling	crying
turn out	end in the result that
nervous breakdown	mental illness

Chapter Practice

Objective Questions

• Multiple Choice Questions

1. Mr. Braun believes that Einstein does not believe in the education system. Select the option that explains it.
(a) Einstein does not believe in learning facts.
(b) Einstein is not interested in school.
(c) Einstein believes that the education system is faulty.
(d) Einstein feels that the school teaches unnecessary things.

Ans. (a) Einstein's statement that he does not believe in learning facts makes Mr. Braun believe that Einstein does not believe in the education system. For Mr. Braun, facts are central to learning and education.

2. What was Albert's theory of education?
(a) Learning all important facts
(b) Memorising
(c) Writing everything
(d) Ideas behind things

Ans. (d) According to Einstein, education should focus on ideas and not on facts. Facts can be looked up in books but ideas are required to be understood.

3. Select the option that lists the feelings Einstein fostered about the school.
  (i) Expensive   (ii) Faulty
 (iii) Torturous   (iv) Hostile
  (v) Dejected
(a) (i) and (ii)   (b) (ii) and (iii)
(c) (iii) and (iv)   (d) (iv) and (v)

Ans. (b) Einstein felt going to school to be torturous as he did not like the current education system which relied on facts.

4. Einstein's misery was .... the atmosphere around his lodgings.
(a) subdued by
(b) alleviated by
(c) intensified by
(d) dominated by

Ans. (c) Einstein was already miserable due to his school. This misery increased because of the place where he lived.

5. The 'slum violence' referred to by Einstein included
(a) children howling
(b) children being beaten by parents
(c) drunken landlord
(d) All of the above

Ans. (b) Einstein refers to his landlady beating her children as one of the instances of slum violence he has encountered at his lodgings.

6. "But at least you have a room of your own, which is more than I can say,"

Through the given lines, Yuri is .... Einstein.
(a) comforting   (b) admonishing
(c) onfronting   (d) helping

Ans. (a) By stating that Einstein has a room of his own, Yuri wants him to understand that he is in a much better condition. Yuri had to share a room with uncivilised students.

7. Select the suitable option for the given statements, based on your reading of 'Albert Einstein at School'.
  (i) Yuri sounds bitter, almost envious of Einstein.
 (ii) Yuri was Einstein's only fried in Munich.
(a) (i) is false but (ii) is true.
(b) Both (i) and (ii) are true.
(c) (ii) is a fact but unrelated to (i).
(d) (i) is the cause for (ii).

Ans. (a) It is true that Yuri was Einstein's only friend in Munich.

8. "And these are the students." With what feeling does the speaker utter these words?
(a) Exasperation   (b) Disgust
(c) Shoc   (d) Annoyance

Ans. (b) When Einstein gets to know about the killing of a boy and the reaction of the other boy he feels disgusted at the state of students.

9. As per Einstein, what was good enough reason to study something?
(a) If the reader likes it
(b) If it is a part of the curriculum
(c) If the reader is forced to study it
(d) If the reader is able to justify his knowledge

Ans. (a) According to Einstein, one should study or read something only if one likes it, just like him who reads Geology, a subject that wasn't taught in the school.

10. Classify (1) to (4) as Fact (F) or Opinion (O), based on your reading of 'Albert Einstein at School.'

1. Yuri really supported Einstein in his plan.
2. Yuri was reluctant to offer Einstein his help.
3. Yuri is Einstein's only friend in Munich.
4. Einstein cared for Yuri and thus met him on his last day in Munich.

(a) F-1, 3, 4; O-2
(b) F-2, 3; O-1, 4
(c) F-1, 3 ; O-2, 4
(d) F-3, 4; O-1, 2

Ans. (c)

11. Albert was .... about his appointment with the doctor.

(a) annoyed   (b) worried
(c) passive   (d) thrilled

Ans. (b) Albert Einstein was nervous about meeting the doctor as he did not know what he was going to say to the doctor.

12. How did Albert plan to get into a college?

(a) By giving an entrance exam
(b) Through his father's reference
(c) By getting a reference from his history teacher
(d) By getting a reference from his mathematics teacher

Ans. (d) Einstein had planned on furthering his studies at an institute in Italy by getting a referral from his Mathematics teacher.

13. Mr. Koch offered the reference willingly to Einstein. Select the option that explains it.

(a) Mr. Koch also wanted Einstein to leave as he disturbed the class.
(b) Mr. Koch felt that Einstein knew everything that he could learn from school.
(c) Mr. Koch could see that Einstein was a special child and wanted to help him.
(d) Mr. Koch did not want the future of a child to get spoilt because of the school.

Ans. (b) Mr. Koch appreciated Einstein and wrote a reference for him because he believed that Einstein had learned everything he could at school. In fact, he knew more than what mathematics the school could teach him.

14. What sort of a student Einstein was according to Mr. Braun?

(i) Insincere   (ii) Rebellion
(iii) Troublesome   (iv) Obedient
(v) Notorious   (vi) Talkative
(a) (i), (ii) and (iii)   (b) (ii), (iii) and (iv)
(c) (iii), (iv) and (v)   (d) (i), (iv) and (v)

Ans. (a) According to the teachers of the school, Einstein was an insincere and a rebellious child. His presence was troublesome to the class as teachers could not teach and students could not learn.

15. Select the suitable option for the given statements, based on your reading of 'Albert Einstein at School'.

(i) Albert Einstein hated the town as much as he hated the school.
(ii) Einstein's misery was caused by the slum violence and the constant insults he got from his teachers.

(a) (i) is false but (ii) is true.
(b) Both (i) and (ii) are true.
(c) (ii) is a fact but unrelated to (i).
(d) (i) is the cause for (ii).

Ans. (b) Einstein's hatred for the town and the school comes from the misery he suffered because of the violence he had seen and the insults he had borne from his teachers.

• Extract Based MCQs

1. Read the extract given below and answer the questions that follow.

"I can't see any point in learning dates. One can always look them up in a book."

Mr Braun was speechless for a few moments.

"You amaze me, Einstein," he said at last. "Don't you realise that one can always look most things up in books? That applies to all the facts you learn at school."

"Yes, sir."

"Then I suppose you don't see any point in learning facts."

"Frankly, sir, I don't," said Albert.

"Then you don't believe in education at all?"

"Oh, yes, sir, I do. I don't think learning facts is education."

(i) By stating that he does not believe in learning facts he is .... his perspective.

(a) clarifying   (b) negotiating
(c) amplifying   (d) rectifying

Ans. (a) When Einstein tells his teacher that he does not believe in learning fact, he is clarifying why he does not want to learn facts from the book.

(ii) Select the correct inference from the given options on the basis of the extract.

(a) Mr. Braun hated Einstein for his lack of interest in history.
(b) Mr. Braun was irritated with Einstein for his disinterest in learning facts.
(c) Mr. Braun did not want Einstein to stay in the school after this incident.
(d) Mr. Braun did not appreciate Einstein negating all of his views.

Ans. (b) Mr. Braun disliked the fact that Einstein was not at all interested in learning dates or in general facts about anything.

(iii) Which of the following qualities can be associated with Einstein on the basis of the given extract?

    (a) Daring   (b) Frank

    (c) Honest   (d) Sincerity

Ans. (c) The given extract shows that Einstein was an honest child who answered his irritated teacher's questions without any hesitation or hint of lie.

(iv) Select the option that correctly states the views of Mr. Braun.

    (a) Education systems focus on what is taught in schools and colleges.

    (b) Education system does not give any space to one's opinions.

    (c) Education system is based on learning facts.

    (d) Education system is qualitative and does not need students like Einstein to question it.

Ans. (c) From the given extract, it can be gathered that Mr. Braun believes that education should be based on learning facts.

(v) Einstein says that he does not believe that education is about learning facts.

Which of the following correctly states Einstein's perspective regarding education?

    (a) Views behind events   (b) Ideas that lead to creation

    (c) Opinions   (d) All of these

Ans. (d) Einstein believed that education system shows focus on ideas, views and perspectives behind any event. It should not focus on learning facts.

2. Read the extract to attempt the questions that follow:

"At least you live among civilised human beings, even if they are all poor students," said Albert.

"They are not all civilised," Yuri replied. "Did you not hear that one of them was killed last week in a duel?"

"And what happens to the one who killed him?"

"Nothing, of course. He is even proud of it. His only worry is that the authorities have told him not to fight any more duels. He's upset about this because he hasn't a single scar on his face to wear for the rest of his life as a badge of honour."

"Ugh!" exclaimed Albert. "And these are the students."

"Well, you'll be a student one day," said Yuri.

(i) How is Einstein feeling in the given lines?

    (a) Surprised   (b) Annoyed

    (c) Shaken   (d) Disgusted

Ans. (d) Einstein feels disgusted in the given lines at the savage behaviour of the students.

(ii) Yuri is trying to ……….. Einstein in the given lines.

    (a) show his care for   (b) calm and comfort

    (c) cheer up   (d) help

Ans. (b) In the given lines, Yuri is trying to calm Einstein and provide comfort to him when he feels miserable.

(iii) How did Yuri achieve his purpose?

    (a) Yuri compared his situation with Einstein's.

    (b) Yuri distracted him with a news from his locality.

    (c) Yuri told him about how he feels suffocated.

    (d) Yuri told him about how he would have a better future.

Ans. (a) Yuri had wanted to calm Einstein and for the same he compared his own situation to that of Einstein.

(iv) What can be said about the boy who killed another boy in the duel?

    (a) Arrogant   (b) Barbaric

    (c) Gutsy   (d) Egoist

Ans. (b) The boy who had killed another boy can be called barbaric as he was not at all ashamed of his act. He was even proud of it and was regretful for having no scar from the duel.

(v) "Well, you'll be a student one day," said Yuri.

What effect does the above lines have on Einstein?

    (a) Fills him with disgust

    (b) Intensifies his misery

    (c) Makes him disbelieve in the education system

    (d) Both (a) and (b)

Ans. (d) Einstein is disgusted at the savage behaviour of the students. The whole aspect of facing such scenario increases his misery.

PART 2

Subjective Questions

• Short Answer Type Questions

1. Why did Einstein say—"I can't see any point in learning dates?"

Ans. Einstein said this when the history teacher asked him about the dates of the Waterloo battle. He replied honestly that he did not like learning dates at all as there is no use of it. In fact he didn't see any point in learning facts. He never considered learning facts as education. Rather, he believed in learning ideas or getting insight of a concept.

2. What was Einstein's view on education?

Ans. Einstein believed that the existing system of education was incapable of meeting the purpose of education. He believed that memorising dates and facts was not education. Ideas, that come from critical thinking and analysis, form real education.

3. Do you think Einstein was being impolite while answering the history teacher?

Ans. I think Einstein was not being rude or impolite while answering his history teacher. He just wanted to express his frank opinion about education. As his views did not match with that of the teacher's, he was scolded and punished.

4. What made Einstein unhappy at school?

Ans. Einstein had arguments with his teachers, got frequent punishments and was ridiculed by them over his ideas of education. He was considered a 'disgrace' for expressing his frank opinion instead of obeying his teachers and learning dates and facts, which made him unhappy at school.

5. Einstein was ruthlessly insulted by his history teacher. Comment.

Ans. Einstein was considered to be a nuisance in the class by his history teacher, Mr Braun. The teacher was sarcastic and cruel with him the day they had an argument. He punished Einstein but remarked that it would not help in any way. He called Einstein a disgrace. Further, he called Einstein an ungrateful boy who should be ashamed of himself.

6. What does Yuri tell Einstein about the accommodation which he shared with other students?

Ans. Yuri tells Einstein that he was lucky to live in a separate room of his own, whereas Yuri was living with fellow students who always indulged in violence and fighting. In fact, one of the students killed another student in a fight and was even proud of it afterwards. But he was not even punished for this, only was told by the authorities not to fight anymore.

7. Who was Elsa ? What advice did she give to Einstein ?

Ans. Elsa was Einstein's cousin and lived in Berlin. She sometimes came to Munich and met Einstein.

Einstein told her that he doubted if he could pass the exams for the school diploma. Elsa told him that she had seen boys who were more stupid than Einstein who had passed the diploma exam. She advised him to learn like a parrot and repeat it in the exam so that he would pass.

8. Why did the author refer to Einstein's interest in music as his only comfort?

Ans. Einstein used to feel miserable both at his school as well as at where he stayed in Munich. The school atmosphere was oppressive, and did not give any opportunity for creativity. 'Slum violence' was depressing where he stayed in Munich. So playing music only provided Einstein some comfort in this unpleasant environment.

9. Why did Einstein want to get a medical certificate?

Ans. Einstein was miserable at school. He knew that if he went home, his father would send him back to Munich. It was unreasonable for him to stay there and waste his father's money and everybody's time. He wanted to get a medical certificate so that he could go away from school in Munich and his father wouldn't send him back.

10. Yuri calls Einstein 'the world's worst liar'. Is it a compliment or an insult to Einstein?

Ans. It was a compliment. Einstein believed in truth and honesty. He was unable to tell a deliberate lie. Even if he tried to lie, his face betrayed it and people could make out that he was lying.

11. How was Einstein comforted by the doctor when he met him for the medical certificate?

Ans. Dr Ernst comforted Einstein when he met him by saying that he understood Einstein's feelings because he was also a student until recently. Dr Ernst also discussed Einstein's plans about what he wanted to do after leaving school. Both these factors comforted Einstein when he met the doctor.

12. Who was Dr Ernst Weil ? How did he help Einstein?

Ans. Dr Ernst Weil was an old acquaintance of Yuri. He had recently qualified as a doctor.

When Einstein asked Yuri for help to get a medical certificate, he recommended Dr Ernst Weil's name. As the doctor had just stopped being a student himself, he could understand Einstein's condition very well. So, he asked Einstein for how long he wanted to stay away from school and gave Einstein the medical certificate he wanted.

13. What did Einstein plan to do after leaving the school and how did he plan to achieve it?

Ans. Einstein wanted to go to Italy for higher studies in maths, where his parents lived and wanted to take admission in an Italian institute for this purpose. But for this, he must have a reference from his teacher. So, he went to his maths teacher, Mr Koch, who had firm faith in Einstein's abilities and held him in high esteem. He gave Einstein the required reference.

14. 'Einstein' felt the medical certificate almost burning a hole in his pocket." Why?

Ans. Einstein gave a treat to Yuri as he had helped him get the medical certificate. Finally, it wasn't needed as the head teacher himself asked Einstein to leave. Einstein felt that he took all the trouble for nothing and that the certificate was not even needed.

15. How did Einstein leave his school after spending five years?

Ans. Einstein left his school without saying goodbye to any teacher or student. He was not feeling ashamed for being asked to leave the school. He himself wanted to be away from the system of education which this school represented. So he left the school with his head held high.

• Long Answer Type Questions

1. Do you think that one should raise one's voice against the deplorable education system? Discuss with reference to the chapter 'Albert Einstein at School'.

Ans. It is true that education is an important part of our lives. The future of a child totally depends on the quality of education it gets. But sometimes the students don't get what they deserve in the school. One of the reasons is that nowadays education is based more on facts than ideas. Students are being taught but not in a result oriented manner.

Even if Einstein didn't find history classes interesting, it was his teacher's responsibility to make him realise that it is also important. Rather than taking an innovative way to teach Einstein, he thought of punishing him. Such a situation could have been avoided if the teacher had been understanding.

One should not tolerate this kind of system; rather, one should raise one's voice against such a deplorable education system and must have enough courage to stand up against it and express our views like Einstein did.

2 What do you understand about Einstein's nature from his conversation with his history teacher, his mathematics teacher and the head teacher? **(NCERT)**

Ans. Einstein's nature appears to be that of a rebel. He did not believe in the prevailing rote learning system of education. Thus, he found memorising facts and dates useless. Ideas interested him more than facts because of which he had an argument with his history teacher.

From his conversation with the maths teacher, we come to know that he was a genius at maths, because his maths teacher frankly told him that Einstein could even teach maths soon to the teacher himself.

Thus, Einstein can be recognised as a person of rebellious nature, who is very honest and straightforward about his thoughts. He is also a genius at maths and thus, his history teacher's comment about him being a disgrace and ungrateful is incorrect. Later, when he confronts the head teacher, we find him defensive at the beginning and carefree at the end of the meeting.

His interaction with the head teacher shows him as a mature person who doesn't want to get into pointless arguments.

3. Suppose you are Einstein. Write a letter to your friend describing the present education system in Germany. Also express your views about how the education system can change.

Ans. 30 Hudson Colony, Munich

26th December, 19XX

Dear John

How are you? I hope that you are doing much better than me. You wrote in your last letter that you wanted to know what my school was like. But frankly, my experience at this school has been quite shocking.

Here, school education is totally unproductive. The teachers believe that learning facts is education. They don't want to use innovative ideas to make their subject interesting. I am not criticising all the teachers of my school. In fact, my maths teacher, Mr Koch, is quite different from the rest. He understands our problems and always tries to help us.

In contrast, my history teacher, Mr Braun, punished me just because I could not tell the year when Prussia defeated France at Waterloo. His approach is quite primitive. What I hate the most is that he discourages new ideas presented by the students. When I told him that I don't feel that learning these facts would be of much importance, he insulted me.

I hope to get rid of this hateful place as soon as possible.

Yours truly

Einstein

4. Today's school system curbs individual talent and ignores the genius in students, imposing a teacher—school centred approach upon the students. Discuss in the context of the chapter 'Albert Einstein at School'.

Ans. Einstein studied in a school in Munich where he was unhappy with the teaching system. Einstein liked maths, which required reasoning to be applied. But he was averse to rote learning which emphasised learning without understanding just to pass the examination. When Einstein's history teacher asked him the dates of specific battles, he could not remember them as he was not interested in memorising dates. His history teacher got annoyed and refused to listen to his views about what education should be. In fact, he punished Einstein for disobedience.

An understanding teacher would have at least listened to his point of view and tried to reason with the student. Further, the head teacher considered himself supreme and was equally unconcerned about the student. He took the most extreme measure of expelling the student without giving him an opportunity to express his point of view.

It was really ridiculous that a teacher centred approach failed to recognise the genius of Einstein.

5. Discuss Einstein's relatively poor performance in school in terms of what that might mean to students today who may not do as well as they are capable of doing.

Ans. In Einstein's time, most of the teachers emphasised on learning facts. According to them, education was about rote learning and memorising facts and figures. Obviously, a young student will get bored with such type of education and that's what happened to Einstein too.

It is well said that if "you judge a fish by its ability to climb a tree, it will spend the rest of its life believing that it is stupid". We all know that Einstein was one of the greatest physicists who ever lived. Still his school grades said otherwise. His poor grades can be attributed to the fact that some of his teachers failed to recognise his true potential because of their primitive thinking.

In short, we can say that grades are not the right criteria to measure one's ability. We are not good at everything. Students today are suffering from the same problem. It is the responsibility of their teachers to understand the special abilities of their students and bring out their latent talents.

● Extract Based Questions

1. Read the extract to attempt the questions that follow.

"In that case," said the history teacher with heavy sarcasm, "perhaps you will be so kind as to tell the class the Einstein theory of education."

Albert flushed.

"I think it's not facts that matter, but ideas," he said. "I don't see the point in learning the dates of battles, or even which of the armies killed more men. I'd be more interested in learning why those soldiers were trying to kill each other."

"That's enough," Mr Braun's eyes were cold and cruel. "We don't want a lecture from you, Einstein. You will stay in for an extra period today, although I don't imagine it will do you much good. It won't do the school any good, either. You are a disgrace. I don't know why you continue to come."

(i) Do you think Mr. Braun is offended by Albert?

(ii) What is the concept of education as proposed by Einstein?

(iii) Mr. Braun cannot accept Einstein's opinions regarding education. Comment.

(iv) Do you approve of teachers of Mr. Braun? Justify.

(v) Why do you think Einstein is in the school even when he does not approve of the education system?

Ans. (i) Yes, I feel that Mr. Braun is offended by Albert for not believing in learning fact as the basis of education system.

(ii) Einstein proposes that education is not at all about learning fact. According to him, it is the ideas, perspectives and beliefs behind the things that matter.

(iii) Mr. Braun cannot accept Einstein's opinions regarding education because since he has been teaching he had been told that learning facts constitute education. In this light, Einstein perspective comes in stark contrast and thus he cannot accept it.

(iv) No, I do not approve of teachers like Mr. Braun who cannot accept other's opinions and go on to insult the students for negating his opinion.

(v) Einstein has to come to school because his father had send him to Munich to get a School diploma and would not call him back until he had got it.

2. Read the extract to attempt the questions that follow:

"Only that you want me to think you have had a nervous breakdown, and say that you mustn't go back to that school."

"Oh dear." Albert's face fell. "He shouldn't have told you that."

"Why not? Isn't it true, then?"

"Yes, that's the trouble. Now you'll say there's nothing wrong with me, and you'll tell me to go back to school."

"Don't be too sure of that," said the doctor. "As a matter of fact I am pretty sure you are in a nervous state about that school."

"But I haven't told you anything about it," said Albert, wide eyed. "How can you know that?"

(i) Why had Einstein visited Dr. Weil?

(ii) "He shouldn't have told you that." Who is 'he' in this line?

(iii) Do you think Dr. Weil is right in giving the certificate to Einstein?

(iv) Albert feels dejected when he gets to know that Yuri had told the truth to the doctor. Explain.

(v) How does the Dr. justify his action to Einstein?

Ans. (i) Einstein visited Dr. Weil to get a medical certificate that would get him out of school for a longer period with his father's consent.

(ii) 'He' refers to Yuri, Einstein's only friend in Munich. He told Dr. Weil what Einstein need from him.

(iii) Ethically, it is not correct for a Doctor to give a fake medical certificate but Dr. Weil believes that Einstein is actually on the verge of a nervous breakdown. So yes, I think Dr. Weil is right in giving the certificate to Einstein.

(iv) Albert feels dejected when he gets to know that Yuri had told the truth to the doctor because he feels that the doctor would not help him in his idea and then he would have to stay in the school.

(v) The doctor tells Einstein that the fact that Einstein has to do such things to get out of school is indicative of how close he was to a nervous breakdown and thus, he was going to give him the medical certificate.

3. Read the extract to attempt the questions that follow.

He soon found out. Before he had a chance to ask for an interview with the head teacher, he was summoned to the head's room.

"Well, it saves me the trouble of having to wait an hour or two outside," he thought.

He hardly bothered to wonder why he had been sent for, but vaguely supposed he was to be punished again for bad work and laziness. Well, he had finished with punishments.

"I'm not going to punish you," the head teacher said, to Albert's surprise. "Your work is terrible, and I'm not prepared to have you here any longer, Einstein. I want you to leave the school now."

"Leave school now?" repeated Albert, dazed."

(i) What did he found out?

(ii) Do you think Einstein considered the fact that he was going to be expelled?

(iii) What does the given extract tell us about what his teacher thought about him?

(iv) Why does the head teacher ask Einstein to leave?

(v) Justify the significance of the given lines.

Ans. (i) Einstein found out how Mr. Koch knew about him leaving soon, even before he himself knew.

(ii) No, I don't think Einstein considered even the chance that he would be expelled. He felt that he was getting summoned for some punishment.

(iii) The given extract shows us that the teachers did not really appreciate Einstein as a student. They felt that he was a lazy boy who did no good staying in the school.

(iv) The head teacher asks Einstein to leave because his presence was interrupting the learning of other pupils.

(v) The given lines are significant because they not only state how the education system ignores the needs of unique students like Einstein but also how Einstein's work to get the medical certificate had gone waste.

Mother's Day

—by JB Priestley

In this Chapter...

- Chapter Summary
- Word Meaning
- Chapter Practice

Chapter Summary

Chapter Sketch

This humorous play portrays the status of a mother in the family. The author brings out the plight of the mother very realistically in the play. Mrs Annie Pearson, the mother, is not treated well by her husband and children. With the help of her neighbour, Mrs Fitzgerald and a magic spell which temporarily allows them to interchange their roles, she stands up for her rights. Mrs Annie Pearson's family is shocked at the change, but they learn to behave properly with her so that she gets the respect that she deserved.

Introduction of Mrs Annie Pearson and Mrs. Fitzgerald

Mrs Annie Pearson and Mrs Fitzgerald are next door neighbours. Apart from this, there is no similarity between them. Annie is a pleasant and nervous looking woman in her forties. Fitzgerald is an older and heavier woman with a strong personality. Annie has a soft voice whereas Mrs Fitzgerald has a deep, throaty voice.

Mrs Fitzgerald is a fortune-teller and is reading Annie's fortune. She advises Annie to be strict and become the 'boss' in her family.

Annie or Mrs. Pearson had been taken granted by her family. Her husband, son and daughter are so spoilt that they don't do any work or help their wife or mother. Instead, they treat her disrespectfully and ungratefully. Mrs. Fitzgerald is enraged at such a treatment and asks Mrs. Pearson to take action. However, Mrs. Pearson is reluctant. Even though she wants others in her family to respect her, she cannot be unpleasant with them. So she is constantly worried about them.

Mrs Fitzgerald Outlines the Plan to Reform Annie's Family

Mrs Fitzgerald, suggests that they should temporarily exchange their personalities by using a magic spell that she had learnt in the East. She takes Annie's hand and chants a spell. A transformation takes place and the personality of Mrs Fitzgerald shifts into the body of Annie and *vice-versa*.

Annie is scared, but Mrs Fitzgerald assures her that the change is reversible. Mrs Fitzgerald, now in the body of Annie, stays at Annie's house and sends Annie (in Mrs Fitzgerald's body) to her house where she can relax.

Doris Gets a Shock

Doris, the daughter of Mrs Annie Pearson, a beautiful 20 year old girl enters the house. She gets shocked at seeing her mother smoking and playing cards alone. She enquires about tea and her yellow silk dress but gets a rude reply from her mother. Annie tells her to make tea for herself and iron her clothes herself too. She tells Doris that she works much more than her and does not even get a pay.

Further, when Doris informs her mother about her plans with Charlie Spence, Annie makes fun of him. She calls him buck teeth and half-witted. Annie also tells Doris that if she were her age, she would have found someone better.

All of this hurts Doris who runs away crying.

Cyril also gets a Shock

After Doris leaves, Cyril, Annie's son enters the room, asking for tea, when Annie tells him it isn't, he gets annoyed and angry. He tells his mother to get the tea ready as he doesn't have much time but Annie doesn't do anything. Even when he asks about his clothes, Annie refuses to do anything.

Cyril gets anguished by his mother's strange behaviour. He tells her that she was not talking nicely. His mother coldly replies that they all talk to her like that. They do what they want to do and now she has joined them.

Just then Doris enters the scene wearing a shoulder wrap. She had been crying. Annie, upon seeing Doris, remarks that she was looking terrible. Dories tells her mother that it was because she made her cry. Annie now goes to get stout to drink.

Discussion between Doris and Cyril

Both Doris and Cyril are filled with horror and shock at their mother's behaviour. Both wonder what has happened to their mother suddenly. Doris thinks that she got hit on her head by something. She says that the manner in which their mother spoke hurt her the most and made her cry. Both start giggling at the thought of what will happen if their mother keeps behaving in this weird manner in front of their father.

Annie's Remarks About her Family

When Annie sees Doris and Cyril giggling she remarks that it was high time they grew up. Doris then asked her if they had done something wrong. Annie tells them that it is actually their behaviour that bothered her the most. They always came, asked for something and went without bothering to know whether she wanted to go out or how she was feeling. She always does her best to keep everybody happy but all three of them were not bothered about her.

Annie also remarks that while the three of them do a job of eight hours a day with two days off at the weekend, she goes on working seven days round the clock. She informs them that on weekends, she might also be going away.

Doris is really worried about what will happen if her mother takes a holiday on weekends. However, Annie assures Doris that she would do some work on Saturday and Sunday only when she is requested and thanked for whatever she does. She adds that she might go out for weekends as she was fed up of staying in the house. When Dorris enquires about it, Annie tells her that she is just going to be like them. The only difference will be that she will be able to look after herself.

Hearing this, Dorris expresses her concern but Annie rudely shuts her down.

Mr George Pearson is Shocked at his Wife's Behaviour

Mr George Pearson now enters the house. He is about 50 years old and considers himself as a very important person. He gets annoyed at his wife who is sipping stout when he enters. He tells her that he does not want any tea as he has to go to the club for supper. Annie tells him that she has not prepared any tea anyway. At this, George gets annoyed that his wife is not bothered about him.

Annie continues to rebuke him, telling him that he is not respected in the club where he keeps going every day. She tells him that people at the bar in the club call him 'Pompy-ompy Pearson' due to his self-important behaviour. George cannot believe what Annie says and confirms the truth from his son, Cyril.

When Cyril tells his mother that she has hurt their feelings, Annie tells him that it does people good to have their feelings hurt. She also tells Cyril that he has no future. Just then there is a knock. Cyril checks on the door and reports that it was the 'silly old bag' Mrs Fitzgerald. Hearing this, Annie rebukes him and asks him to let her in.

The Real Mrs Annie Pearson Returns

Mrs. Fitzgerald (actually Mrs. Pearson) is worried for her family. When she expresses it, Cyril rudely answers her. Such a disrespectful behaviour earns a scolding from Annie (Mrs. Fitzgerald). After Cyril leaves, Mrs. Fitzgerald and Mrs. Pearson start talking. Annie says that she is putting everyone in their places telling them how they really are.

While they are talking, George enters the room and gets angry and rude towards Mrs. Fitzgerald for entering their quarrel. He is also angry at Annie for ruining their mood. But Annie remains unaffected. In fact, she tells him to be respectful and mannerful in front of guests and neighbors. Hearing this George is enraged which gets Annie to threaten him. Seeing his angry wife, George is intimidated.

Doris again enters the scene. She, like her brother and father, is also disrespectful towards Mrs. Fitzgerald and thus gets reprimanded too.

Mrs Annie Pearson and Mrs Fitzgerald Go Back to their Original Personalities

The real Mrs Annie Pearson (now Mrs. Fitzgerald) gets really disturbed and wants everyone to leave as she wants to talk in private with Annie (the real Mrs. Fitzgerald).

She tells Mrs. Fitzgerald that she can see all of them are miserable and now it is time to change back into their true selves. Mrs. Fitzgerald agrees and they again get back to their own selves. After they come back in their original forms, Mrs. Fitzgerald tells Mrs. Pearson to be firm and strict, if required. She even warns her not to give any apology or explanation, otherwise they will again start treating her indifferently. She must wear a tough look and talk to them rudely if she wanted them to behave in the right manner.

Mrs. Fitzgerald wants Mrs Pearson to test it out. When she leaves, she calls the family inside and hides herself to hear/see the change.

The Changed Pearson Family

When Doris, Cyril and George enter the room, they get relieved seeing Mrs. Pearson smile. She tells her family that she wants to play a game of rummy with her family. After that, the children can prepare supper while she talks to George. Everyone agrees while Doris is hesitant. However, a sharp tone of Mrs. Pearson makes her agree.

The play ends with the family surrounding Mrs. Pearson ready to do whatever she suggests.

Word Meanings

The given page numbers correspond to the pages in the prescribed NCERT textbook.

Word	Meaning
Page 32	
suburb	outlying area of a city
muslin-covered	covered with a muslin curtain
settee	sofa
Page 33	
sinister	strong
flurried	nervous and confused due to overwork
Cockney	style of speaking of people living in the East end of London
Irish	style of speaking of people living in Ireland
fortune teller	person claiming to have magic powers
out East	in the British colonies in Asia
Page 34	
Lieutenant Quartermaster	non-commissioned officer in British Army
put your foot down	be very strict
mistress	woman with authority
apologetically	as if feeling sorry
treating 'em like dirt	showing lack of respect
dubiously	in an unsure manner
unpleasantness	quarrelling
have it out	settle it finally
good gracious	an expression of surprise
Page 35	
got the idea	understood me
gimme	give me
Page 36	
go lax	looking like they are dead
puffing	smoking

Word	Meaning
complacently	feeling happy and satisfied
Page 37	
patience	a card game played by a single person
taken anything in	understood what is going on
square meal	full and satisfying meal
Page 38	
indignantly	with annoyance
be seen dead	like to be seen
buck teeth	upper set of teeth sticking out
half-witted	stupid
masculine counterpart	brother
Page 39	
off-colour	not feeling well
get cracking	work quickly
aggressively	forcefully
put my things out	lay out my clothes
laconic and sinister	briefly and meaningfully
wear that face	look so bad
Union	association of employees
bar	stop
movement	association of employees
Page 40	
never you mind	don't bother
stout	strong beer
clot	idiot
in a huddle	come close together to talk
barmy	insane
fathead	idiot
concussion	serious injury to her head
guffaw	laugh loudly
Page 41	
be your age	behave properly as per your age
do with	appreciate
Page 42	
a bit thick	unreasonable
airily	carelessly
Page 43	
aghast	horrified
passionately	with much emotion
blubbering	crying like a baby

Word	Meaning
bulge	stick out
Page 44	
bewildered	confused, puzzled
distaste	dislike
Page 45	
indignantly	in a displeased tone
standing jokes	permanent amusements
Page 46	
greyhound races	races run by tall, slender dogs
dirt tracks	racing courses for motorcycles
ice shows	entertainment shows performed by ice skaters
sulkily	showing an irritated feeling
old bag	unpleasant elderly woman
smacking	bringing together with force so they make a sound
piecan	stupid person
Page 47	
putting 'em in their places	making them behave properly

Word	Meaning
doing 'em all a world of good	helping them to learn how to behave properly
eating out of your hand	completely under your control
crying her eyes out	crying uncontrollably
Page 48	
at sixes and sevens	in total confusion
Page 49	
tiddly	slightly drunk
in despair	hopelessly
a flash of temper	sudden anger
ticking her off	reprimanding her
Page 50	
'cos	because
Page 51-52	
go soft on	treat gently
spirit	enthusiasm
apprehensively	anxiously
rummy	a card game
cluster round	surround

Chapter Practice

Objective Questions

• Multiple Choice Questions

1. What is the play 'Mother's Day' about?
(a) It is about a family celebrating Mother's Day
(b) It is about a family's treatment of the mother
(c) It depicts the sick mother and her struggles
(d) It depicts the status of Mrs. Fitzgerald in her family

Ans. (b) The play 'Mother's Day' is about the Pearson family and their treatment of the mother, Mrs. Pearson.

2. Choose the statement(s) that is/are correct about the play.
  I. Mrs. Fitzgerald learnt the art of fortune telling in the East.
  II. Mrs. Pearson was very happy with her family.
  III. Mrs. Fitzgerald looked aiding and has a high-pitched voice.
(a) Only I (b) Only II (c) Only III (d) I and III

Ans. (a) It is true that Mrs. Fitzgerald learnt the art of fortune telling in the East but she had a sinister looking face and a deep voice. Mrs. Pearson was not very happy with her family's treatment of her.

3. "Besides I'm so fond of them even if they are so thoughtless and selfish."

In the given line, Mrs. Pearson is trying to
....
(a) Defend her family members
(b) Defend her own disposition
(c) Blame her subservient personality
(d) State that she won't be able to do anything

Ans. (b) By stating that she is fond of them, Mrs. Pearson is trying to defend her position as a subservient mother and wife.

4. In what endeavour does Mrs. Fitzgerald help Mrs. Pearson?
(a) To see future
(b) To make her family treat her well
(c) To run errands
(d) None of the above

Ans. (b) Mrs. Fitzgerald helps Mrs. Pearson by making sure that her family learns to treat her well by teaching them a lesson.

5. How does Mrs. Fitzgerald plan to help Mrs. Pearson?
(a) By talking to Mrs. Pearson's family
(b) By listening to Mrs. Pearson's rants
(c) By swapping personalities with Mrs. Pearson
(d) Both (a) and (b)

Ans. (c) Mrs. Fitzgerald plans to help Mrs. Pearson by swapping personalities with her and then teaching the family a lesson.

6. Mrs. Pearson was ...... about Mrs. Fitzgerald's plan.
(a) excited (b) hesitant
(c) sure (d) envious

Ans. (b) Mrs. Pearson was hesitant about Mrs. Fitzgerald's plan to swap personalities.

7. Select the suitable option for the given statements, based on your reading of 'Mother's Day.'
 (i) Mrs. Pearson is not appreciative of the fact that Mrs. Fitzgerald wants to teach her family a lesson.
 (ii) Mrs. Fitzgerald wants Mrs. Pearson to get respect from her family members.
(a) (i) is false but (ii) is true
(b) Both (i) and (ii) are true
(c) (ii) is a fact but unrelated to (i)
(d) (i) is the cause for (ii)

Ans. (a)

8. Select the suitable option for the given statements, based on your reading of 'Mother's Day.'
 (i) Doris is used to her mother doing everything for her.
 (ii) Doris's dominating attitude is a reflection of Mrs. Pearson's submissive behaviour.
(a) (i) is false but (ii) is true
(b) Both (i) and (ii) are true
(c) (ii) is a fact but unrelated to (i)
(d) (i) is the cause for (ii)

Ans. (d) Doris is dominating because her mother is subservient to her and does every little thing for her.

9. 'Cyril Pearson is a male version of Doris Pearson.' Select the option that explains it.
(a) They both are similar in nature- arrogant.
(b) They both do not treat their mother with respect.
(c) They both want Mrs. Pearson to do their work.
(d) All of the above

Ans. (d) All the options explain the given statement.

10. Cyril says, 'that's different'. What is he talking about?

(a) Working day (b) Way of talking
(c) Overall behaviour (d) His behaviour

Ans. (a) Cyril believes that his working day is different from his mother's working day.

11. What was George's reaction when he saw his wife drinking stout during the daytime?

(a) He did not like it
(b) He did not mind
(c) He accompanied her
(d) He ignored her

Ans. (a) George was furious and expressed that he did not like his wife drinking stout during the day time as he saw her doing so.

12. Choose the correct statements about the play.

I. Cyril asks his mother to snap out of her new change.
II. Doris gets a red eye as she cries immensely.
III. George is well-respected at the club he goes to.
IV. Mrs. Pearson was drinking coffee as she was smoking.

(a) I and III (b) I and II
(c) II and III (d) III and IV

Ans. (b) Out of the above statements, only I and II are correct as George is ridiculed by the club members in his absence and Annie wasn't drinking coffee while smoking.

13. Classify (1) to (4) as Fact (F) or Opinion (O), based on your reading of 'Mother's day.'

1. Mrs. Pearson should not have told George what people thought about him.
2. Mrs. Pearson, actually Mrs. Fitzgerald, went overboard in insulting the Pearson family.
3. Mrs. Fitzgerald's entry led to the climax of the play.
4. Mrs. Fitzgerald, actually Mrs. Pearson, should have let her family alone for some more hours.

(a) F-1, 3, 4; O-2
(b) F-2, 3; O-1, 4
(c) F-2; O-1, 3, 4
(d) F-3, 4; O-1, 2

Ans. (c)

14. The family members are annoyed at Mrs. Pearson, but commonly for a few reasons. Identify them.

I. Mrs. Pearson made no tea for them.
II. Mrs. Pearson was busy talking to her friends on the phone.
III. Mrs. Pearson expected them to change their selfish behaviours.

(a) I and III (b) I and II
(c) II and III (d) Only II

Ans. (a) The Pearson family members are mad at Mrs. Pearson for two common reasons. Firstly, she did not prepare any tea for them and secondly, she expected them to respect her work and change their selfish behaviours towards her.

15. What message does the author of 'Mother's Day' try to convey?

(a) To work hard for your mother
(b) To spend time with family
(c) To appreciate wives/ mothers for their work
(d) To respect everyone

Ans. (c)

• Extract Based MCQs

1. Read the extract given below and answer the questions that follow.

"[As she is about to rise, Mrs. Fitzgerald reaches out across the table and pulls her down.]

Mrs. Fitzgerald Let 'em wait or look after themselves for once. This is where your foot goes down. Start now. [She lights a cigarette from the one she has just finished.]

Mrs. Pearson [Embarrassed] Mrs. Fitzgerald—I know you mean well—in fact, I agree with you—but I just can't—and it's no use you trying to make me. If I promise you I'd really have it out with them, I know I wouldn't be able to keep my promise.

Mrs. Fitzgerald Then let me do it.

Mrs. Pearson [Flustered] Oh no—thank you very much, Mrs Fitzgerald—but that wouldn't do at all. It couldn't possibly be somebody else— they'd resent it at once and wouldn't listen— and really I couldn't blame them. I know I ought to do it—but you see how it is? [She looks apologetically across the table, smiling rather miserably.]

Mrs. Fitzgerald [Coolly] You haven't got the idea."

(i) What is the contrast in the personalities of the two women?

(a) Polite vs Assertive
(b) Gentle vs Sensible
(c) Scared vs Brave
(d) They have nothing to contrast

Ans. (a) The two women, Mrs. Pearson and Mrs. Fitzgerald contrasts the former's politeness and the latter's assertiveness. While Mrs. Pearson thinks about dropping hints and being polite to explain to her family about some things, Mrs. Fitzgerald believes in being assertive and confrontational about it.

(ii) Which of the following explains "This is where your foot goes down"?

(a) To physically fix your foot down to the floor
(b) To restraint yourself against a strong person
(c) To adopt a firm policy when faced with opposition or disobedience
(d) To give into what is expected

Ans. (c) The phrase 'to put your foot down' means to adopt a firm policy when faced with opposition or disobedience. Herein, it means to teach a lesson to the family about respecting her.

(iii) Who are the women talking about in the passage above?

    (a) About a neighbouring family
    (b) About Mrs. Fitzgeralds's family
    (c) About a group of their friends
    (d) About Mrs. Pearson's family

Ans. (d) The women are talking about Mrs. Pearson's family and how they would not comply or even listen to Mrs. Pearson.

(iv) What does Mrs. Fitzgerald mean by 'let me do it'? Select the option that explains it.

    (a) She wants to confront Mrs. Pearson's family
    (b) She has an unusual solution to the problem
    (c) It is unclear that she wants to help
    (d) She wants to teach confrontational skills to Mrs. Pearson

Ans. (b) Mrs. Fitzgerald certainly has an unusual solution to the problem as when Mrs. Pearson tries to clarify what her neighbour had meant, Mrs. Fitzgerald says that Mrs. Pearson had no idea.

(v) Why does Mrs. Fitzgerald's idea embarrass Mrs.Pearson?

    (a) Because she knows her family will disrespect her
    (b) Because she knows that it would be useless
    (c) Because she does not want anything to change
    (d) Because she hadn't expected such a solution

Ans. (b) Mrs. Pearson gets embarrassed at Mrs. Fitzgerald's suggestion because she knows that it would not help the situation. In fact it would deteriorate it making it useless.

2. Read the extract to attempt the questions that follow.

"**Mrs. Pearson** I might. Who d'you think?

Doris [Staring at her] Mum—what's the matter with you?

Mrs. Pearson Don't be silly.

Doris [Indignantly] It's not me that's being silly— and I must say it's a bit much when I've been working hard all day and you can't even bother to get my tea ready. Did you hear what I said about my yellow silk?

Mrs. Pearson No. Don't you like it now? I never did.

Doris [Indignantly] Of course I like it. And I'm going to wear it tonight. So I want it ironed.

Mrs. Pearson Want it ironed? What d'you think it's going to do—iron itself?"

(i) Identify the tone in which Mrs. Pearson talks.

    (a) Cool and incisive
    (b) Flattering and apologetic
    (c) Brave and strong
    (d) Taunting and angry

Ans. (a) The tone with which Mrs. Pearson (as Mrs. Fitzgerald in her body) talks is cool and incisive.

(ii) Why is Doris consistently reacting 'indignantly' towards her mother Mrs. Pearson?

    (a) The mother is not listening to her
    (b) The mother is angry at her as well
    (c) The mother is acting unusual
    (d) All of the above

Ans. (c) Doris is consistently reacting with anger towards her mother, Mrs. Pearson as she is acting unusual and is not complying to Doris.

(iii) Choose the words that describe Doris's personality, on the basis of the passage.

    I. Spoilt   II. Independent
    III. Bad tempered   IV. Kind

    (a) I and II   (b) I and III   (c) II and IV   (d) II and III

Ans. (b) Doris was a spoiled brat of a child, who expected her mother to do everything for her. She is bad tempered as well, as she gets irritated very easily.

(iv) What does the passage reflect upon the relationship between Doris and Mrs. Pearson?

    (a) Doris only talks to her mother to get her work done
    (b) Doris cherishes her mother and likes to spend time with her
    (c) Doris uses her mother's dresses to look better
    (d) Both (b) and (c)

Ans. (a) Doris is a selfish child, who only talks to her mother to get her work done. She takes her mother for granted and the passage reflects that.

(v) Mrs. Pearson is ………… Doris for getting over dependent on her.

    (a) taunting   (b) scolding   (c) hinting   (d) comical

Ans. (b) Mrs. Pearson (actually Mrs. Fitzgeral(d) wants Doris and other family members to treat Mrs. Pearson with respect. For the same, she scolds and even berates everyone so that they understand how they had taken Annie for granted.

PART 2

Subjective Questions

• Short Answer Type Questions

1. How did Mrs. Fitzgerald utilise her husband's posting in the East?

Ans. Mrs. Fitzgerald's husband was posted in the East (meaning the British colonies in Asia) for twelve years. She utilised her time there by learning fortune-telling and how to use magic spells to exchange personalities. She used this knowledge in temporarily exchanging her strong personality with the weak personality of Mrs. Annie Pearson to help her resolve her problems with her family.

2. What advice did Mrs. Fitzgerald give to Annie?

Ans. Mrs. Fitzgerald was very bold and dominating in nature; she knew how to control the family members. So, Mrs Fitzgerald felt that it was time for Annie to set her family right and teach them a lesson. Mrs. Fitzgerald advised her to put her foot down and be the 'boss' in her family.

3. How was Annie responsible for her own fate?

Ans. To a certain level, Annie was herself responsible for her own fate. She was soft, loving and caring. Unfortunately her children and husband never acknowledged her role and failed to understand her worth. She wanted to correct them but could not do so due to fear of hurting their feelings.

4. What was wrong in Mrs. Annie Pearson's family?

Ans. The members of the Annie's family, George (her husband), Doris and Cyril (her children) were self-centred and took Annie for granted, whereas she took care of all their needs without demanding anything. Annie tolerated their behaviour but she wanted her presence and work to be acknowledged by all family members.

5. "Then let me do it." What did Mrs Fitzgerald want to do?

Ans. Annie got miserable treatment at home. Her family treated her shabbily. But Annie couldn't even raise her voice, let alone teach her family a lesson. Mrs Fitzgerald cared for her friend and wanted her to earn some respect. She suggested that if Annie couldn't handle them then she would teach them a lesson by temporarily changing her behaviour.

6. Who is the first one to face the mother's ire and how?

Ans. Doris, Annie's daughter, is the first one to face her ire (anger). She comes home and asks about her yellow dress. Mrs. Fitzgerald, in the body of Annie, doesn't even pay attention to her. Doris asks her about tea; Mrs. Fitzgerald replies that she should make it herself. She even ridicules her boyfriend and Doris starts crying at her unusual behaviour.

7. Who is Doris? How does Doris treat her mother?

Ans. Doris is Annie's spoilt daughter. She is a pretty girl in her early twenties. She makes her mother run after her all the time. She expects her mother to do all tasks that she asks her to do without questioning her. She thinks nothing of her mother.

8. Who is Cyril? How does he behave with his mother?

Ans. Cyril is the son of Annie. He treats his mother with indifference. He wants that whatever he commands his mother to do must be done with utmost urgency. He lacks any concern for his mother and tries to show that he is a busy man by working eight hours a day.

9. Mention some remarkable changes in Mrs Annie Pearson's behaviour that shocked both Doris and Cyril. What possible reasons for this change were thought of by her children?

Ans. The remarkable changes in Mrs Annie Pearson's behaviour that shocked both her children were

- She was smoking (which she had never done before her family) and playing cards with herself, both unusual.
- She had not carried out any of the work she normally did, like making tea for the family and ironing their clothes.
- The children thought that either she had hit her head so badly that it affected her brain or that she had gone mad.

10. Do you agree that Doris and Cyril's behaviour with their mother was extremely rude and unheard of?

Ans. Yes, Doris and Cyril were extremely rude to their mother. We generally don't see children speaking to their mother in such a rude manner. Their words 'Is tea ready' and 'you are going to iron it for me' are rude and demanding. This shows the children were extremely selfish, badly behaved and self-centred. They ordered their mother as if she was their servant.

11. How does Annie plan to spend her weekends in future?

Ans. Annie informs her children that she would also work for only eight hours a day and take two days off every week on Saturday and Sunday. She said that on these days she would do some work only and that also will depend how she was treated and if they requested her to do the work.

12. Who is George? How does he treat his wife?

Ans. George is Annie's husband. He thinks too much of himself and makes his wife do whatever he commands. That is why he told her that he did not expect her to drink strong beer at that time of the evening and she should follow his instructions to stop drinking it. George has dominated his wife so far, so he did not expect this changed behaviour from her.

13. George was angry that there was no tea even though he didn't want any. What does this reflect about his character?

Ans. George came home and said that he wouldn't be having tea. However, his wife rudely replied that she didn't bother to prepare any in the first place. He got agitated even though he didn't want to drink tea. This shows that he is overbearing and self-centred, besides expecting his wife to behave like his servant.

14. Describe George's attitude towards his wife. How is he taught a lesson by Mrs. Fitzgerald?

Ans. George's male ego suffers a jolt when he comes to know that his wife has not kept tea ready for him. Whether he needs it or not, she should have kept his tea ready like an obedient servant. He is always at the club at night and spends little time with his wife. After exchanging her personality with Annie, Mrs. Fitzgerald, ridicules him saying that he has become a standing joke for the people at the club.

15. What change can be seen in Annie's family in the end?

Ans. After being treated very rudely and roughly by Mrs. Fitzgerald, all the family members respond properly to Mrs. Annie Pearson's smile and decide to stay back and spend time with her. They also responded properly to whatever she says.

16. Mrs. Annie Pearson and Mrs. Fitzgerald are totally opposite to each other in their attitude. Show the difference in their personalities.

Ans. Mrs. Annie Pearson is submissive, soft-spoken and wears a worried look as she is being treated more like a slave than like a mother or wife.

Mrs Fitzgerald is well-versed in many arts, bold and strong in her opinion and knows how to make people behave properly.

Annie doesn't want to hurt people but Mrs Fitzgerald is willing to take any step to discipline people, even if it hurts their feelings.

• Long Answer Type Questions

1. Mother is the axis around which the family revolves. Mother should always be respected. Elaborate.

Ans. A mother has been expected to contribute her whole life caring for her family. A mother is someone who holds a family together, because it is up to her to provide the love, care, attention and support needed. She is a good listener, problem solver and guide, as well as being always available for her children.

Unfortunately, so many times a mother's love is not reciprocated the way it should have been. Some children do not recognise the importance of what their mother is doing for them. They do not take into account the sacrifices she makes so that her children could be reared in the best possible way.

As children grow up they want to be totally independent and consider mother's concern for them an interference, not wanting to be checked at any point of time. Some children are so self-centred that they even insult their mother, which is totally unacceptable. A mother demands respect and at any cost it should be given by her family members in return for what a mother does for them.

2. Today a woman shoulders all the responsibilities at home as well as outside, but she is still exploited. Write your views on the 'Need for Woman Empowerment'.

Ans. Today's woman shoulders all the responsibilities at home as well as outside as she is educated, responsible and can take independent decisions. But still the subject of empowerment of women is a burning issue all over the world, especially India.

Inequality between men and women and discrimination against women have been age old issues. But women are still exploited, as men refuse to accept the rising status of women.

They try to find ways to insult women and degrade them. People still think of women as a means of entertainment and not as an individual who should be respected. Increasing rapes in the country are an indication of men's poor thinking about women.

Laws are there to protect women. But unless men are taught by their mothers to respect the women in their lives, woman empowerment seems a distant dream.

3. The play, 'Mother's Day' is a humorous and satirical depiction of the status of the mother in the family. Express your relationship with your mother.

Ans. The play very humorously and interestingly depicts the status of the mother in a family. Through the character of Mrs. Annie Pearson, the play very subtly depicts the plight of women, especially the housewives.

Playing of magic, exchange of personalities and the shocking behaviour of Mrs. Annie Pearson's family members are all humorous as well as satirical.

My relations with my mother are very healthy and friendly. We are more like friends and enjoy each other's company.

I try to help my mother in the kitchen as well as in other household work. I realise that my mother keeps busy the whole day taking care of everyone's needs. I try to help her as much as I can and really appreciate her selfless efforts without demanding anything. I respect my mother and have much regard for her.

• Extract Based Questions

1. Read the extract to attempt the questions that follow.

"No doubt about it at all. Who's the better for being spoilt— grown man, lad or girl? Nobody. You think it does 'em good when you run after them all the time, take their orders as if you were the servant in the house, stay at home every night while they go out enjoying themselves? Never in all your life. It's the ruin of them as well as you. Husbands, sons, daughters should be taking notice of wives an' mothers, not giving 'em orders an' treating 'em like dirt. An' don't tell me you don't know what I mean, for I know more than you've told me."

(i) Who is speaking these lines and to whom?

(ii) What is the speaker talking about?

(iii) How will you characterise the Pearson family?

(iv) Do you think the speaker is happy with the listener?

(v) What does the speaker want Mrs. Pearson to do?

Ans. (i) Mrs. Fitzgerald is speaking these lines to Mrs. Pearson.

(ii) The speaker is talking about how Mrs. Pearson's family is ill-treating her.

(iii) The Pearson family can be characterised as selfish and uncaring.

(iv) No, I don't think that the speaker, Mrs. Fitzgerald, is happy with Mrs. Pearson, the listener, as she thinks that Mrs. Pearson is the one who is promoting her family's ill-behaviour.

(v) The speaker wants Mrs. Pearson to stop attending to her family's needs and let them know about their behaviour.

2. Read the extract to attempt questions that follow.

"**Mrs. Pearson** [Coolly] Can't remember. But I doubt it.

Cyril [Moving to the table; protesting] Now—look. When I asked you this morning, you promised. You said you'd have to look through 'em first in case there was any mending.

Mrs. Pearson Yes — well now I've decided I don't like mending.

Cyril That's a nice way to talk — what would happen if we all talked like that?

Mrs. Pearson You all do talk like that. If there's something at home you don't want to do, you don't do it. If it's something at your work, you get the Union to bar it. Now all that's happened is that I've joined the movement.

Cyril [staggered] I don't get this, Mum. What's going on?

Mrs. Pearson [laconic and sinister] Changes."

 (i) How does Cyril react to his mother's changed behaviour?

(ii) 'That's nice way to talk'. Explain the way of talking.

(iii) Does Cyril like 'the way of talking'?

(iv) Why do you think is Mrs. Pearson acting so strangely?

 (v) Mrs. Pearson says 'I've joined the movement'. What does this mean?

Ans. (i) Cyril is not at all happy with his mother's changed behaviour as she is not doing anything that he asks her to.

(ii) The way of talking referred to in the extract is cool and uncaring.

(iii) No, Cyril does not like the way her mother is talking as she is coolly refusing to do anything for him.

(iv) Mrs. Pearson is acting so strangely because she is actually Mrs. Fitzgerald in Mrs. Pearson's body and she had taken a task to teach a lesson to the Pearson family.

 (v) The statement by Mrs. Pearson means that she is also going to be as uncaring as her daughter, son and husband.

3. Read the extract to attempt the questions that follow.

"**Mrs. Pearson** [With spirit] It's all right for you, Mrs Fitzgerald. After all, they aren't your husband and children...

Mrs Fitzgerald [impressively] Now you listen to me. You admitted yourself you were spoiling 'em — and they didn't appreciate you. Any apologies—any explanations—an' you'll be straight back where you were. I'm warning you, dear. Just give 'em a look —a tone of voice— now an' again, to suggest you might be tough with 'em if you wanted to be— an' it ought to work. Anyhow, we can test it.

Mrs. Pearson How?

Mrs. Fitzgerald Well, what is it you'd like 'em to do that they don't do? Stop at home for once?

Mrs. Pearson Yes— and give me a hand with supper...

Mrs. Fitzgerald Anything you'd like 'em to do —that you enjoy whether they do or not?"

 (i) Why does Mrs. Fitzgerald ask Mrs. Pearson to not give any explanations?

(ii) What does Mrs. Pearson feel in the given extract?

(iii) How does Mrs. Fitzgerald want Mrs. Pearson to test the change?

(iv) Do you think the Pearson family would do as Mrs. Pearson says?

 (v) "Just give 'em a look —a tone of voice—." Explain.

Ans. (i) Mrs. Fitzgerald asks Mrs. Pearson to not give any explanations as she feel that it would ruin everything that she had done.

(ii) Mrs. Pearson feels sorry for her family in the given extract and does not feel that any change would come upon her family.

(iii) Mrs. Fitzgerald wants Mrs. Pearson to order her children and husband to do what she wants to do.

(iv) Yes, I think that the Pearson family would do as have Mrs. Pearson says because they have been scared by her unusual behaviour and fear what would happen if she continued with it.

 (v) The given phrase has been uttered by Mrs. Fitzgerald wherein she tells Mrs. Pearson to be rough and angry at her family so that they learn to respect her.

CHAPTER 03

Birth

—by AJ Cronin

In this Chapter...

- Chapter Summary
- Word Meaning
- Chapter Practice

Chapter Sketch

Dr Andrew Manson has just begun his medical practice in the small Welsh mining town of Blaenelly. When he returns from a terrible evening with his girlfriend Christine, Joe Morgan approaches Dr Andrew Manson to help in the delivery of his wife.

Dr Andrew Manson has to put in much labour in the delivery, as the mother requires much attention before she is revived. Further, the baby was not breathing at birth. Using all his knowledge and intuition, Dr Andrew Manson makes more efforts to revive the child. After almost half an hour of frantic efforts, he succeeds and comes away with a sense of achievement.

Chapter Summary

Joe Morgan was Waiting for Dr Andrew

Dr Andrew had recently graduated from medical college. He was practising as an assistant to Dr Edward Page in a small Welsh mining town named Blaenelly. One night he was returning home when he found Joe Morgan waiting for him outside the clinic. He had been there for more than an hour and now was relaxed to see the doctor. He informed that the doctor was needed at their home as his wife was expecting to deliver the a baby.

He was worried for both his wife and child as it was their first child after 20 years of marriage. Hearing Joe, Dr. Andrew who was in his own thoughts, got his bag and went to number 12 Blaina Terrace (Joe's House).

A Tough Case of Mrs. Morgan

On their journey, Andrew felt tired. He had no idea how important this case would be for his career. When they reached their destination, Joe stopped outside the house and requested Dr Andrew to go inside alone. Through a narrow staircase the doctor reached a small and clean but a scantily furnished room. He found two women beside the patient, Susan Morgan's mother, a tall, grey-haired woman of nearly seventy, and an elderly midwife.

Susan's mother offered Dr. Andrew a cup of tea. Upon realising that she felt that he would leave due to the waiting period. Dr Andrew told her to relax. He knew that if he went home he wouldn't be able to relax. So he decided to stay there. After an hour, he checked on his patient and came down. There was absolute silence except for the sound of Joe's hurried footsteps. He could sense the worry of Joe and Susan's mother.

Andrew's Dilemma

While he waited by the Kitchen fire, Dr. Andrew went into his thoughts. He was faced with a dilemma of marriage with his lover, Christine. He loved Christine but at the same time remembered the lives of other married males around him. He remembered Bramwell and Dr. Edward Page, whose marriages are dismal failures. The dilemma of his emotions for Christine and his rational mind made him resentful. He was confused and his thoughts were only filled with Christine.

Hope for the Child

Dr Andrew was so deep in his thoughts that the voice of Susan's mother surprised him. She informed him that her daughter didn't want him to give her chloroform if it would harm the baby. Dr Andrew replied that it would do no harm. Just then he heard the midwife's voice. It was half-past three and according to him, it was time for him to start working on the delivery.

The Delivery

After a harsh struggle of an hour, a lifeless boy was born. This terrified Dr. Andrew who had promised to keep the baby healthy. However, he was in a tough situation. He was divided in trying to resuscitate the baby and his obligation to help Susan who was in a desperate state. He was so hurried in the situation that he gave the baby to the nurse and focused on helping Susan. Susan was losing strength as well as her pulse.

Dr. Andrew hurriedly gave the injection to the mother (Susan). When he felt that Susan was safe, he moved to tend to the child. The nurse had hidden the child under the bed. Dr. Andrew pulled out the child who he diagnosed with asphyxia, pallida (lack of oxygen).

Dr Andrew's Efforts to Save the Child

Dr Andrew recalled a case he had once seen in the Samaritan (a medical journal) and the treatment that was given. He asked the midwife to quickly get hot water and cold water along with two bowls. Then he mixed hot and cold water in the bowls and started as special method of respiration.

Then, he started plunging the child once into the icy water and then into the steaming bath alternately. Fifteen minutes passed and nothing happened.

Dr. Andrew was filled with hopelessness. However, he remembered Susan's longing for the child. He could also feel the dejection of Susan's mother. So, he decided to give one more try. The midwife who has been seeing Dr. Andrew tried to stop him. But, he paid no attention to her.

The Miracle

Dr. Andrew started rubbing the child's chest with a rough towel trying to get breath into the limp body. Then, as if by a miracle, the child slowly started breathing. The sight made Dr. Andrew redouble his efforts. Soon, the child gave a cry.

The Happy News

After the child came alive, Dr. Andrew felt tired. He saw the mess in the room and Susan's mother praying. So, he addressed the nurse and told her that he was leaving and would get his bag later.

He went downstairs, drank water and left the house. At the gate, he gave Joe the happy news and moved ahead. It was morning then and people were going for their morning shifts. Andrew was unaware of his surrounding when he realised that he had first successful case that would change his future.

Word Meanings

The given page numbers correspond to the pages in the prescribed NCERT textbook.

Word	Meaning
Page 65	
mining town	a town where most people work in a coal mine
surgery	operating room
burly	large and strong
driller	a miner who uses a drill machine
missus	wife (informal)
ye	you
before time	the delivery is going to be before the due date
contemplation of	thinking about
perceptive	energetic
premonition	idea
drew up short	stopped
strain	tiredness
Page 66	
stout	strongtly built
midwife	woman trained to help in childbirth
bach	dear
leave the case	not stay till the delivery was completed
overwrought	very tired
snatch	take
lethargy of spirit	lack of enthusiasm
cinder	partly burnt piece of coal
grate	fireplace
muddled	mixed up
obsessed him	dominated his thinking
sordidly	unpleasantly
level, doubting	reasonably doubtful
overflowing	full of emotions
broodingly	worryingly
pursued a different course	followed a different line of thought
Page 67	
awful set upon	very much wanting
ay	yes
fancy	believe
top landing	top of the stairs
elapsed	passed
streaks of dawn	light of morning
strayed past	came through

Word	Meaning
blind	sunshade
still form	lifeless body
torn between	feeling two opposing thoughts
resuscitate	bring back to life
desperate	critical
dilemma	difficulty
instinctively	without thinking
pulseless	not having the pulse of life
not yet out of the ether	not become conscious
ebbing	receding
glass ampoule	sealed glass capsule with liquid medicine
hypodermic syringe	needle used to inject liquid medicine in the bloodstream
unsparingly	without a break
strengthened	started beating properly
in his shirt sleeves	in only his shirt without a jacket over it
brow	forehead
frightened gesture	indication with fear
fishing	searching
sodden	soaked
tallow	animal fat
cord	umbilical cord connecting the mother to the child in her womb
of a lovely texture	with a wonderful feel
lolled	hung loosely

Page 68

Word	Meaning
haggard frown	worried and tried look
asphyxia pallida	an abnormal medical condition in a newly born baby who appears pale and limp, temporarily unable to breathe and having a slow heart action

Word	Meaning
threw out	spoke quickly
basins	large bowls
pallid	pale
ewer	a large jug with a wide mouth
crazy juggler	madman moving the child quickly
raging hopelessness	fierce disappointment
consternation	feeling of anxiety
dashed away	finished
draggled	dirty and wet
sopping	drenched
stillborn	born dead
limp	motionless

Page 69

Word	Meaning
by a miracle	mysteriously
pigmy	small
convulsive	jerky
heave	gasp
turned giddy	became weak
unavailing	ineffective
mucus	viscous liquid
iridescent	sparkling
spinelessly	loosely
blanched	pale
shuddering litter	total mess
soiled	dirty
impaled	stuck
scullery	room for washing dishes
thickly	in a hard to understand tone
footfalls	sounds made by feet while walking

Chapter Practice

Objective Questions

• Multiple Choice Questions

1. Why is the chapter titled 'Birth'?
   (a) Because the doctor is specialist in childbirths.
   (b) Because a lot of childbirths take place.
   (c) Because it is about birth of a child.
   (d) Because it talks about philosophy of life.

Ans. (c) The chapter is titled 'Birth' as it is about the significance of the birth of a child.

2. Joe refuses to enter the house. Why?
   (a) Because he was superstitious.
   (b) Because he didn't want to disturb.
   (c) Because he didn't want to see the child.
   (d) Because he was anxious.

Ans. (d) Joe Morgan was feeling very anxious and thus, did not enter the house.

3. Choose the option that lists the words used by the author to describe Mrs. Morgan's mother.
   I. Unintelligent
   II. Grey-haired
   III. A woman in early-seventies
   (a) I and II
   (b) II and III
   (c) I and III
   (d) All of these

Ans. (b) The author describes Mrs. Morgan's mother as a wise, grey-haired woman in her early seventies.

4. Select the statement(s) that is/are correct on the basis of your reading of 'Birth.'
   (i) Dr. Andrews did not really want to marry Christine.
   (ii) Dr. Andrews was sure he wanted to spend his life with Christine.
   (a) Both (i) and (ii) are correct
   (b) Both (i) and (ii) are incorrect
   (c) (i) is correct but (ii) is incorrect
   (d) (i) is incorrect but (ii) is correct

Ans. (b) Dr. Andrews did want to live a life with his lover Christine but was in the dilemma due to the failed marriage of men around him.

5. Choose the word(s) that suit the condition of the new born baby.
   I. Lifeless
   II. Healthy
   III. Underweight
   IV. Anemic
   (a) Only I
   (b) Only II
   (c) Only III
   (d) III and IV

Ans. (a) The child was born lifeless and was described by the author in the same manner as it was born.

6. What dilemma did Dr. Andrew face?
   (a) Whether the child could be saved or not.
   (b) Whether the treatment would be successful.
   (c) Whether to attend to the child or the mother.
   (d) Whether to inform Joe or not.

Ans. (c) The dilemma was that Dr. Andrew had to decide whether to attend to the child or the mother.

7. The midwife had placed the child under the bed. Select the option that explains it.
   (a) She did not want to break the hopes of the Morgan family.
   (b) She didn't believe that the doctor could save the child.
   (c) She had not expected that the child will die.
   (d) She could not bear the sight of a dead child.

Ans. (b)

8. What did Andrew conclude from the whiteness of the child?
   (a) That he was dead.
   (b) That he suffered from a lack of oxygen.
   (c) That he should be taken to hospital.
   (d) That Andrew couldn't save him.

Ans. (b) Andrew concluded that the child suffered from a lack of oxygen from the whiteness.

9. Choose the method(s) that Andrew applied to save the still born baby.
   I. He used a special method of respiration.
   II. He called Dr. Edward Page.
   III. He took the child to a hospital.
   IV. He proceeded to offer him his blood.
   (a) Only I
   (b) Only II
   (c) Only III
   (d) I and III

Ans. (a) Andrew proceeded to apply a special method of respiration to save the child.

10. Why did the doctor continue his efforts despite the baby not resuscitating?
(a) Fear of failure of his career
(b) Fear of dashing Morgan family's hopes
(c) Fear of reactions of the Morgan family
(d) Fear of the society

Ans. (b) The author feared breaking the hopes and promises made to the Morgan family and so he continued his efforts.

11. Choose the statement(s) that apply to the chapter.
   I. It took Andrew forty-five minutes to yield results.
   II. Eventually, Andrew gave up on the lifeless child.
   III. Andrew proceeded to change the course of mid-wife's behaviour.
(a) Only I
(b) Only II
(c) Only III
(d) None of these

Ans. (d) It took Andrew half an hour to yield the results, which ended in Andrew saving the life of the stillborn. At no point does Andrew attempt to change the course of mid-wife's behaviour.

12. What does the author refer to as 'a miracle'?
(a) Life getting into the stillborn
(b) Morgan family welcoming a child
(c) Susan getting consciousness
(d) None of the above

Ans. (a) The miracle refers to the act of life getting into the stillborn child of the Morgans.

13. Why did Andrew get oblivious to all the work he had done in Blaenelly?
(a) Because he got all hopeless.
(b) Because he did something extraordinary that night.
(c) Because he was leaving Blaenelly.
(d) Because he got tired.

Ans. (b) Andrew got oblivious to all the work he had done in Blaenelly because he did something truly extraordinary that night.

14. In the end, Dr. Andrew exclaims, "I've done something; oh, God! I've done something real at last." Explain.
(a) He felt happy finishing the task that took forever.
(b) He felt like he truly accomplished something.
(c) He felt anxious at the fame which was to follow his actions.
(d) He felt sad at finishing a task.

Ans. (b) He realised that he had truly saved a life that night, fulfilling the purpose of his profession. For the first time Dr. Andrew felt that he had done something 'real', something worthwhile.

15. What can you say about Dr. Andrew after reading 'Birth'?
(a) He did not put all his efforts.
(b) He fulfilled his obligations well as a doctor.
(c) His skills were not enough.
(d) He was arrogant.

Ans. (b) One can see that Dr. Andrew truly fulfilled his obligations well as a doctor after the reading of this chapter.

• Extract Based MCQs

1. Read the extract given below and answer the questions that follow.

"THOUGH it was nearly midnight when Andrew reached Bryngower, he found Joe Morgan waiting for him, walking up and down with short steps between the closed surgery and the entrance to the house. At the sight of him the burly driller's face expressed relief. "Eh, Doctor, I'm glad to see you. I been back and forward here this last hour. The missus wants ye—before time, too."

Andrew, abruptly recalled from the contemplation of his own affairs, told Morgan to wait. He went into the house for his bag, then together they set out for Number 12 Blaina Terrace. The night air was cool and deep with quiet mystery. Usually so perceptive, Andrew now felt dull and listless. He had no premonition that this night call would prove unusual, still less that it would influence his whole future in Blaenelly."

(i) Explain: "The missus wants ye—before time, too."
(a) The pregnant lady went into labour before expected.
(b) The pregnant lady was awfully scared.
(c) The pregnant lady wanted assistance before labour as well.
(d) It is unclear from the passage.

Ans. (c) The pregnant lady, Mrs. Susan Morgan, demanded for Dr. Andrew to be present even before her labour began for more support and asked her husband, Joe Morgan to fetch him before time.

(ii) What does the expression "walking up and down with short steps" signify about Joe Morgan's feelings?
(a) He was stressed out
(b) He was more calm
(c) He was impatient
(d) He was angry

Ans. (a) The expression of walking up and down with short steps points that Joe Morgan was stressed out and anxious as he waited for Dr. Andrew to appear.

(iii) Despite feeling dull, Dr. Andrew decides to take the case. What does this highlight about him?
(a) He is dedicated
(b) He is underwhelmed
(c) He is patient
(d) He is boring

Ans. (a) Showing his motivation towards his case, he takes the case despite feeling dull. This shows that he is truly dedicated towards his work.

(iv) Identify the literary device used in the last line of the passage.
(a) Metaphor
(b) Personification
(c) Foreshadowing
(d) Simile

Ans. (c) 'Foreshadowing' is a literary device which predicts the event to occur in the story ahead. In the last line, the writer is focusing on the importance this case would bring to him and foreshadows this in the beginning of the chapter.

(v) The contemplation referred to in the extract refers to
(a) Thoughts about his career
(b) Thoughts about a medical case
(c) Thoughts about his lover, Christine
(d) Thoughts about marriage

Ans. (c) Dr. Andrews throughout the lesson worries about his lover, Christine.

2. Read the extract given below and answer the questions that follow.

Inside, a narrow stair led up to a small bedroom, clean but poorly furnished and lit only by an oil lamp. Here Mrs Morgan's mother, a tall, grey-haired woman of nearly seventy and the stout, elderly midwife waited beside the patient, watching Andrew's expression as he moved about the room.

"Let me make you a cup of tea, Doctor, bach," said the former quickly, after a few moments. Andrew smiled faintly. He saw that the old woman, wise in experience, realised there must be a period of waiting that, she was afraid he would leave the case, saying he would return later.'

"Don't fret, mother, I'll not run away."

(i) Choose the statement(s) that elaborate the description of the room.
  I. The room is very bright and welcoming.
  II. The room has dim lighting and a faint feeling.
  III. The room is highly hygienic.
  IV. The room is huge with poor furniture in it.
  (a) I and II   (b) I and III
  (c) Only II   (d) III and IV

Ans. (c) The room can be described as one with dim lighting and a faint feeling.

(ii) Why does Dr. Andrew focus on the room more than the pregnant Mrs. Susan Morgan?
  (a) Because he is quickly assured that she does not need attention right away.
  (b) Because he does not want to interrupt the midwife.
  (c) Because the room is grand and beautiful to captivate him.
  (d) Because he is bored and finds the details in the room more interesting.

Ans. (a) Dr. Andrew figures as soon as he read the expressions of the two women that Mrs. Susan Morgan does not need his assistance immediately and thus, his focus shifts to other things in the room.

(iii) What are the old woman's fears in the passage?
  (a) That her daughter would not be healthy.
  (b) That her grandchild would die.
  (c) That the doctor was not interested in the case.
  (d) That the doctor would leave.

Ans. (d) The doctor's movement points that he might just leave the case and go and this scares the old woman who looks at him, demanding assurance.

(iv) What is the meaning of 'bach' in this context?
  (a) Baby   (b) Child
  (c) Dear   (d) Love

Ans. (c) Bach is a Welsh term for Dear, which is said after the name of a person to show care.

(v) "Don't fret, mother, I'll not run away." Why did Andrew say this?
  (a) To reassure Mrs. Morgan's mother
  (b) To fulfill his obligations
  (c) To break the silence
  (d) To handle a critical situation well

Ans. (a) Andrew said to reassure Mrs. Morgan's mother.

PART 2
Subjective Questions

• Short Answer Type Questions

1. Who was Dr Andrew ? Where was he working?

Ans. Dr Andrew was a young graduate who had just passed from medical school.

He was working as an assistant to Dr Edward in the small Welsh mining town of Blaenelly.

2. Who was Joe Morgan? Why was he waiting for the doctor when he returned at midnight?

Ans. Joe Morgan was a miner working as a driller.

He was waiting for the doctor because his pregnant wife needed medical attention. He was worried for her as she was going to deliver her first child after 20 years of marriage.

3. Did the doctor accompany Joe Morgan? How do you assess the doctor here?

Ans. Yes, the doctor, without any complaint, accompanied Joe Morgan, though he was physically and mentally very tired due to his unhappy love life.

The doctor was thoroughly professional. For him duty came first and no personal problem could come in the way of attending his duty.

4. Dr Andrew had no idea that this particular night would influence his future career in Blaenelly. How did it do so?

Ans. When Dr Andrew accompanied Joe Morgan at midnight, he had no idea that this particular night was going to affect his whole future career. The doctor did his best to save Susan Morgan and revived the child. This was his first successful case and thus, a huge contribution to his medical career.

5. Who was the old lady? Why was she afraid?

Ans. The old lady was Susan Morgan's mother, a tall, grey-haired woman of nearly seventy. She was wise in experience. She realised that there must be a period of waiting before the delivery. She was afraid that the doctor might leave the case saying he would return later.

6. Dr Andrew was good enough to wait at Joe Morgan's house till everything was over. Why did he decide this?

Ans. Dr Andrew had reached Joe Morgan's home at midnight. He was distressed and upset. He knew that if he went back home, he would not be able to sleep even for an hour though he needed much rest and sleep. Moreover, as the case was complicated and needed all his attention, he decided to remain there until everything was over.

7. Why was Dr Andrew in a conflicting state of mind?

Ans. Dr Andrew loved his girlfriend Christine and thought of leading a peaceful life with her by marrying her. But he had been thinking of many unsuccessful marriages. People like Bramwell, Edward or Denny were all living unhappily due to problems in their marriages. So he was in a very conflicting state of mind.

8. Why did Dr. Andrew shiver with horror?

Ans. Dr. Andrew shivered with horror because, after a long harsh struggle, the child that was born was lifeless. He remembered the promise to keep the child and the mother safe, but the situation was not in his favour.

9. Why was Dr Andrew in a state of conflict when the child was born?

Ans. Dr Andrew was in a state of conflict as he was torn between two desires. The dilemma before him was whether to save the mother first or her child. The dilemma was so urgent that he couldn't solve it consciously.

10. What did the elderly midwife think of the young doctor in the beginning?

Ans. The midwife remained doubtful about the young doctor's abilities and pessimistic about the child's survival. Her act of keeping the child under the bed shows that she never believed that the doctor would be able to revive the child at any stage.

11. Why did Dr Andrew want to save the child?

Ans. The child looked lifeless when born. Dr Andrew realised, due to his medical knowledge, that the child suffered from an abnormal medical condition which made it look dead, but there was a chance of it being revived. So he made frantic efforts to save the child.

12. What efforts did Dr Andrew make to save the lifeless-looking boy at birth?

Ans. When Dr Andrew saw the lifeless-looking boy, he realised that the boy's whiteness meant that he was suffering from *asphyxia pallida*, which required a particular method of revival. So, he began a special method of respiration. So, he plunged the child into a basin of icy water followed by plunging him into very hot water repeatedly. Then, in one last desperate effort, he rubbed the boy, crushing and releasing his chest, trying to get breath into his limp body. Suddenly the child's chest started going up and down, some mucus came out of its nose and finally the boy gave a cry.

13. What was the condition of the room after Dr Andrew had saved both the mother and the child?

Ans. The room was in a mess full of soiled newspapers, towels, blankets and soiled instruments. The floor was full of mud and water, as the doctor had used two basins full of water. The hypodermic syringe was stuck in the linoleum on the floor, the jug was knocked over and the kettle was on its side. On the huddled bed, the mother was lying unconscious.

14. How did Dr Andrew feel after saving the lives of Susan Morgan and her child? What was Dr Andrew's reaction and why did he say so?

Ans. Dr Andrew made frantic efforts to save both the mother and her baby. It is really a very tough job to concentrate on anyone because he had to focus on both the lives. So, when he got success in it, he uttered, "I have done something; oh God! I've done something real at last." He thanked God and felt a sense of relief. He was satisfied that as a doctor he did something strong and consequential.

15. Describe the case that called all of Dr. Andrew's attention.

Ans. The case that called all of Dr. Andrew's attention is of the Morgan family. Joe and Susan Morgan are expecting their first child after 20 years of marriage. Consequently, the case was complicated. When the child was born, it was lifeless and the health of the mother was also bad. Dr. Andrew had to make a choice and save both their lives.

16. "Sometimes instincts play a vital role along with bookish knowledge." Comment in reference to 'Birth'.

Ans. Yes, it is true that sometimes instincts play a vital role over bookish knowledge. In the chapter, 'Birth', Dr. Andrew, a medical graduate, uses his instincts to get over the dilemma of saving the life of the mother or the child. Instincts help him resuscitate the child as well as save the life of his mother.

• Long Answer Type Questions

1. "For doctors, the duty towards the patients is foremost, irrespective of their own personal affairs." Discuss with reference to the excerpt, 'Birth'.

Ans. There is a saying that after God, it is the doctor only who can save the life of someone. A patient comes to a doctor with the hope that he would cure his illness. But we should not forget that a doctor himself is a human being. Troubles and miseries are part of his life also. He can also feel distressed and depressed. In spite of all these, a doctor has to give his duty the topmost priority.

We saw in the chapter how Dr Andrew made frantic efforts to save the lives of Mrs Susan Morgan and her child. Dr Andrew also used his intuition and medical knowledge to save the lifeless child when there was no hope.

Though he was really upset before coming to Joe Morgan's house, Dr Andrew stayed there, as the case demanded all his attention. He could barely see his own future but was diligent enough to realise his call of duty. Hence, we can say that even though being preoccupied with his own personal affairs, he did not forget his duty and made sincere attempts to succeed.

2. No matter what your profession is, moral values always play an important role in making you a complete human being. Explain with reference to the chapter 'Birth'.

Ans. One of the most challenging and complex of life's areas is the realm of moral issues and decisions. Every day of our life, in whatever profession we may be, we make moral choices and decisions that reflect our own moral orientation.

In the chapter 'Birth', Dr Andrew considered it his moral duty to attend to a patient inspite of his mental agony and tiredness. He spent the whole night in saving two lives. He used all his knowledge as well as instincts to revive the child and finally succeeded in making the family happy. In the end he emerged as a distinct human being who went all out to save precious lives not out of greed but because he considered it his moral duty to do his best. His efforts were applauded and he himself indulged in self-appraisal 'on doing something' really good. His moral values helped him in achieving this feat.

3. "I have done something; oh, God! I've done something real at last." Why does Andrew say this? What does it mean? **[NCERT]**

Ans. Dr Andrew utters these words after he was able to bring an almost stillborn child back to life, although it seemed impossible in the beginning. The child was born to Susan Morgan with a peculiar breathing problem called *asphyxia pallida* in medical terminology. After feverish efforts to revive the child with the known treatment for this condition, he brought the child to life.

He spoke these words out of a deep satisfaction on achieving the seemingly impossible task. He had been able to apply his medical knowledge and skill to revive a newborn child, which was a great achievement for him. He felt that God had used him as a medium to grant life to the child and Andrew acknowledged this with his words.

And also helped his career by successfully attempting his first case ever.

4. There lies a great difference between textbook medicine and the world of a practising physician. Discuss. **[NCERT]**

Ans. For a long time, we have been hearing that there is a lot of difference between theory and practice. This is true. Theoretical information gathered from books does not provide solutions to all problems. The medical textbook provides information about the treatment of various diseases but at times, doctors face a dilemma which cannot be solved by any theory.

In this chapter, Dr Andrew undergoes the same experience. When the mother and son both needed his attention, he had to make a decision about who to take care of first. In this decision-making, no medical textbook could have helped him. In this case, Dr Andrew acted instinctively. He first saved the mother and then the child. He treated the mother with the traditional treatment and the child with a mixture of traditional and intuitive treatment. The net result was that both survived and his efforts were successful.

If Dr Andrew would have gone by the textbook, he might have not been able to save the mother as well as the child. According to the textbook, the child was born lifeless.

But Dr Andrew was successful in reviving it. Hence, we see that there lies a great difference between textbook medicine and the world of a practising physician.

• Extract Based Questions

1. Read the extract given below and answer the questions that follow.

"It was a conclusion which, in his present state, made him wince. He wished to consider marriage as an idyllic state; yes, he could not otherwise consider it with the image of Christine before him. Her eyes, shining towards him, admitted no other conclusion. It was the conflict between his level, doubting mind and his overflowing heart which left him resentful and confused. He let his chin sink upon his chest, stretched out his legs, stared broodingly into the fire. He remained like this so long, and his thoughts were so filled with Christine, that he started when the old woman opposite suddenly addressed him. Her meditation had pursued a different course."

(i) What does the author think about marriage?

(ii) Do you think the author's wants to marry?

(iii) How does the author's thought impact him?

(iv) How will you connote the dilemma faced by the author?

(v) "Her meditation had pursued a different course." Explain.

Ans. (i) The author does not believe in marriages as the men around him didn't have very successful marriages.

(ii) I feel that the author does want to marry his lover, Christine, but is dissuaded by the failure of marriage around him.

(iii) The author's thoughts fill him with a dilemma because of which he is confused and resentful.

(iv) The dilemma faced by the author was between his heart and emotions that wanted to marry Christine and his brain which saw the failed marriages around him.

(v) The given line means that the old lady (Susan Morgan's Mother) was worried about her daughter and her child's safety which was much different from what the author had been thinking.

2. Read the extract given below and answer the questions that follow.

"The dilemma was so urgent he did not solve it consciously. Blindly, instinctively, he gave the child to the nurse and turned his attention to Susan Morgan who now lay collapsed, almost pulseless, and not yet out of the ether, upon her side. His haste was desperate, a frantic race against her ebbing strength. It took him only an instant to smash a glass ampule and inject the medicine. Then he flung down the hypodermic syringe and worked unsparingly to restore the flaccid woman. After a few minutes of feverish effort, her heart strengthened; he saw that he might safely leave her. He swung round, in his shirt sleeves, his hair sticking to his damp brow."

  (i) What dilemma is referred to in the extract?

  (ii) What did the nurse do with the child?

  (iii) "He swung round, in his shirt sleeves, his hair sticking to his damp brow." Explain.

  (iv) How was the doctor's dilemma solved?

  (v) What is the significance of the given lines?

Ans. (i) The dilemma referred to in the extract is the confusion between trying to resuscitate the lifeless child and the helping the mother whose health was deteriorating.

  (ii) The nurse put the child beneath the bed in the middle of some newspapers.

  (iii) The given line explains the condition of the author after he had saved the life of Susan Morgan who had just given birth.

  (iv) The doctor's dilemma was solved instinctively. He handed the child to the nurse and turned his attention to the mother who lay faint.

  (v) The given lines are significant as they show how practical knowledge wins over theoretical or bookish knowledge.

3. Read the extract given below and answer the questions that follow.

"A desperate sense of defeat pressed on him, a raging hopelessness. He felt the midwife watching him in stark consternation, while there, pressed back against the wall where she had all the time remained — her hand pressed to her throat, uttering no sound, her eyes burning upon him —was the old woman. He remembered her longing for a grandchild, as great as had been her daughter's longing for this child.

All dashed away now; futile, beyond remedy… The floor was now a draggled mess. Stumbling over a sopping towel, Andrew almost dropped the child, which was now wet and slippery in his hands, like a strange, white fish. "For mercy's sake, Doctor," whimpered the midwife. "It's stillborn." Andrew did not heed her. Beaten, despairing, having laboured in vain for half an hour, he still persisted in one last effort, rubbing the child with a rough towel, crushing and releasing the little chest with both his hands, trying to get breath into that limp body."

  (i) Why was there a raging helplessness in the situations?

  (ii) What was the midwife's reaction?

  (iii) Why were the old woman's eyes burning upon the author?

  (iv) Why did the doctor not heed to the nurse's comment?

  (v) Did the doctor's efforts become successful?

Ans. (i) There was a raging helplessness in the situation because the doctor's efforts were not yielding any result.

  (ii) The midwife was looking at the doctor and his efforts in fear.

  (iii) The old woman's eyes were burning upon the doctor because she wanted the doctor's efforts to be successful for she was also hoping for her grandchild.

  (iv) The doctor did not heed to the nurse's comment because he wanted to give his every effort to save the child and the hopes of the Morgan Family.

  (v) Yes, the doctor's efforts became successful as the child started breathing soon.

Section Test (Literature)

Prose

Objective Questions

1 In the chapter 'The Ailing Planet' what does the three-year study conducted by the United Nations state?
   (a) Environment has deteriorated that it is critical in eighty-eight countries.
   (b) Forests are being cut down at an alarming rate.
   (c) There is not much of drinking water left.
   (d) Fossil fuels are getting extinct at a fast rate.

2 In the chapter 'The Ailing Planet' what is the transcending concern?
   (a) The survival of the planet
   (b) The survival of forests
   (c) Global warming
   (d) To save water

3 What does Mrs. Crocker - Harris ask Taplow to do?
   (a) To leave
   (b) To get the prescription made
   (c) To read his book
   (d) Both (a) and (b)

4 In the chapter 'Silk Road' why was the protagonist facing communication problems in Darchen?
   (a) As he never wanted to talk to locals.
   (b) As he was always busy in his meditation.
   (c) As no one knew English.
   (d) None of the above

5 Why did Norbu want to do Kora?
   (a) Because he wanted to become a monk.
   (b) Because he wanted peace.
   (c) As he was practising meditation from so long.
   (d) Because he was writing an academic paper on Kailash Kora.

Extract Based Questions

FRANK: And your considered view is that the Agamemnon is muck?

TAPLOW: Well, no, sir. I don't think the play is muck — exactly. I suppose, in a way, it's rather a good plot, really, a wife murdering her husband and all that. I only meant the way it's taught to us — just a lot of Greek words strung together and fifty lines if you get them wrong.

FRANK: You sound a little bitter, Taplow.

TAPLOW: I am rather, sir.

FRANK: Kept in, eh?

TAPLOW: No, sir. Extra work.

FRANK: Extra work — on the last day of school?

(i) What does the given passage tell us about Crocker Harris?

(ii) Do you think Taplow dislikes his teacher?

(iii) Why is Taplow kept in for extra work?

(iv) Why do you Frank is surprised when he gets to know that Taplow had come for extra work?

(v) What does Taplow really think about Agamemnon?

Short Answer Type Questions

1 Why and how is Earth considered as a living organism?

2 Why are the millions of living species still unnamed not yet catalogued?

3 When Mr. Frank says "there's one comfort", what does he mean?

4 Do you think Mr Crocker-Harris was too strict in assigning extra work after school hours and not being available at the time he promised. Why?

5 How does the author describe the atmosphere and sky when they were leaving Ravu?

6 How did Tsetan know when they were approaching a herd of wild asses?

Long Answer Type Questions

1 In some places, firewood has become more expensive than food Who do you think is responsible for this situation? How can you contribute in controlling the situation?

2 "It is just not only the survival of the people which is at stake but also of the planet." Explain with suitable examples.

3 Do you feel that the forecast of life for future generations is not looking good? What is the current ecological scenario?

4 Mr Frank encourages a discussion with Taplow about a colleague. Is it a violation of professional ethics? Give reasons.

5 What do you learn about the system of education and values followed by British schools of that time from the chapter 'The Browning Version'?

6 Describe how the environment near Lake Manasarovar and at Darchen has been neglected by the authorities. Suggest three steps they should have taken to ensure that it did not deteriorate.

Poetry

Objective Questions

1 In the poem 'The Voice of The Rain' why does the poet compare the rain with a song?
   (a) Because she beautifies the Earth
   (b) Because she provides life on Earth
   (c) As they both share a common journey
   (d) None of the above

2 In which of the following phrases has the literary device hyperbole being used?
(a) Bottomless sea
(b) I am the poem of Earth
(c) Soft-falling shower
(d) Voice of the rain

3 What did the poet conclude about his lost childhood at the end of the poem?
(a) It went to another dimension.
(b) It moved away with time.
(c) It went to some forgotten place.
(d) It shifted to his younger sibling.

4 Which poetic device has been used in the following line-
Was it when I found my mind was really mine.
(a) Alliteration
(b) Simile
(c) Metaphor
(d) Personification

5 In his attempt to find his childhood, the poet seems __________
(a) Desperate
(b) Frantic
(c) Disdain
(d) Both a and b

Extract Based Questions

And who art thou? said I to the soft-falling shower,
Which, strange to tell, gave me an answer, as here translated:
I am the Poem of Earth, said the voice of the rain,
Eternal I rise impalpable out of the land and the bottomless sea,
Upward to heaven, whence, vaguely form'd, altogether changed, and yet the same,

(i) Why was it strange for the poem?

(ii) Does the soft falling shower really reply to the poet?

(iii) Why do you think that the rain calls itself the 'Poem of Earth'?

(iv) Explain 'vaguely form'd, altogether changed, and yet the same'.

(v) The rain says that its rises eternally. Comment.

Short Answer Type Questions

1 Is it normal that a conversation can take place between a human being and the rain? Why/ Why not?

2 How does rain give life to its origin?

3 In the poem 'Childhood' why does the poet think that he had lost his childhood?

4 Why does the poet mention Hell and Heaven in the poem 'Childhood'?

5 How are adults different from children according to poet in the poem'Childhood'?

Long Answer Type Questions

1 Why does the poet call rain "Eternal."? How is the eternal nature of rain useful for mankind?

2 Rain has been described as giving life to Earth. Discuss the importance of rain in the context of the poem 'The Voice of the Rain'.

3 Discuss your experience of reaching the stage of adulthood from childhood. When did you realise that you are growing towards adulthood?

4 Today's materialistic society is responsible for loss of innocence and childhood. Comment.

Supplementary

Objective Questions

1 How much did the doctor charge from Albert?
(a) Asked Albert to invite him for a meal.
(b) Asked Albert to invite Yuri for a meal.
(c) High amount
(d) His normal consultation fees

2 For how long was Albert supposed to stay away from school as per the certificate?
(a) One month
(b) Two months
(c) Six months
(d) One year

3 Mrs. Pearson is characterised in the play as .... personality.
(a) Ignorant and Dominating
(b) Compliant
(c) Considerate
(d) Both (b) and (c)

4 Which of the following is the correct message of the play 'Mother's Day'?
(a) To give respect to every family member.
(b) To appreciate wives/ mothers for their work.
(c) To maintain healthy relationships is important.
(d) To give equal importance to each family member.

5 Why did Andrew get oblivious to all the work he had done in Blaenelly?
(a) Because he got all hopeless.
(b) Because he did something extraordinary that night.
(c) Because he was leaving Blaenelly.
(d) Because he got tired.

Extract Based Question

MRS PEARSON: Going up to the bar and telling 'em you don't want a glass of beer but you're annoyed because they haven't already poured it out. Try that on them and see what you get.

GEORGE: I don't know what you're talking about.

MRS PEARSON: They'd laugh at you even more than they do now.

GEORGE: [indignantly] Laugh at me? They don't laugh at me.

MRS PEARSON: Of course they do. You ought to have found that out by this time. Anybody else would have done. You're one of their standing jokes. Famous. They call you Pompy-ompy Pearson because they think you're so slow and pompous.

GEORGE: [horrified] Never!

(i) Why is Mrs. Pearson behave in this manner with her husband?

(ii) Do you think that the name given to George suits him?

(iii) Do you feel that the revelation would change George? How?

(iv) How would you translate George reaction to the revelation?

(v) What complaint does Mrs. Pearson have of George?

Short Answer Type Questions

1 Comment on Einstein's 'Unthinking Honesty' while replying to the history teacher.

2 Do you think Einstein's father would have been happy to see Einstein leaving the school without a serious reason?

3 What was the problem of Mrs Annie Pearson as found out by Mrs Fitzgerald?

4 How does Mrs Fitzgerald plan to deal with the family of Mrs Annie Pearson?

5 Describe the case that called all of Dr Andrew's attention.

6 Why did Joe Morgan prefer to stay outside his house?

Long Answer Type Questions

1 "A friend in need is a friend indeed." What impression do you form of Yuri in the light of this statement?

2 Compare and contrast the opinions of the maths and history teachers about Einstein to bring out the different values that they displayed.

3 Do you think Mrs Fitzgerald played fairly in exchanging her personality with Mrs Annie Pearson? What lesson did Annie teach to her children and husband?

4 Every mother and wife demands respect from her children and husband. Discuss this statement in the context of 'Mother's Day' chapter.

5 Why was Dr Andrew so emotionally attached to his efforts to bring the seemingly lifeless baby back to life?

6 Dr Andrew was undergoing an emotional crisis, but still managed to perform his duties as a doctor very well. Emotional instability should never be a hurdle in one's profession. Comment.

Practice Paper 1*
(Unsolved)

General Instructions

■ Time : 2 Hours
■ Max. Marks : 40

1. The question paper contains three sections A, B and C.
2. **Section A** Reading section has Reading Comprehension and Unseen passage for Note-Making and summarisation attempt as per specific instruction for each.
3. **Section B** Writing has 3 question. Attempt questions as per specific instructions. Grammar section has 4 questions. Attempt question as per specific instructions.
4. **Section C** Literature section has extract based questions, short answer type questions and long answer type questions. Internal choice is given for individual questions.
5. Marks are mentioned against each question.

** As exact Blue-print and Pattern for CBSE Term II exams is not released yet. So the pattern of this paper is designed by the author on the basis of trend of past CBSE Papers. Students are advised not to consider the pattern of this paper as official. It is just for practice purpose.*

Section A   Reading Comprehension

1. Read the passage given below.

1. Reform — but not needlessly. That's the message for Indian education policymakers from the research findings of two Indian economists — Sandip Datta of Delhi School of Economics and Geeta Gandhi Kingdon of University College London. The fiscally-strapped Indian state can save around Rs 1.5 trillion a year on education spends if it acts on data and evidence instead of preconceived notions, the paper says.

2. Conventional wisdom in India and abroad has led experts, economists, academics and even parents to believe that large class sizes in schools have an adverse effect on learning. Low learning outcomes have typically been blamed on the inability of a single teacher to teach students who are at different learning levels, but in the same grade; the huge administrative burden most senior teachers in the government school system grapple with; and large class sizes. It is widely known that in many government schools there are 60-80 pupils in a single classroom.

3. Hence, huge resources have been directed at reducing class sizes in both public and private schools. Between 2010 and 2017, the total number of elementary schoolteachers rose by 0.4 million, and the corresponding total teacher salary bill swelled by \$3.6 billion in 2017-18. But research by Kingdon and Datta shows that class sizes can be increased to an optimal level of 40-odd for science subjects and 50-odd for non-science subjects with no detrimental effect on learning levels. In fact, peer learning that happens in larger class sizes implies that classes can reach an optimal level to enhance learning outcomes.

4. Datta and Kingdon further suggest that there is scope for increasing class sizes in India from the current 22.8 to 40 in science and 50 in non-science, without hurting student learning. Their findings have been published in two papers — a RISE working paper titled "Class Size and Learning: Has India

Spent Too Much on Reducing Class Size?", and another paper published by the IZA Institute of Labour Economics earlier this month titled "Teacher Shortage in India: Myth or Reality?". The study based on rigorous econometric analysis was possible due to the availability of data from Lucknow's City Montessori School chain with 57,000 students spread over 18 branches in the city, of which Kingdon is president.

5. The findings have huge policy implications for India and other countries that are reforming their education systems. India spent an estimated \$3.6 billion in 2017-18 on the salaries of the 0.40 million additional teachers it appointed between 2010 and 2017, which reduced the pupil-teacher ratio (PTR) in elementary public schools from 31.2 (in 2010) to 22.8 (in 2017-18), and to 27.9 in secondary education the same year. The Right to Education Act mandates a maximum pupil-teacher ratio of 30, but adjusting for fake enrolments, the true PTR now is a low 19.8.

Based on your understanding of the passage, answer **any eight** out of the **ten** questions by choosing the correct answer.   **(8 Marks)**

(i) Select the correct inference with reference to the following, 'huge resources have been directed at reducing class sizes in both public and private schools.'

(a) The efforts are being made to reduce the burden on a teacher who cannot teach multiple students together.
(b) More no. of versatile students in a single class hampers the chances of individual attention being given by the teacher.
(c) More no. of students in a single class gives more revenue to the school.
(d) A teacher is best judged on the basis of her/his way of handling any students' doubts in the class.

(ii) According to the passage, which papers have been published by Kingdon and Datta?
(a) A RISE working paper and paper published by the IZA Institute of Labour Economics.
(b) Lucknow's City Montessori School working paper and paper published by the IZA Institute of Labour Economics.
(c) The econometric analysis paper and paper published by the IZA Institute of Labour Economics.
(d) Both (a) and (c)

(iii) Pick the option that lists statements that are TRUE according to the passage.

1. There is a scope for increasing class sizes in India without hampering the students' learning in all streams.

2. India spent an estimated 360 crore rupees in 2017-18 on the salaries of the 4 lakh additional teachers it appointed between 2010 and 2017.

3. Most of the senior teachers in the government school system face a burden of more no. of students in the class.

4. Most of the schools have different set of students divided on the basis of their grades and performances.
(a) 1 and 2   (b) 3 and 4
(c) 2 and 4   (d) 1 and 4

(iv) Based on your reading of the passage, select the counter-argument to the given argument.

Argument: The Right to Education Act mandates a maximum pupil-teacher ratio of 30.
(a) According to the Right to Education Act 2009, the pupil teacher ratio should be 30:1.
(b) The RTE Act does not restrict the school to have a ratio of 30:1.
(c) Under the Right to Education act, pupil teacher ratio for primary classes and upper primary classes are 30: 1 respectively.
(d) Under the Right to Education Act 2009, which covers children between 6-14 years of age, the stipulated pupil-teacher ratio for primary classes and upper primary classes is 30:1.

(v) Select option that displays the correct cause-effect relationship.

(a) I handle more than 35 students in my class. — I find it bit difficult to give attention to the queries of my students.
(b) I have 25 students in my class below the age of 10. — I cannot handle them and need a coordinator for my class.
(c) My school needs to focus----------------- on the guidelines of the education policy given by the government. — I need to plan the ratio of each class with 40:1 ratio of the student and the teacher.
(d) I always focus on group study in my every class. — My students do not interact much and I am planning to withdraw the peer study methodology soon.

(vi) According to passage, which of the statements is one of the reasons why in government schools there are 60-80 pupils in a single classroom?
(a) Because of the administrative decision of the schools, most senior teachers in the government school system grapple large class sizes.
(b) Lack of space does not allow schools to expand or split their existing divisions.
(c) Lack of good facilities and curriculum hinders the growth in the expansion of the school.
(d) Because of the pressure of the decision of the government, schools focus more on increasing the admissions to generate revenue.

(vii) The statement 'peer learning that happens in larger class sizes implies that classes can reach an optimal level to enhance learning outcomes' refers that-
  (a) Some students, especially weaker students, need more time to think over concept test questions.
  (b) Advantages of peer teaching include gains in better coaching among the students in the class.
  (c) Peer learning is mutually beneficial and involves the sharing of knowledge, ideas and experience between the participants.
  (d) Peer coaching can be ineffective and a burden for teachers if there are more no. of students in the class.

(viii) Read the two statements given below and select the option that suitably explains them.

  1. Huge resources have been directed at reducing class sizes in both public and private schools.

  2. But research by Kingdon and Datta shows that class sizes can be increased to an optimal level to enhance the peer interaction.
  (a) (1) is the problem and (2) is its solution
  (b) (1) is false but (2) correctly explains it
  (c) (2) elaborates on (1)
  (d) (1) is true and (2) is the reason for (1)

(ix) Find the word similar in meaning to "detrimental" in paragraph 3.
  (a) Fruitful   (b) Damaging
  (c) Favourable   (d) Admonishing

(x) Find the word opposite in meaning to "fake" in paragraph 5.
  (a) Bogus   (b) Counterfeit
  (c) Genuine   (d) Acrimonious

2. Read the passage given below and answer the questions that follow:

  1. When planning to go on a vacation, the tendency is to make sure that the travel plans are hassle free, before stepping out of one's doors. This involves booking by train, bus or even by air to one's chosen destination. Yet the greatest holidays can be enjoyed by going on foot and I am not referring to trekking expeditions into the wilds. Any holiday can be made into a walking trip by opting out of a bus ride or a train journey or a taxi drop, by selecting to go on foot. Besides, walking is a great form of exercise and above all, helps you to go deep into the local culture, the daily lives of people, their food and their music.

  2. Walking helps you enhance the adventurous streak in you. If you are out on a beach holiday, instead of workouts at the gym, head out to the water for your exercise. Resort pools are a great way to have fun and stay fit and are suitable for all ages. Wake up early to start your day with a swim and you can also recruit family and friends to join in to make the activity even more interesting.

  3. The best holiday destinations need not be those that the travel brochures advertise. It can be one of your own search, if you take advantage of what an area is known for and then set out to explore it on your own terms. Thus, you can learn tai chi when on a trip to China or smarten up your dancing skills by trying out flamenco when in Spain.

  4. In order to enjoy a walking holiday to the hilt, one needs to be physically in form. Thus, one needs to keep a tab on one's diet. The travel brochures give you a choice of tried-out brands with a peppering of local options. But whatever be your choice, it is smart to stick to the rule book. In every place you are sure to find fresh and healthy high-protein, high- fibre options to fill you up. That will keep you away from opting for the high sugar, processed foods and simple carbohydrates.

  5. These simple rules would ensure that your walking holiday was not only enjoyable but also one that left you feeling fully in command of your holiday mood and proved economical as you did not waste a single moment nursing an upset belly or a sluggish day or a boring ride across acres of, non-stimulating countryside, cooped in a taxi or jostling on a train.

(i) On the basis of your reading of the above passage, make notes on it, using headings and subheadings. Also supply an appropriate title to it.   **(2 Marks)**

(ii) Write a summary of the passage in about 80 words.   **(3 Marks)**

Section B Creative Writing Skills and Grammar

Creative Writing Skills

3. On the occasion of World Heritage Day, design a poster to be put on your school notice board highlighting the need to preserve old monuments which are a testimony to history. You are Sarla/Sharan, the President of the History Club of your school.   **(3 Marks)**

Or

Your locality has started a Reader's club for the benefit of the children of the locals. Prepare a suitable poster for display in the colony.   **(3 Marks)**

4. You are Anuj Dixit of Chitra Senior Secondary School, Pandav Puram, Delhi, you are captain of the Hockey Team of your School. You have no playground in your school. Write a letter to the Principal, requesting him to arrange playground facility from neighbouring school for practice of your team. **(2 Marks)**

Or

You are interested in doing a course in fashion design. For this you want to join NIFT. NIFT holds a competitive examination for admission. Sapphire Academy, Dadar, Mumbai gives coaching for the admission test. Write a letter to the Director, Sapphire Academy requesting him to provide you with all the necessary information. You are Karan / Kirti, 48 Fort Apartments, Pune.

5. "Brain drain is not a bane for a developing country like India." Write a debate either for or against the motion. **(3 Marks)**

Or

"The Internet cannot replace a classroom teacher." Write a debate either for or Gramman against the motion. **(3 Marks)**

Grammar

6. Choose the correct option to fill in the blank.

(2 Marks)

(i) Despite the material donations from the local shops, the school still needs ...... more equipment such as video players, cassette players and computers.

(a) a few   (b) many   (c) some   (d) plenty

(ii) In recent decades, the efficiency of the United Nations by a growing number of countries.

(a) will have been questioned   (b) would be questioned

(c) has been questioned   (d) had been questioned

7. Transform the given sentence as directed without changing their meaning. **(2 Marks)**

(i) No other spa is as good as the Golden Spa. (on the basis of determiners)

(a) Golden spa is better than other spas.

(b) Golden spa is one of the good spas.

(c) Golden spa is a lot good than many spas.

(d) No other spa is better than Golden spa.

(ii) She has an eager interest in athletics. (Change into Present Perfect Tense)

(a) She had have an eager interest in athletics.

(b) She had had an eager interest in athletics.

(c) She has an eager interest in athletics.

(d) She has had an eager interest in athletics.

Section C Literature

8. Attempt anyone of the following. **(3 Marks)**

Since the tropical forest is, in the words of Dr Myers, "the powerhouse of evolution," several species of life face extinction as a result of its destruction. It has been well said that forests precede mankind; deserts follow. The world's ancient patrimony of tropical forests is now eroding at the rate of forty to fifty million acres a year and the growing use of dung for burning deprives the soil of an important natural fertiliser. The World Bank estimates that a five-fold increase in the rate of forest planting is needed to cope with the expected fuelwood demand in the year 2000.

(i) Why is Tropical forest called 'the powerhouse of evolution'?

(ii) "Forests precede mankind; deserts follow." Explain.

(iii) Do you think the given lines mention the reason for decreasing forestry?

Or

TAPLOW: (imitating a very gentle, rather throaty voice) "My dear Taplow, I have given you exactly what you deserve. No less; and certainly no more." Do you know sir, I think he may have marked me down, rather than up, for taking extra work. I mean, the man's hardly human. (He breaks off quickly.) Sorry, sir. Have I gone too far?

FRANK: Yes. Much too far.

TAPLOW: Sorry, sir. I got carried away.

FRANK: Evidently. (He picks up a newspaper and opens it) - Er Taplow.

TAPLOW: Yes, sir?

FRANK: What was that Crocker-Harris said to you? Just - er - repeat it, would you?

TAPLOW: (Imitating again) "My dear Taplow, I have given you exactly what you deserve. No less and certainly no more."

(i) Do you think Taplow is criticising his teacher Mr. Crocker Harris?

(ii) What can you make out of Mr. Crocker Harris on the basis of the extract?

(iii) What do you make of Frank's wanting Taplow to imitate Crocker Harris the second time?

9. Attempt anyone of the following. (3 Marks)

And who art thou? said I to the soft-falling shower,

Which, strange to tell, gave me an answer, as here translated:

I am the Poem of Earth, said the voice of the rain. (The Voice of the Rain)

(i) Do you think that the poet was expecting the soft falling shower to answer?

(ii) Explain 'Poem of the Earth'.

(iii) Do you really think that the rain is answering? Give reason for your answer.

Or

Where did my childhood go?

It went to some forgotten place,

That's hidden in an infant's face,

That's alii know. (Childhood)

(i) Why does the poet to know the whereabouts of his childhood?

(ii) Do you think the poet is asserting that we must maintain the childhood qualities as an adult?

(iii) Why does the poet say that it has gone to some forgotten place?

10. Attempt anyone of the following. (3 Marks)

"We don't want a lecture from you, Einstein. You will stay in for an extra period today, although I don't imagine it will do you much good. It won't do the school any good, either. You are a disgrace. I don't know why you continue to come. "It's not my wish, sir," Albert pointed out. "Then you are an ungrateful boy and ought to be ashamed of yourself. I suggest you ask your father to take you away." Albert felt miserable when he left school that afternoon; not that it had been a bad day- most days were bad now, anyway - but because he had to go back to the hateful place the next morning. He only wished his father would take him away, but

there was no point in even asking. (Albert Einstein at School)

(i) What was the lecture given by Einstein?

(ii) Do you think Mr. Braun accepts Einstein ideas even intrinsically?

(iii) Why does Einstein think that there was no point in asking his father to take him away?

Or

MRS FITZGERALD: I did. Twelve years I had of it, with myoid man rising to be Lieutenant Quartermaster. He learnt a lot, and I learnt a lot more. But will you make up your mind now, Mrs. Pearson dear? Put your foot down, once an' for all, an' be the mistress of your own house an' the boss of your own family.

MRS PEARSON: [Smiling apologetically] That's easier said than done. Besides I'm so fond of them even if they are so thoughtless and selfish. They don't mean to be ... (Mothers day)

(i) Mrs Fitzgerald says 'I learnt a lot more'. Comment.

(ii) Why does Mrs. Fitzgerald ask Mrs. Pearson to put her foot down?

(iii) Do you think Mrs. Pearson is defending her family? Is yes, why?

11. Attempt any one of the following. (3 Marks)

(i) What was the author's purpose in the journey to Mount Kailash in 'Silk Road'?

Or

(ii) What happens when it rains after a long hot spell of weather? Answer with reference to the poem 'The Voice of the Rain'.

12. Attempt any one of the following. (3 Marks)

Was Albert really a nuisance in the class, considering how he behaved with his History teacher ? Explain.

Or

How does Doris treat her mother in Mother's Day?

Answers

1. (i) (b)　(ii) (a)　(iii) (a)　(iv) (b)　(v) (a)　(vi) (a)　(vii) (c) (viii) (a)　(ix) (b)　(x) (c)

Practice Paper 2*
(Unsolved)

General Instructions

- Time : 2 Hours
- Max. Marks : 40

1. The question paper contains three sections A, B and C.
2. **Section A** Reading section has Reading Comprehension and Unseen passage for Note-Making and summarisation attempt as per specific instruction for each.
3. **Section B** Writing has 3 question. Attempt questions as per specific instructions. Grammar section has 4 questions. Attempt question as per specific instructions.
4. **Section C** Literature section has extract based questions, short answer type questions and long answer type questions. Internal choice is given for individual questions.
5. Marks are mentioned against each question.

*** As exact Blue-print and Pattern for CBSE Term II exams is not released yet. So the pattern of this paper is designed by the author on the basis of trend of past CBSE Papers. Students are advised not to consider the pattern of this paper as official. It is just for practice purpose.**

Section A   Reading Comprehension

1. Read the passage given below.

1. Indian cinema has influenced the youth of this country from generations. It was introduced in 1913 when the first movie "Raja Harishchandra" was made. Since then, Cinema has started making a major impact on the thinking and perspective of people about different things. It is scientifically proven that watching movies reduces stress, watching horror movies can burn our calories too.

2. You can find many movies that remind us about our culture and values and tells us the difference between wrong and right. Movies like "Baghban" and "Swades" are some of the examples that made an impact on me when I was a kid. As the time is changing and the society is modernizing, Indian Cinema is evolving too, now it is giving us movies like "Padman"," Dangal"," Hindi Medium"," Article 15", etc, which are creating awareness and breaking negative stereotypes of the society. Positive thoughts like gender equality, social rights, etc, are spread through these movies.

3. Most of the Indian parents want their children to be an engineer or a doctor, but this stereotype is changing these days because of some movies like "3 idiots"," Mary Kom", etc. Some movies like "Zindagi Na Milegi Dobara" are influencing youth to concentrate on their career but at the same time live life to its fullest.

4. Though watching movies helps us to relax it also helps us in knowing what is going on in the world, But, at the same time, the "modern cinema" have started picturing adult scenes and making adult movies to attract the viewers. There is no restriction to do that but the problem starts when kids who are underage, get to see them (as there are so many ways these movies can be accessed

illegally). It puts a negative effect on them and they mentally become more mature according to their age. Not only kids, but even youth also try to copy their favourite actors including their way of talking, hairstyle, dressing sense, and so on.

5. Crimes are being portrayed in movies these days and eve-teasing is also shown as a heroic act and some people take it in the wrong way because of which the number of crimes and harassment cases is increasing. In some movies, women are being objectified by adding item songs and scenes which are demeaning to women where on the other hand, ironically, they are preaching gender sensitivity.

6. Nepotism in Indian cinema is also a big concern. Indian cinema runs on nepotism, because of which a lot of new talent is being wasted. Children of movie stars are getting easy exposures, movies, and money, and on the other side, struggling actors from middle and lower-class families have to face rejection.

Based on your understanding of the passage, answer **any eight** out of the **ten** questions by choosing the correct answer.   **(8 Marks)**

(i) Which movie as mentioned in the passage teaches the youth to strike a balance between their personal and professional lives?
(a) Mary Kom
(b) Zindagi Na Milegi Dobara
(c) 3 Idiots
(d) Hindi Medium

(ii) A phrase is a small group of words standing together as a conceptual unit.

The writer mentions that 'watching horror movies can burn our calories too.'

Select the words from the options that is a correct phrase using 'burn'.
(a) Burn the midnight oil   (b) Burning wish
(c) Burning matter   (d) Burning the candle to eat

(iii) Select the option that suitably completes the given dialogue as per the context in paragraph IV.

X: What do you wish to become in life?

Y: I wish to be famous. (1) ....

X: But becoming a hero in the movies can give you more fame?

Y: (2) It's an ....
(a) (1) I want to become a doctor (2) shortcut to earn money and name.
(b) (1) I wish to become a teacher (2) simple way to serve the society.

(c) (1) I wish to become a businessman (2) informal way to earn more money in life.
(d) (1) I wish to become an army officer (2) easy way to earn name, money and fame.

(iv) Which option/options represents the movies that has been favourite of the writer when he was young?
(i) Padman and Mary Kom
(ii) Dangal and Article 15
(iii) Baghban and Swades
(iv) Swadesh and 3 Idiots
(a) Options (i) and (ii)   (b) Options (ii) and (iii)
(c) Options (iii) and (iv)   (d) Options (iii) only

(v) Select the option that is correct with reference to the given passage.
(a) Most of the Indian parents want their children to be an engineer or a doctor today.
(b) Many movies remind us about our culture and values and tells us how to differentiate between wrong and right.
(c) The youngsters are easily influenced by the stardom shown in the movies and they chose wrong means to debut in the films.
(d) Both a) and b)

(vi) What is the relationship between (1) and (2)?
(i) As the time is changing and the society is modernizing, Indian Cinema is evolving too.
(ii) Now it is giving us movies which are creating awareness and breaking negative stereotypes of the society.
(a) (ii) is the cause of (i)
(b) (i) and (ii) are independent of each other
(c) (ii) elaborates upon the premise of (i)
(d) (i) sets the stage of (ii)

(vii) 'Nepotism in Indian cinema is also a big concern.' What does the word 'nepotism' mean in the context of the passage.
(a) A form of favoritism   (b) A form of impartiality
(c) A form of meritocracy   (d) A form of fairness

(viii) Which of the following reason as per the passage attracts the children towards their stars in the movies and puts a negative effect on them?

1. The children force the parents to buy the things that their favourite stars eat and wear.

2. The children emulate their favourite stars and they mentally become more mature according to their age in course of doing so.

3. The heroic images of the film stars influences the children to save the world like them.

4. Children being immature in nature and age are easily enticed towards the negative things shown in the movies.

(a) Option 1   (b) Option 2
(c) Option 3   (d) Option 4

(ix) Which quote best summarises the writers' description about the impact of movies on people?

  (a) "I think cinema, movies, and magic have always been closely associated. The very earliest people who made film were magicians."

  (b) "Cinema is a cultural expression, a cultural transaction between the filmmaker and the audience."

  (c) "Cinema reflects culture and there is no harm in adapting technology, but not at the cost of losing your originality."

  (d) "Cinema, radio, television, magazines are a school of inattention: people look without seeing, listen in without hearing."

(x) "Indian cinema runs on nepotism, because of which a lot of new talent is being waste." What does the writer mean to say in this statement?

  (a) Nepotism is trying hard to stop the new talents but it is getting failed due to the unstoppable spirit of new generation talents.

  (b) Nepotism negates talents, abilities, merits and efficiency.

  (c) Nepotism adversely affects the general credibility of the public servants and makes the general masses to become cynics.

  (d) While the Indian film industry struggles to produce a league of good actors, nepotism has allowed many emerging actors to find their real talent.

2. Read the passage given below and answer the questions that follow.

Good decoration reflects the personality of the people who live in the home. It should, first of all, be distinctive, just as each person is distinctive. A home should have unity not only within each room but also throughout the house. Rooms should, to some degree, harmonize with each other. The colour and styling of each room, particularly, should fit into the colour and styling of the rooms which run out of it.

Attractive home furnishings set the stage for pleasant living. If they are an expression of yourself, you will have a feeling of satisfaction every time you enter your home and friends will share your enjoyment.

However, furnishings and surroundings expressive of just the right note of restfulness, gay informality, or elegant simplicity are not often assembled by accident. Even enthusiasm alone is not enough. For most home decorators, it takes poring over plans, trying colour schemes, finding ingenious ways to make the best of what you have, and shopping around to search out just the right purchases at prices you can afford to pay. But there is keen pleasure in striving for the perfect result and great satisfaction in achieving it.

A successful house and successful rooms will depend upon the proper relationship of each element in it to the others and to the whole. Therefore, in selecting each piece it is well to consider the background, the usage, the draperies, the floor covering, the upholstering materials, the woods, shapes, colour scheme and the 'feeling' you prefer for the room.

Work and plan to enjoy your house. Limit the expenditures of time, effort and money to the extent of your abilities, so that just running the house doesn't dominate your life. Elegance and delicate things may be a drain you can afford only in a limited way. If you can't afford outside help, select a house and furnishings that require less care. Plan your activities so that tumult and upset are limited to a few rooms-an activity room or a bedroom or a comer of the dining room.

You'll get more pleasure out of a house if you have a hobby connected with it-collecting glass or antiques, gardening or indoor flower growing ceramics, art, cooking, decorating, flower arrangements, etc. And you'll get more satisfaction and a great deal of help from studying household activities.

You can select a pleasing combination of colours from a wallpaper, a fabric, an oriental mug, a flower or scene or even a picture in a magazine. If you don't already have the furniture or mugs, it is a good idea to make up a colour scheme in this way. Let one colour predominate. limit a colour scheme to two or three colours, with white or gray tones.

(i) Make notes on the passage in any suitable format. Use abbreviations, wherever necessary. Give a suitable title. **(2 Marks)**

(ii) Make a summary of the passage. **(3 Marks)**

Section B   Creative Writing Skills and Grammar

Creative Writing Skills

3. National Book Trust is organising an exhibition displaying books on yoga on the occasion of International Yoga Day on 21st June. Design a poster highlighting the advantages of developing the habit of yoga for the occasion. **(3 Marks)**

Or

Design an attractive and instructive poster on behalf of the Delhi Police to educate and warn the people against any suspicious or unclaimed objects in public places/trains/buses to avert bomb blasts.

4. You have borrowed some books from your school library. Unfortunately you have to go away to visit a sick relative and cannot return the books in time. Then you find that you cannot even locate them. Write a letter to the library incharge. Explain what has happened and propose what you can do in this regard.

Clues

- Details of books
- Issue date and due dates
- Reason for not returning
- Pardon for inconvenience
- Way for compensation **(2 Marks)**

Or

You plan to join an advanced course in English Speaking offered by the Vocational Training College, New Delhi. You are Anil/ Shobha Gupta of Dhruva Apartments, Patparganj. Write a letter to the Director, English Language Teaching Division of the college, requesting to send you the information on the courses offered, fees and duration of the courses etc.

5. "The policy of no detention till class VIII is not in the interest of students." Write a debate either in favour of or against the motion. **(3 Marks)**

Or

A career counsellor (not you yourself) is the best person to guide you in the choice of a career. Write a debate either for or against the motion.

Grammar

6. Transform the given sentence as directed without changing their meaning. **(2 Marks)**

(i) The girl was too clever to be taught.

   (a) The girl is very clever.

   (b) The girl was so clever that she could not be taught.

   (c) The girl is not as clever as other girls.

   (d) The girl is a lot clever than expected.

(ii) Change into Simple Past tense.

   But I have had my revenge at last.

   (a) But I had had my revenge at last.

   (b) But I had have my revenge at last.

   (c) But I had my revenge at last.

   (d) But I have my revenge at last.

7. Rearrange the following into meaningful sentences. **(2 Marks)**

(i) P : a five star hotel with

   Q : next week, I will

   R : Shah Rukh Khan

   S : be having dinner at

   (a) RPQS   (b) RSQP   (c) QSRP   (d) QSPR

(ii) P : the man to

   Q : addressed the letter

   R: was dead

   S : whom he had

   (a) PQSR   (b) PSQR   (c) SQRP   (d) QSRP

Section C   Literature

8. Attempt any one of the following. **(3 Marks)**

TAPLOW: Mr Crocker-Harris. The funny thing is that in spite of everything, I do rather like him. I can't help it. And sometimes I think he sees it and that seems to shrivel him up even more-

FRANK: I'm sure you're exaggerating.

TAPLOW: No, sir. I'm not. In form the other day he made one of his classical jokes. Of course nobody laughed because nobody understood it, myself included. Still, I knew he'd meant it as funny, so I laughed. Out of ordinary common politeness, and feeling a bit sorry for him for having made a poor joke. Now I can't remember what the joke was, but suppose I make it. Now you laugh, sir.

(i) Explain 'in spite of everything' with reference to the given lines.

(ii) How can you characterise Taplow on the basis of the given lines?

(iii) Even though Crocker Harris is not physically present in the play, his presence is felt throughout. Comment.

Or

They were completely fearless of our vehicle, shooting straight into our path, causing Tsetan to brake and swerve. The dog would make chase for a hundred metres or so before easing off, having seen us off the property. It wasn't difficult to understand why ferocious Tibetan mastiffs became popular in China's imperial courts as hunting dogs, brought along the Silk Road in ancient times as tribute from Tibet. It wasn't difficult to understand why ferocious Tibetan mastiffs became popular in China's imperial courts as hunting dogs, brought along the Silk Road in ancient times as tribute from Tibet.

(i) Give a brief physical description of the dog mentioned in the extract.

(ii) What characteristics made the dog popular in China's imperial courts?

(iii) How would the dog react upon seeing an car near them?

9. Attempt any one of the following. **(3 Marks)**
When did my childhood go?
Was it the day I ceased to be eleven,
Was it the time I realised that Hell and Heaven,
Could not be found in Geography,
And therefore could not be,

(i) How would you characterise the poet's drive to know about his childhood?

(ii) Explain the significance of the reference to Hell and Haven.

(iii) Do you think that he was able to find his childhood?

Or

And forever, by day and night, I give back life to my own origin, And make pure and beautify it; (For song, issuing from its birth-place, after fulfilment, wandering Reck'd or unreck'd, duly with love returns.)

(i) Explain 'I give life to my own origin'.

(ii) How does it carry out the task of purification and beautification?

(iii) Why do you think that the last lines of the extract are given in brackets?

10. Attempt any one of the following. **(3 Marks)**
MRS PEARSON: [Promptly] Nothing but come in, ask for something, go out again, then come back when there's nowhere else to go.

CYRIL:[Aggressively] Look -if you won't get tea ready, then I'll find something to eat myself ...

MRS PEARSON:Why not? Help yourself.
[She takes a sip of stout.]

CYRIL:[Turning on his way to the kitchen] Mind you, I think it's a bit thick. I've been working all day.

DORIS:Same here.

MRS PEARSON: (Calmly) Eight hour day!

CYRIL:Yes-eight hour day -an' don't forget it.

MRS PEARSON: I've done my eight hours.

CYRIL:That's different.

DORIS:Of course it is.

MRS PEARSON: [Calmly] It was. Now it isn't. Forty-hour week for all now. Just watch it at the weekend when I have my two days off.

(i) Why do you think that Cyril and Doris are reacting in such a manner?

(ii) What change can be seen in Mrs. Pearson's behaviour?

(iii) Do you agree with Cyril saying that their work is different?

Or

Andrew handed her the child. He felt weak and dazed. About him the room lay in a shuddering litter: blankets, towels, basins, soiled instruments, the hypodermic syringe impaled by its point in the linoleum, the ewer knocked over, the kettle on its side in a puddle of water. Upon the huddled bed the mother still dreamed her way quietly through the anaesthetic. The old woman still stood against the wall. But her hands were together, her lips moved without sound. She was praying.

(i) What was the condition of the child?

(ii) Why did Andrew feel weak and dazed?

(iii) How will you translate the actions of the old woman?

11. Attempt any one of the following. **(3 Marks)**
What did the poet realise when he had reached the age of eleven years?

Or

Write the meaning of the statement made by Margaret Thatcher, "No generation has a freehold on this Earth. All we have is a life tenancy- with a full repairing lease."

12. Attempt any one of the following. **(3 Marks)**
Describe the characteristic traits of Mrs. Pearson in the chapter Mother's day.

Or

"For doctors the duty towards the patients is foremost, irrespective of their own personal affairs." Discuss with reference to the excerpt, 'Birth'.

Practice Paper 3*
(Unsolved)

General Instructions

- Time : 2 Hours
- Max. Marks : 40

1. The question paper contains three sections A, B and C.
2. **Section A** Reading section has Reading Comprehension and Unseen passage for Note-Making and summarisation attempt as per specific instruction for each.
3. **Section B** Writing has 3 question. Attempt questions as per specific instructions. Grammar section has 4 questions. Attempt question as per specific instructions.
4. **Section C** Literature section has extract based questions, short answer type questions and long answer type questions. Internal choice is given for individual questions.
5. Marks are mentioned against each question.

** As exact Blue-print and Pattern for CBSE Term II exams is not released yet. So the pattern of this paper is designed by the author on the basis of trend of past CBSE Papers. Students are advised not to consider the pattern of this paper as official. It is just for practice purpose.*

Section A   Reading Comprehension

1. Read the passage given below.

1. News of the telephone spread quickly in Sweden. In 1885, Stockholm had the greatest telephone penetration in the world. Nowhere else were there as many phones in use. Expansion of telephone service outside the capital also started quickly, thanks to the many local telephone associations.

2. Only a few years after the telephone was first demonstrated in Stockholm in 1877, the general public was thus aware of the new invention. At first, phones were found in general stores, telegraph offices and drug stores. The general store received a telephone number such as 1 or 2 and acted as a news centre for the village. People went to the store and asked if anyone had phoned. If so, the proprietor would read the message.

3. Not everyone was thrilled by these developments, however. The telephone was often viewed with scepticism and not a little fear. There was something magical about sounds coming from a thin wire, and many people were afraid that the contents of the lines would spill out in some way if there was a break. Many elderly persons refused to touch a telephone for fear of electrical shock. Others tried to take advantage of the telephone, relates Peter Andersson in his book, "Telecommunications yesterday and today." In some town's persons suffering from rheumatism went to the telephone stations in the hope that the electrical impulses received by their bodies would cure them.

4. The greatest fear, however, was that the telephone was in some way able to attract evil spirits, or at least thunder and lightning. In one town it was in fact difficult to obtain premises and to recruit a manager for the telephone station, since there was widespread concern about the possible effects of the telephone lines and electricity in the station.

5. The build out of the telephone network quickly became evident to rural residents, who saw telephone poles being set in the ground and "telephone acrobats" climbing the poles to draw lines that crisscrossed the countryside. In the cities, lines were drawn across the roofs, creating over time an extensive network of telephone antennas and lines above the rooftops.

6. The telephone thus provoked anger. There were farmers, land owners and property owners who refused to allow this nuisance to pass over their land or buildings or who simply pulled down lines and destroyed them. Theft and sabotage were common as the telephone network expanded. And in the churches, the preachers likened the telephone to an instrument of the devil.

Based on your understanding of the passage, answer **any eight** out of the **ten** questions by choosing the correct answer.   **(8 Marks)**

(i) When was the telephone invented as mentioned in the passage?
(a) After the first demonstration in Stockholm in 1877.
(b) After the first demonstration in Stockholm in 1876.
(c) After the first demonstration in Stockholm in 1878.
(d) None of the above

(ii) A phrase is a small group of words standing together as a conceptual unit.

The writer mentions that 'The telephone thus provoked anger.'

Select the words from the options that is a correct phrase/idiom using 'anger'.
(a) To bristle with anger   (b) To open with anger
(c) Amber in anger   (d) Green in anger

(iii) Select the option that suitably completes the given dialogue as per the context in paragraph III.

X: What is this in your hand?

Y: It's called a telephone (1) ....

X: How do you speak through this?

Y: (2) Well, ...
(a) (1) It's new invention in the market (2) It has a wire attached to it
(b) (1) It's new discovery in the market (2) It operates on a battery
(c) (1) Would you like to speak using it? (2) I think it I do not know how to use it.
(d) (1) Hope I can easily speak to my friends now (2) You need to wait for your chance.

(iv) Which option/options represents the feelings of the people towards the telephone when it came into existence?

(i) Conviction and trust
(ii) Incredulity and Cynicism
(iii) Agitation and Disbelief
(iv) Apperhension and consent
(a) Options (i) and (ii)   (b) Options (ii) and (iii)
(c) Options (iii) and (iv)   (d) Options (iv) only

(v) Select the option that is correct with reference to the given passage.
(a) In the churches, the telephone was linked to be an instrument of the devil.
(b) The telephone was welcomed warm-heartedly by all the levels and age groups of people once it came into existence.
(c) The telephone was often viewed with faith and not a little fear.
(d) Incidents of theft and sabotage came to an end once the telephone network expanded.

(vi) What is the relationship between (1) and (2)?
(i) In one town it was in fact difficult to obtain premises and to recruit a manager for the telephone station.
(ii) Many elderly persons refused to touch a telephone for fear of electrical shock.
(a) (ii) is the cause of (i)
(b) (i) and (ii) are independent of each other
(c) (ii) elaborates upon the premise of (i)
(d) (i) sets the stage of (ii)

(vii) 'In some town's persons suffering from rheumatism went to the telephone stations.' What does the word 'rheumatism' mean in the context of the passage?
(a) Arthritis   (b) Stress
(c) Depression   (d) Aberrations

(viii) Which of the following reason mentions why the elderly persons refused to touch a telephone as described by the writer in the passage?
(i) In the fear of getting an electric shock.
(ii) The telephone is able to attract evil spirits.
(iii) In the fear of theft and sabotage.
(iv) The telephone attracts thunderstorms and shocks.
(a) Option (i)
(b) Option (ii)
(c) Option (iii)
(d) Option (iv)

(ix) Which quote best summarises the writers' description about the importance of phone?
(a) "Utility is when you have one telephone, luxury is when you have two, and paradise is when you have none."
(b) "If you don't love telecommunication, you are either a pessimist or an orthodox."
(c) "I will not be at the mercy of the telephone!."

   (d) "Technology gives us the facilities that lessen the barriers of time and distance - the telegraph and cable, the telephone, radio, and the rest."

(x) "There were farmers, land owners and property owners who refused to allow this nuisance to pass over their land or buildings." What does the writer mean to say in this statement?

   (a) The farmers, land owners and property owners raised their objection to spread the cable network crossing through their belongings.

   (b) The farmers, land owners and property owners raised their objection to spread the cable network crossing through their homes.

   (c) All the common residents raised welcomed the idea of communication through the cable network.

   (d) Most of the common people were afraid of the electricity cables running over their homes due to fear of electric shock.

2. Read the passage given below and answer the questions that follow:

1. Jahangir was born on 30th August, 1569, to Akbar, the Mughal Emperor, and his Hindu wife, Jodha Bai. He was crowned on 24th October, 1605. In the twenty-two years, he was Emperor, till his death on 28th October, 1627, he had many battles to fight and many rebellions to suppress. But he always found time for his greatest hobby-the study of animals and plants. He was an avid bird watcher or an ornithologist as he would be called now, and a keen naturalist. The care and accuracy with which Jahangir described various characteristics of animals and birds, their geographical distribution and behaviour, would have done credit to a full-time naturalist. His observations are recorded in his memoirs, the Tuzuk-i-Jahangiri.

2. Jahangir had a small zoo and he would spend hours-sometimes days and nights together-on his observations. For the first time in the history- of ornithology, he noted how sarus cranes mate brood over their eggs in turn, and how chicks are hatched and taken care of. He also observed one human quality in this bird: the parents love not only their eggs and chicks but also each other.

3. The Emperor had several famous painters in his court. When he came across a rare animal, bird or plant, he would instruct an artist to draw it. The painter who excelled in this art was Ustad Mansur. For modern ornithologists, Jahangir's collection of paintings provides a strikingly accurate description of the natural history of the day. Unfortunately, most of these paintings are no longer to be found in India. With the disintegration of the Mughal Empire, foreign adventures looted this treasure. Most of the paintings were thus lost.

4. In 1958, a Russian researcher, A Ivanoc, created a sensation when he discovered, a rare portrait of the dodo, a large non-flying pigeon-like bird, which became extinct about three centuries ago. This portrait was found in a collection of paintings at the Institute of Orientalists of Soviet Academy of Sciences. There was no way of identifying the painter, but the style, without doubt was that of Ustad Mansur. Now there is evidence to show that it was the portrait of Mauritian dodo that was presented to Emperor Jahangir around 1624. Over three centuries after their death, Jahangir and his dodo made a dramatic reappearance in the world of ornithology!

5. Jahangir also loved gardens, but his dissertations in botany and horticulture were mostly confined to how a lotus traps hornets or how saffron sprouts from soil. However, he was responsible for the cultivation of high altitude trees such as the cypress, juniper, pine and Javanse sandal in plains.

6. Jahangir had many other scientific interests. He once conducted an experiment to show that the air of Mahmudabad (in Gujarat) was healthier than that of Ahmadabad. He was fascinated by the movement of the stars and the planets and used to regularly record the occurrence of solar and lunar eclipses. When a comet made its appearance, he recorded the growth and decay of its tail.

(i) On the basis of your reading of the above passage, make notes on it in points. Also, suggest a suitable title. **(2 Marks)**

(ii) Write a summary of the passage in not more than 80 words using the notes made. **(3 Marks)**

Section B Creative Writing Skills Grammar

Creative Writing Skills

3. CBSE Board exams are just round the corner and as an educationist you can feel the pressure on students. Design a poster on behalf of CBSEto be displayed in schools asking students to take the help of the counselors. **(3 Marks)**

Or

Your school is organising a fete to aid the earthquake victims. Design a poster for your school in about 50 words.

4. As the Head Boy of your school, write a letter to the Principal requesting him/her to arrange programmes of career counselling for the students of classes XI and XII. Request him to invite experts from several professions to speak to the students to give insights and information.

Or

You would like to join NDA coaching classes. Write a letter to the Director Model Coaching Centre, Andheri, Mumbai to enquire about the coaching classes for the next examination. Ask for all necessary details. You are Sunita / Suraj, 4 Grant Road, Dadar.

5. 'Private cars should be banned in the congested commercial areas of the cities.' Write a debate in 150- 200 words either for or against the motion. **(3 Marks)**

Or

Our large population is not a cause of poverty but an asset, a resource.' Write a debate in 150-200 words either for or against the motion.

Grammar

6. Choose the correct option to fill in the blank. **(2 Marks)**

(i) The police found …… counterfeit money as well as guns at the gang's headquarters.
(a) several more (b) a large amount of
(c) only a few (d) a number of

(ii) We no problems whatsoever with the dam since it forty years ago.
(a) were having / was being constructed
(b) have had / was constructed
(c) had had / had been const~ucted
(d) are having / is constructed'

7. Rearrange the following into meaningful sentences. **(2 Marks)**

P:; mainstream offerings

Q : a stimulating contrast

R : their works are

S : to a lot of
(a) PQSR (b) SRPQ
(c) RPSQ (d) RQSP

Or

P : both poles of the Universe

Q : and Earth. man becomes

R : in the space between Heaven

S : the conduit of communication between
(a) SQPR (b) RPSQ
(c) RQSP (d) QSRP

Section C Literature

8. Attempt anyone of the following. **(3 Marks)**

My initial relief at meeting Norbu, who was also staying in the guest house, was tempered by the realisation that he was almost as ill-equipped as I was for the pilgrimage. He kept telling me how fat he was and how hard it was going to be. "Very high up," he kept reminding me, "so tiresome to walk." He wasn't really a practising Buddhist, it transpired, but he had enthusiasm and he was, of course, Tibetan. Although I'd originally envisaged making the trek in the company of devout believers, on reflection I decided that perhaps Norbu would turn out to be the ideal companion.

(i) With reference to the given lines, explain the narrators' initial relief upon meeting Norbu.

(ii) Why does the narrator feel that Norbu would be an ideal companion for him?

(iii) How do you the narrator finally completed his kora?
Or

We have begun to take a holistic view of the very basis of our existence. The environmental problem does not necessarily signal our demise, it is our passport for the future. The emerging new world vision has ushered in the Era of Responsibility. It is a holistic view, an ecological view, seeing the world as an integrated whole rather than a dissociated collection of parts. Industry has a most crucial role to play in this new Era of Responsibility. What a transformation would be effected if more businessmen shared the view of the Chairman of Du Pont, Mr Edgar S. Woolard who, five years ago, declared himself to be the Company's "Chief Environmental Officer." He said, "Our continued existence as a leading manufacturer requires that we excel in environmental performance."

(i) What does 'holistic view' and 'Era of Responsibility' indicate in the given lines?

(ii) How can the environmental problem be our passport of future?

(iii) 'Industry has a most crucial role to play in this new Era of Responsibility.' Explain with reference to the statement given by Mr. Edgar S. Woolard.

9. Attempt anyone of the following.   (3 Marks)

Eternal I rise impalpable out of the land and the bottomless sea,

Upward to heaven, whence, vaguely form'd, altogether changed, and yet the same,

I descend to lave the droughts, atomies, dust-layers of the globe,

And all that in them without me were seeds only, latent, unborn;

(i) Do you find any characteristic of rain in the extract? Is yes, state them.

(ii) Explain 'vaguely form'd, altogether changed, and yet the same.'

(iii) How does the given extract justify the rain's comparison with a poem?

Or

When did my childhood go?

Was it when I found my mind was really mine,

To use whichever way I choose, Producing thoughts that were not those of other people

But my own, and mine alone

Was that the day!

(i) Explain 'my mind was really mind.'

(ii) In talking about a stage in the process of growing up, the extract also highlights some qualities of adults. Comment.

(iii) Can you find the use of a literary device in the given extract? If yes, state which one?

10. Attempt anyone of the following.   (3 Marks)

Get me hot water and cold water," he threw out to the nurse. "And basins too. Quick! Quick But,

Doctor-" she faltered, her eyes on the pallid body of the child. "Quick! " he shouted. Snatching a blanket, he laid the child upon it and began the special method of respiration. The basins arrived, the ewer, the big iron kettle. Frantically he splashed cold water into one basin; into the other he mixed water as hot as his hand could bear. Then, like some crazy juggler, he hurried the child between the two, now plunging it into the icy, now into the steaming bath.

(i) Why do you think that the doctor was desperate to save the child?

(ii) Do you think that the Doctor was successful in his attempts?

(iii) The doctor uses a method that he had seen somewhere to resuscitate the child. Comment.

Or

I'll never go back to that place," Albert assured him. "I'm going to take this certificate to the head teacher tomorrow, and that will be the end of it." "Don't forget to get a reference in writing from your mathematics teacher first," Yuri reminded him. Mr Koch willingly gave Albert the reference he wanted. "If I say I can't teach you any more, and probably you'll soon be able to teach me, will that be all right?" he asked. "That's saying too much, sir," said Albert. "It's only the truth. But alright. I'll put it more seriously." (Albert Einstein at school)

(i) Why does Einstein say that he is never going back to the school?

(ii) Explain the reference to 'this certificate.'

(iii) How will you translate Mr. Koch's words in comparison to Mr. Braun words for Einstein?

11. Attempt anyone of the following.   (3 Marks)

What do you learn about the 'system of education in old British schools from the play 'The Browning Version'?

Or

Why does rain call itself 'impalpable' in the poem 'The Voice of the Rain'?

12. Attempt any one of the following.   (3 Marks)

He had no premonition that this night call would prove unusual, still less that it would influence his whole future in Blaenelly. Comment with reference to the chapter Birth.

Or

How did Albert hope to get admission to an Italian college without a diploma from the GErman School?

Printed by Libri Plureos GmbH in Hamburg,
Germany